Honest Ogden

American Decision Series

*In the American Revolutionary War,
a Leading American Patriot's Story of His Struggle
to Regain His Lost Respect*

By William (Bill) R. Truran

Copyright © 2024 William (Bill) R. Truran All rights reserved

The characters and events portrayed in this book are fictitious. Any similarity to real persons, living or dead, is coincidental and not intended by the author.

No part of this book may be reproduced, or stored in a retrieval system, or transmitted in any form or by any means, electronic, mechanical, photocopying, recording, or otherwise, without express written permission of the publisher.

ISBN: 979-8-8693-7229-1

Cover design by: Miblart

Dedication

This book is dedicated to the people of America.

I hope that my interpretation of the life of Robert Ogden II shows his integrity to the truth and his bonified desire to carry on a good name for himself and his family. This desire by Ogden is a human trait and one that had inspired many of our Founding Fathers to "do the right thing" when they fought for and made the rules and laws of our new country. I hope that Ogden's desire to be "a good man" provides the people of America today a person that they might admire and whose qualities they might want to consider for their own.

Preface

The study of history has always been a passion of mine. To understand what has come before us provides us experience vicariously with which to gain wisdom.

World-shaking events can give us a broad foundation on how humans have developed. We can also grow and improve by studying our local history. This is in part the reason for this book.

Within about a five-mile radius of my mostly rural county, there have been some large figures in history whom we can study. Robert Ogden II is one of these people.

An important player in the American Revolution and from New Jersey, Ogden may provide an example of one who had a Faustian dilemma. He was threatened with death and agreed not to reveal who the perpetrators were. This conflicted with the great respect of the people. He was known as an honest lawyer who was respected for his truthfulness.

There's not too much of his life with which to write a book, so I created a novel, a historical novel. This also allows me to inject many of the myths, legends, and stories of our area from that time and develop a reasonable picture that can include these other players and events.

This book is part of a three-book series that I call *American Decision*. All three men were influential in the Revolutionary War, and their many descendants also played some key parts in the development of our nation. Along with Judge Ogden, I will include a book on the military leadership of Colonel John Seward from Snufftown Mountain, his development, and the changing character of his outlook on life.

The third book is on a signer of the Declaration of Independence, Lewis Morris III. All three of these important men were near my home and were instrumental in the struggle for our new nation.

I hope you enjoy the story that I tell.

Bill Truran

Foreword

This book is about history, historical fiction, myths, and legends.

I have chosen to write about people from my local home area who were, in their time, accomplished and resourceful men. They made crucial decisions during the American Revolutionary War. The outcomes of those decisions were seen immediately in that time period, and the vestiges of those decisions still echo today.

They do have a story that is valuable to tell.

But there does not exist much factual information on them today, most having been lost due to a time that had less writings and documentation and also due to the fact that they were more or less fugitives from the dominant British who wished to see them dead. The ravages of time also must have taken factual evidence away with the gusts and sweeping of the winds of time. So, I needed to fill gaps and make the men real, if not, necessarily, accurate.

There are several tales, myths, and legends that are from the same Revolutionary War period that could be woven into the story. These legends involve Loyalist James Moody, the cowboy Claudius Smith, and other individuals and deeds that are remembered but not well documented. I chose to weave these people in as well, and it did seem that they fit a puzzle well to help support my writing about the primary characters.

I hope you will appreciate a book that has real people from the time and with reasonable embellishments to their lives and actions.

Thank you,
Bill

Moral & Theme

Moral of the story: To portray the character of "A Good Man," what that may be, and which may be defined through Christian values.

Theme of the work: A man's steadfast desire to maintain the outward appearance of honesty while striving to resolve inner conflict of competing values that strain the concept of honesty.

> *"I am so unhappy as to find that my conduct ... has made me the object of too general a resentment."*
> Mr. Ogden's letter resigning his seat in the New Jersey Royal Assembly Legislature

Robert Ogden Headstone:
"In public life both in Church and State he filled many important offices with ability and integrity. In his private business ... he was upright, eminently useful, active and diligent. He was temperate and humane. A friend to the poor, hospitable and generous. A most faithful, tender and indulgent husband and parent, and above all, his life and conversation from his youth was becoming a professor of religion and a follower of blessed Jesus."

Introduction

The series *American Decision* looks at the lives of three important men during the American Revolutionary War. In *Honest Ogden*, we examine the life of Judge Robert Ogden II. He came from a venerable family line. They were well known in colonial America as outstanding citizens and civic leaders. Through several generations and hundreds of years, these men were held in well-deserved esteem. Judge Ogden was a greatly respected lawyer, to the point that he held the moniker of Honest Ogden.

The reader may take note of the respectability and contrast this with the unexpected difficulties that collided with the judge. He was a smart man and took these challenges to heart and struggled with the dichotomy of being honest with the need of being safe. This is what we today might call cognitive dissonance. Deviating either way will upset his respectability.

I think we all can understand and empathize with this dilemma. I hope realizing this can help the reader gain a feeling of the judge's moral chaos that is finally resolved.

Table of Contents

Dedication	3
Preface	5
Foreword	7
Moral & Theme	8
Introduction	9
ACT I OGDEN'S RETREAT	15
Chapter 1 Unrest in Elizabethtown	17
Chapter 2 Rider at the Bridge, 1777 Spring	21
Chapter 3 Washington's Tent, 1777 Spring	27
Chapter 4 Respected & Proud	32
Chapter 5	
Ogden Inspects His Country Home and Learns of Moody	39
Chapter 6	
Ogden Escapes From Elizabethtown, 1777 Summer	45
Chapter 7 Passing by of Pastor Constant Hart	55
Chapter 8 Settling in at Ogdensburg	60
Chapter 9 Church Service	63
Chapter 10 Attackers at the Door, Winter 1778	63
ACT II OGDEN'S DILEMMA	79
Chapter 11 Robbery Aftermath	81
Chapter 12 Jailbreak in Newton	85
Chapter 13 Jailbreak Questioning	91
Chapter 14 Blowing up Powder Stores at Suckasunny	95
Chapter 15 Ogden Questioned on Gunpowder	100
Chapter 16 Breakout Gov Franklin, 1778	104
Chapter 17 Sheriff Comes to Call	108
Chapter 18 Stirling to Ogden on Governor	114
Chapter 19 Talk About Town in the Burg	119
Chapter 20 Kidnap Gov Livingston, May 10, 1780	122
Chapter 21 Judge at the Fire	128
Chapter 22 Plot to Steal America's Treasure	131
Chapter 23 Stealing the Declaration of Independence	135
Chapter 24 Judge in His Library	143
Chapter 25	
Imprisoned at West Point, Battle Stony Point July 16, 1779	146
Chapter 26 Sir Henry Clinton	154
Chapter 27 Ogden to Reveal June 23, 1780	159
Chapter 28 Judge Goes to Morristown	162

Table of Contents

ACT III HONESTY & TABLES TURN	167
Chapter 29	
Washington's Tent for the Battle of Springfield, June 23, 1780	169
Chapter 30 Battle of Springfield With Ogdens	180
Chapter 31	
Newburgh GW & R Weathersfield, CT, June 22,1781	185
Chapter 32	
Chain of Express and Deception, around June 1781	190
Chapter 33 Moody's Gift to Clinton	196
Chapter 34	
Spy-GW Messages on Siege of NYC, around June 1781	199
Chapter 35 Yorktown Secret Information	207
Chapter 36 Battle of Yorktown 10/1781	211
Chapter 37	
Abduction of Admiral Digby & Prince William Henry, March 28, 1782	218
Chapter 38 Smith's Clove	224
Chapter 39 The Smith Gang	229
Chapter 40 Claudius on the Gallows, January 22, 1779	237
Chapter 41	
Matthias Ogden in France, Aaron Ogden as Governor, and the Judge	248
Chapter 42 Ogden's Redemption	251
Chapter 43 Moody's Reflections	253
What's next?	257
More to read…	258
Acknowledgements	259
The life of an author	261
References	264
Index and Endnotes	266

If you would hearken to my commandments,
your prosperity would be like a river,
and your vindication like the waves of the sea;
Your descendants would be like the sand,
and those born of your stock like its grains,
Their name never cut off
or blotted out from my presence.

– Isaiah 48: 17-19

ACT I
OGDEN'S RETREAT

"The best inheritance that a father can leave to his children, and which is superior to any patrimony, is the glory of his virtue and noble deeds: to disgrace which ought to be regarded as base and impious."

– Cicero

Chapter 1
Unrest in Elizabethtown

The morning sun rose from the east here in colonial America, 250 years ago, shedding its golden beams across Manhattan and beyond the busy harbor full of ocean-going sail ships and making a mark in brightening the city of Elizabethtown, New Jersey. Here lay a beautiful, small urban area, with many wooden and stone houses, some standing out as elegant estates with proper lawns and long, straight fences. Polite men and ladies kindly greeted one another. The community exuded a feeling of the steady rhythm of successful business and fortune. Commerce wagons delivered goods to stores, and people went about their shopping on foot and in carriages. All this effect reflected a dignified picture of gentrified surroundings.

As the sun climbed in the sky, ship traffic commenced in the waters of Newark Bay and the adjoining sound, carrying the product of a burgeoning society. And out to the sound the Elizabeth Town River casually flowed, with Staten Island a short ferry ride to the east. The river came from farther inland, meandering through pretty meadows and still pastures that made for a patchwork of green around the stately homes of prominent citizens of the town. A fine road led from the courthouse to the sound and a mile or so from the governor's mansion now known as Liberty Hall where Governor Livingston resided.

Around this road and the river were several city estates of a well-known family—the Ogden clan. These were mainly clustered near each other, with a large piece of property having been subdivided from prior generations. Chief among them in these early days of the Revolutionary War was the home of Robert Ogden II[i], a wonderful estate with plowed fields, pasture, and an orchard. It backed up to the Red Store along an easy bend in the river. The Ogdens were near a mill that stood along the river and a thriving tannery.

From more primitive surroundings and distilled social life during past days, Elizabethtown now was buzzing with major change and hard choices. A ripping of the cloth of society was at hand. It was the time of the American Revolutionary War, and the life-changing choice of remaining a "Loyalist" to the British or to be a "Patriot" with the fight for freedom. This struggle was particularly felt by Robert Ogden II. In his large home along the river and amidst the orchard and fine fencing, he could be seen this fine day treading a groove into his parlor, head down anxiously and moving back and forth. He was deep in contemplation about his social condition.

"Phoebe[ii]" he said to his wife, who was knitting in the chair along the wall, "I am beside myself in anguish." He said this as he stopped to look at her.

She sighed, lowered the thread, and offered some consolation. "Robert, dear, you have been earnest all your life, giving what you can to society to make the world a better place."

"That may have been my intention, but the world has been rejecting me in my current life." He strutted forward again, saying, "The Ogden family has been very respected all these years, shining with a stellar heritage. But now …"

"Oh dear, Robert, you certainly are disturbed."

"And well I should be," he said as he kept up his pacing. "The Ogden family has been here for well over a hundred years and in fine standing. Now the name is stained."

Phoebe was born a Hatfield. Both the Ogden and Hatfield families had been pillars of the community over the years. The Hatfield homestead was just up the street, and the extended clans occupied several nearby streets with only friendly fences separating them.

"And it's ruined now, my name is tarnished," he said while wearing a hole in the fine floor rug as he paced in the elaborate parlor. "Me, a fifth descendent of the honored John Ogden the Pilgrim."

This was true. John Ogden the Pilgrim was the first to the town. It was stated that he "was a pilgrim in obedience to God's will," the person known as to "lay the cornerstone of Elizabethtown" in 1666. The town was the first capital of the state, and John acted as the justice of the peace. He was "possessed with courage and moral fiber." He was widely known as "a true patriot, and a genuine Christian." It had been said that John Ogden's deeds "justly entitled him to rank with the "Pilgrim Fathers." He was now buried stately in the quiet graveyard of the First Presbyterian Church of Elizabeth.

Robert's grandfather Jonathan Ogden was a large landowner and was keeper of the family will. He participated in the release of Lewis Morris, whose extended family was currently of significant service to the new nation.

Robert's father, Robert Senior, owned much land, which was important for voting. He filled many offices and was of great repute. Truthfully put upon his tombstone was that he was "a pillar of church and state."

The Ogden family also prospered in Elizabethtown, owning over three hundred acres in the citified land. The family's influence was strong as well.

"Your family has had a great impact on our town, and in fact the whole colony of New Jersey. All men have an equal chance in life, and your family—and you—have done the best with your chances."

"Well," replied the judge, "I know that I started out fine."

Robert was the commissary and barrack master for the king's troops back in the day when the Americans lived peacefully with those loyal to the Crown. Now, the British troops were camped on property of the Ogden family throughout Elizabethtown.

"And my dear, you remind me of your grandfather John who was also sheriff when the New York royal governor Andros asked him for the surrender of New Jersey, as if he were the governor. Your rich strain of blood might also give through our sons more governors in the future."

"I don't think that my sons could be blessed as such after my demonstrated ill will having been sewn, having been planted to grow like a wicked weed."

In contrast, Phoebe said, "As we recall from Job, you will 'go to the grave at a ripe old age, like a sheaf of grain harvested at the proper time.'"

"That could never happen now, now that I have ruined the family name."

"Sure, it can happen," responded Phoebe, maintaining a cheerier perspective. As Abraham said in Genesis, "I will bless thee, and make thy name great, and thou shalt be a blessing."

The pacing continued. The judge was totally occupied and disturbed by his drop in standing in the community. He was unable to see a return to his previous good repute.

This Ogden parlor was not the only place of discontent. Elizabethtown was also being torn asunder. The colony, and in fact the whole continent, was blighted with a polarizing stigma; the need to be either a Loyalist or a Patriot. There seemed no middle ground.

Elizabethtown was not alone in its division. This malaise could be found along the highways and byways of the land.

Chapter 2
Rider at the Bridge, 1777 Spring

"What need the bridge much broader than the flood?
The fairest grant is the necessity."
— William Shakespeare, Much Ado About Nothing

Lieutenant James Moody[iii] watched the horse and rider as it moved quickly along the rural landscape of gentle rolling hills and smooth fields of grain. Galloping down the road, the messenger hustled to deliver the important bulletin that was stuffed in his saddlebag for General Washington.

Corporal Joseph Lowery[iv], [v][vi] was beside Moody, and he eyed the horse as it thundered toward them. The steed arched its back and straightened out its forelegs, reaching ahead in his stride. The hooves pounded the hard roadway dirt that then rose up in little brown puffs as the rider's topcoat trailed behind him in the wind. Moody watched as he sped by the green pastures and the grazing cows, the messenger's legs banging against the horse's sides and the saddlebags laden with correspondence slapped against the horse's sweating hips. Because of the gusty headwind, Sullivan, the messenger, had to keep raising his hand to hold his blue tricorn hat snug on his head so it wouldn't blow off behind him.

The rider looked anxious. He was riding fast—he rode bent over the saddle horn with the stallion's mane flying up and tickling his nose.

***

As Private Patrick "Red" Sullivan[vii] neared the bridge, the eyes of the horse widened, and his teeth showed fear. The steed yawed back and came to a walk. The horse slowed further and then reached a measured step while approaching the small bridge where a meandering stream trickled underneath. The old, wooden bridge looked in need of repair, and a blockade was the reason for the horse's instinct to have taken over. Two workers, one small and one tall, were on the bridge, bent over at the waist intently working on a plank that was raised up and which made passage impossible.

Realizing the reluctance of the horse and the obvious impediment to travel, Sullivan asked the smaller of the workers, "Sir, will I be able to pass?"

The man wore a round, black hat with a flat brim. He looked up and said, "Surely sir. You look in a hurry."

"That I am," said the rider. "I am Red Sullivan, a private in the army, and I am on my way to Morristown on official business."

"You are with the American Patriot Army, sir? I just want to make sure."

"Yes," said Private Sullivan. He was very willing to talk as he was proud of his uniform and the importance placed upon him. "As an honest person, I must admit that I am of Irish descent. I am really Patrick O'Sullivan, but I try to fit in here in America and thus drop the 'O' and would rather the moniker of "Red" as it more accurately fits my identity."

"You may not be a Red Coat as the British are, but you sure have a pinkish appearance," said the taller man.

The shorter one turned to him and said, "That's enough, Lowery."

"That's why they call me Red, sir," Private Sullivan said, trying for a genial tone. But he felt oddly uncomfortable. He was holding some very important communication from General Washington. His way forward was impeded, and he wished to speed things up. "I'm on an urgent errand, if you please," he said to the workers.

The one who's told Lowery to quiet down now held the plank. He seemed to unfold vertically as he stood up and stretched to over six feet. He was lanky and looked like he could use a meal. His lengthy arms dangled by his side. He wore tall, leather boots that rose up his long legs, ending at the knee. He looked like a gaunt tall tree in winter.

The shorter one motioned to his partner who then placed the plank back down into place. It was a prompt action that seemed to be done in a courteous fashion. Sullivan saw how quickly the men worked on his behalf. His way forward was now clear.

Sullivan nodded his thanks as they completed the task, and he dismounted the horse since the structure was doubtful to hold both a horse and its rider on top. Walking over the narrow bridge Red looked back at his horse sucking wind and steaming from his urgent travel as the small man and the man called Lowery stepped aside to allow him through.

The passage made, Sullivan now safely on the other side, he turned to thank the two men who had helped him.

"Thank you, sirs," he said. "Forgive me for taking your valuable time."

Sullivan stood by his horse and looked more closely at the two workers. The fellow who had been holding the plank now stood still for Red's observation. He wore his round, brimmed hat well and was nicely dressed while the one called Lowery seemed a bit shaggy and in need of a bath.

Lowery had leaned a little forward and said to Sullivan, "That's a fine-looking hunting knife on your belt. I'd not mind one like that for myself."

Red was vaguely alarmed by the statement, but then shook it off.

"That's enough, Lowery," said the other one. Then looking at the Red, he said, "Don't mind him." Sullivan watched as the small one laughed slightly and reached out to shake the messenger's hand. This was apparently a pleasant meeting of like-minded Americans, not always common with the Revolutionary War in full swing.

"Moody's the name for you to remember," he said. He grinned and showed a silver tooth in the front of his mouth.

The messenger was on guard. Something was afoot, and he was wary. Even his horse seemed to sense something. Then, without warning, the man called Lowery smashed the messenger in the face with his fist.

Red fell backward into to the tall, brown grass that grew beside the highway. The impact crushed several stalks of chicory, leaving pretty, cerulean blue flowers smiling out from beneath his motionless form. The only movement was the trickle of blood coming down Red's dimpled cheek, oozing from a gruesome cut.

"Good work, Lowery," said Moody. "He's out cold."

"That he is!" said Lowery. He removed his leather cap and slapped it against his distinctive high boots. He looked at the Patriot who now was laid prone on the ground.

"Hold the horse," said Moody. "It's surprising how naïve the messenger was."

As Lowery took the horse's reigns, Moody rifled through the messenger's bags.

"I have to tell you, Lieutenant Moody," said Lowery "You really had him fooled into thinking that we were just workmen."

"You are an idiot, Lowery."

"What do you mean?" he asked, clearly wounded by the insult.

"Don't be a bumbling fool. Telling a man you admire his knife and wish to have one of your own. That's a good way to raise suspicion. If you want to rob and loot, you must do so with more class. Discretion, my friend. Use discretion. We are lucky he was so trusting."

Lowery glanced skyward at some geese flying in a V-pattern. To Moody, he seemed as though he hadn't heard a word.

"Someday, you will betray me, I swear it," said Moody with dismay.

"I would never, Moody. You know better than to say that," Lowery said. He looked at the geese as they landed in a small pond below the meandering stream that descended from under the bridge.

"Let me tell you this," said Moody. "Deviousness such as this could win the war for our Loyalist friends. Enough of these small incidents could yield large returns in information."

As usual, Lowery was preoccupied and said nothing. This always angered Moody. But as he searched through the bag, he remained quiet. Then all at once, Moody let out a whoop.

"And here it is. A message to General Washington[viii]. I need to get this to the British authorities, and hopefully General Howe can act on it." He looked up to his companion who was holding the reigns of the horse. "Let's go, Lowery."

Lowery hovered over the messenger's body. "Hold on, Lieutenant Moody. I want that knife." Lowery ripped the knife from the limp messenger's belt. "That's a fine blade, long and broad," he said.

"Come on, let's get going. If we're caught, they'll hang us both."

Standing beside the hard pack dirt road, Lowery kept looking at the knife, rubbing the blade against his thumb.

"I can put a nice sharp point on this when we get to the grist stone back at Sharpsboro."

"You do that," said Moody.

"And then it's payback to all of those who've pushed me down."

"That's you, always looking to steal and rob and then show

everyone the spoils of your looting," Moody said. "Whereas I am the intelligent one, you see. I shall devise more of these plots for benefit of the British Army."

Lowery frowned. Then he said, "But I have the knife, and all for the price of a sucker punch. How much do you think the British general will give us for this letter?"

"I will bet no less than a hundred guineas for this stolen mail. There's a quarter ounce of gold for every guinea," said Moody. "That's real money."

Lowery and Moody paused to look at the man in blue, the young Patriot soldier with the pink face and freckles and blood streaming down, lying flat and motionless by the bridge.

"So, what's next?" asked Lowery.

Moody, the obvious leader between the two men, was silent for a long moment. Then he looked at Lowery. "I don't know about you, but I plan on capturing the governor—Governor Livingston—and taking him away just as was done with our royal governor, William Franklin."

Lowery, Moody noticed, looked quizzical. He was dumb as an ox, and Moody worried that one day Lowery would get them both in trouble.

Moody said, "You know, Governor William Franklin, Benjamin Franklin's estranged son. It was that conniving Lord Stirling who took him away."

Moody bent down and picked up a reed. Pausing to chew on it, he said, "I have a lot of plans, Lowery. But the biggest is to sneak into the Continental Congress and steal their documents."

Lowery seemed impressed to Moody's estimation. "That is a bold plan."

"Yes, it is," gloated Moody. "I can see it now, the satisfaction of getting all the acclaim as I hand the Declaration of Independence over to General Howe."

"You will be a hero, sir, that is true. Or you may be dead."

But Moody was dreaming. He said in a far-off voice, "The Patriots won't even have their founding documents anymore."

"And," said Lowery, "there will be reward money. Lots of reward money."

"Come on," said Moody, snapping out of his reverie. "Sullivan looks like he's coming to. Let's get out of sight."

"Steal his horse, sir?"

Moody stopped. Intriguing idea. But then he said, "Let's let the man have some dignity." He walked off with Lowery behind him. Lowery was a scoundrel who drank too much and liked the ladies too keenly. Moody shook his head, thinking that man might get him in trouble one day.

Chapter 3
Washington's Tent, 1777 Spring

"Few men have virtue to withstand the highest bidder."
– George Washington

Private Red Sullivan was still groggy from the sucker punch as he staggered out of General Washington's large, white war tent in Morristown, rubbing his head, replacing his tricorn, and dropping the canvas tent flap behind him as he left. He felt worse than sorry that he failed in his duty to bring in the mail. He should have known better. Especially with the one called Lowery. That man was scandalous to be sure.

Morristown, a small village in north central New Jersey, was known as a main hub, and in fact was a crossroads of the Revolution. It was a strategic enough location that Washington would set up his winter encampment there two times during the war.

"This news troubles me greatly," said General Washington as he spoke to General William Alexander, known as Lord Stirling, who was one of his most trusted advisers.

Due to his heroic exploits, Lord Stirling had been termed "the bravest man in America" for his fearless strength in facing danger, and for his boldness. He was also one of General Washington's most loyal military men. The two had known each other from twenty years before when they both served in the French and Indian Wars. Congress had commissioned Lord Stirling as a brigadier general in 1776. As a general, he provided a significant and heroic act by holding off the British troops during the Battle of Long Island early in the war. This rear-guard action, and its almost suicidal heroism, allowed Washington's main force to escape through the foggy night across the waters to Manhattan Island. It was a vital feat performed with the Maryland and Delaware regiments under Stirling's command that perhaps saved the Revolution during a low point.

Washington knew Stirling as a somewhat colorful officer, well acquainted with politics and the social skills needed to work his way through crowds and brethren as he gabbed away and made connections. People liked him. His personality was as bold as his prowess. He was a man of action. His attractiveness was accentuated by his own personally supplied, keen uniform. If Washington had any complaints, it was the man's drinking; something he did quite heavily.

"It had to have been Moody. He and one of his scoundrels took the message that was intended only for me," said General Washington. He sat down on his worn chair and sighed.

"What was the message. How bad is it?" asked Stirling.

"It concerned sensitive matter about enemy troop movements. And it left Private Sullivan with a fat lip, loose tooth, and a noticeable knife wound tear on his face. He will wear that scar till the end of his days."

"Yes," said Lord Stirling. "If the stolen message was not encrypted and in plain text, they may now know and then capture our own spies or kill them. If it is encrypted, the British could work to decipher it and put at risk our entire network. In either case, it is not good."

"I am worried that we could lose the campaign in the North," said Washington. "You know how important I think spying and ciphering are to our winning the war."

"Right, sir," said Stirling. "But don't forget, they may use the sensitive information to hit us in different ways, like stealing away important men or learning how to sneak up on us here and at Jockey Hollow or slipping past your life guards and reaching you. Those British sympathizers are smart and crafty. James Moody is a key one to watch. A brilliant spy. In truth, I wish he were one of ours."

Washington considered Lord Stirling's words thoughtfully. It was vitally important that that his guards protected him from the fifty or so British-leaning Tories that had formed a secret organization early in the war to assassinate him.

"Yes, my faithful General Alexander, or Lord Stirling[ix] as you aspire to be," said Washington. "I'd hate to see them steal away our current New Jersey governor. I would not want any harm coming to your brother-in-law."

"Nor I," said Stirling, his lips curling from the inference his commander made. He was a proud man. Indeed, Stirling was considered the male heir to the Scottish line and was granted as such by the Scottish court. But the House of Lords, may they be damned, took it away from him. Whenever he thought of it, his gout flared up, as did his rheumatism. It was his wife who told him he shouldn't drink so much. "The pain is caused by the liquor," she'd said many times, not nagging, but sweetly. He told her that was nonsense. Deep down, though, he knew she was right.

Earlier, Washington considered how New Jersey Royal Governor William Franklin[x], Benjamin Franklin's son, and the royal governor before the war, was against their cause and said he was in favor of supporting the Loyalists. This war was a complicated one.

"According to the messenger rider's description," said Stirling, "of those who ruffled through his saddlebag and retrieved the bulletin from him, there were two men. The messenger's valuable hunting knife was ripped from his belt and stolen from him after the tall man in leather boots jealously noted its worth. The other fellow was short, wore a round brimmed hat, and had a silver tooth."

Washington pondered, but not for long, while reading the report on the table. "I am sure it was the Loyalist Lieutenant James Moody and one of his men, Lowery."

He knew William Franklin favored scoundrels like Moody whom he called "the best Partizan" they had for helping the royal governor.

"They've both individually created havoc in North Jersey and southern New York Colony," said Stirling. "They are a menace. We've got to stop it from happening again."

Several continental army officers were busy within the tent, each on special tasks related to demands of the war. General Washington arose for another discussion of planning with them. He stood tall and straight, and his white hair was the highest point in the tent except for the long, vertical poles holding up the white canvas roof. Washington looked forward at several of Erskine's maps along with some of Gardiner's and Alexander's surveys that were spread across a table in the middle of the tent. His forehead furrowed as he pored over the symbols and figures, and he put both hands onto the table. He moved a little closer to the maps, as his eyes were growing wearier and weaker as the war had progressed. He was coming to the realization that incidents like this, small interactions of a clandestine nature, could damage the chances for the Americans to win the war.

He leaned across the table and looked up to Stirling with a serious and concerned expression, slowly saying, "That villain Moody."[xi]

Several officers pulled up the flap of the tent and entered, bringing with them a large dose of bright sunlight. The yellow light spread before them as they approached the general. The wind puffed out the soft canvas tent walls, and then sucked in, as if this headquarters of the continental army were a living, breathing being. General Washington saw the officers come directly toward him and took a deep breath, anticipating bad news.

"Well," said Washington, putting an end to the conversation with Stirling, "we have many other matters to concern us in prosecuting this war."

Just then Washington's slave, Billy Lee[xii], who acted as his assistant and secretary, came running in before the flap closed. He was a short, young, black man wearing his trademark red felt hat with peacock plumage stabbing skyward, the feathers fluttering.

"General Washington, it's time for vespers," Billy said. "And Mrs. Ford is preparing tea in the mansion. I can escort you, sir."

"We can use some spiritual inspiration," the general said. "Who might be preaching today?"

Immediately, one of Washington's life guards stepped up from his formal duty along the edge of the tent. It was Major Matthias Ogden[xiii]. Ogden was a trim and fit young man, smartly wearing his blue Continental Army uniform. He looked ornate with his leather helmet and medium blue cloth binding and white plume, tipped on the left side with "USA" on his uniform buttons.

"Sir," said Ogden proudly, "the preacher today will be my father."

"Ah, Judge Ogden," said Stirling. "The Honest Judge. Your father is quite a devout Presbyterian. I am sure his words will fill us with insight."

"Thank you for the compliment, sir," said Major Ogden. "Father is on his way."

"From the family home? Elizabethtown?" asked Washington.

"Yes, after which he traveled to check on our land in Sussex County."

"Sussex County," said General Washington. "A land of bright opportunity."

He considered briefly the minerals and ore that came from the ground, the water power and plentiful hardwood; all of which were exceptional resources for making iron implements for winning the war. Sussex County had become the new home of the Ogden family, Lewis Morris[xiv]—signer of the Declaration of Independence and his *Morrisvale*—and the brave Colonel John Seward[xv] who had weathered the Battle of Long Island along with Washington and Stirling. Stirling himself owned an iron and zinc mine near the Ogdens.

    The Continental Army officers proceeded from the tent across the richly green grass to the mansion, but General Washington was hailed from behind and pulled back into the tent on additional important matters that would not wait. He had often felt this tether of supreme command reach out to grasp him back.

Chapter 4
Respected & Proud

"Learning to trust is one of life's most difficult tasks."
– Isaac Watts

The men heading to the mansion from General Washington's headquarters tent turned as they heard the rumble of a carriage rolling up in front of the Ford Mansion on the main dirt road from Elizabethtown, Springfield, and other points east.

Judge Robert Ogden and his wife, Phoebe Hatfield Ogden, departed the carriage. Mrs. Ogden was first to be escorted by a life guard into the mansion to talk with Mrs. Ford. The rotund judge tipped the carriage to the side of the footstool, where he hesitated for a moment to collect his balance. This accomplished, he then stepped off and down to the ground as the carriage swayed back to center line. He followed his wife along the gray, slate path leading to the recently built mansion.

General Washington's life guards were quartered across the street from the Ford Mansion. On seeing the carriage, they quickly spilled out from their barracks and assembled in front of the judge. While they knew that Judge Ogden was a friend and fellow Patriot, they had to remain cautious in their prime duty of protecting the general of the army from anyone coming to harm him.

Lieutenant Colonel Mathias Ogden, coming from the headquarters tent, ran to the familiar face.

"Hello, Father dear," said Colonel Ogden, and they clasped in a warm embrace. As death and destruction rained down on the new nation, they knew that each time they met might be the last.

"Hello, my son," Judge Ogden said. "You look splendid!"

Colonel Ogden's face burst open with a wide smile as he snapped to attention before his proud father. Colonel Ogden was slim and fit.

He wore the blue jacket with the white leather strap descending diagonally around his belt. His neatly trimmed buff pants covered a strong frame, and the felt hat sported a tall feather ascending skyward, the vanes ruffling back and forth in the warm breeze. Colonel Ogden assumed an easier position, yet still demonstrated to his father a reflection of his training. The other guards who had assembled returned to their various duties, while those who were able to do so remained.

After a deep breath to capture this moment for posterity, Judge Ogden spoke to the young man in his late twenties. "Son, we just came through Springfield, which you know as Connecticut Farms, and spoke to the dear Reverend James Caldwell[xvi]."

"Wonderful, Father. And how is your old friend?"

"He's doing as well as can be expected in these difficult times. He recently acquired some wonderful hymnals, and they included some of my favorite tunes for the church."

Matthias smiled. "Let me guess. The hymns written by Reverend Isaac Watts[xvii]."

Ogden smiled. "You know me so well, my son. Do you remember the songbooks we once had?" Ogden thought back to the books, printed on the finest paper this side of the Atlantic, published by Benjamin Franklin[xviii]. They were beautiful books filled with his more cherished hymns.

"We spent many days from my youth learning the songs and singing with you. These memories I hold dear."

"Thank you, son. Do you remember this line from Reverend Watts—"

Matthias interrupted his father. *"Learning to trust is one of life's most difficult tasks,"* he sang softly.

Judge Ogden beamed. "Ah, my son." He laughed. "Remember to always equate trust to the ability to be honest, and as being able to bear what is expected of you. This way of living breeds good will and shows valuable bonds with other human beings."

"Thank you, Father, for the words of wisdom. Everyone looks to you for clarity in a complex world."

Several of the young life guards nodded in agreement, each sharing the respect that was due to Judge Ogden for the integrity that he portrayed.

"Son, heed my wisdom and you or your brother may one day grow up to be governor."

"You indeed have words of foresight."

Father and son beheld each other for this short moment of greeting. Then the young Ogden said, "I must report back to my men now. I hope that you remain safe on your way to Sussex County. And take care on your way back to Elizabethtown and our beloved ancestral home."

As his son ran back across the road with the life guards, the judge heard footsteps behind him coming from the Ford Mansion.

Striding out of the house to meet the judge was Lord Stirling. Ogden noticed that he looked quite dapper, replete with his fancy, and personally purchased uniform.

"Greetings, Judge Ogden," said Stirling. "I am honored, sir!"

The ever-prancing Lord Stirling put a foot back and then bowed down with his hat in his hand.

"Oh, General Stirling, thank you," said Judge Ogden. "Coming through Springfield, we saw a load of tar arrive for the men on station there on Hobart Gap ridge between Springfield and Morristown. I've heard rumors ..."

"They are correct," said Stirling. "This is part of my beacon warning system."

"And what is that, I may ask?"

Stirling smiled proudly. "Of course. This is a regional warning system where fires are lit to announce the alarm that the British are coming. We can be warned in a minute's notice. Hence, we shall be called "minutemen" so as to respond quickly like our fellows in Massachusetts. The beacon you saw at Hobart Gap will give us warning here in Morristown if the British Army comes hunting us from their large forces that are massed and stationed on Staten Island."

"It is an ingenious system," said the judge. "I feel that an old man like myself is in good hands with such a daring and resourceful man like you."

"Well, your sons are part of it, sir," said Stirling. "Both Matthias and his brother, Aaron Ogden[xix], are fine young gentlemen. I would say they both would do well as diplomats."

"Or governor someday," said Ogden.

Stirling smiled and sipped some wine that he grabbed on his way through the house. Ogden knew that Stirling was a heavy drinker. "Indeed," said Stirling. "One of your sons could be just like my brother-in-law Livingston is today, as he is now New Jersey governor."

"Yes, both Matthias and Aaron are good sons. They will go far in the politics of our new republic, I am sure."

"And Lieutenant Colonel Matthias Ogden is fighting forces in New Jersey these days? A good soldier who has seen much action, do you agree, Judge?"

Judge Ogden nodded. "Indeed."

Another sip of wine by Stirling. "Yes. He's doing well this day. As you know, he was wounded in the assault of the Battle of Quebec way up north during this war."

"Yes," said Judge Ogden. "Along with his cousin, Aaron Burr, captured and released through exchange by the British in our home of Elizabethtown."

Stirling was silent for a moment. Thoughtfully, he drank more wine. Then he said, "And I believe Matthias is conceiving a plan to capture the British Prince William Henry—a plan that General Washington likes."

Ogden noticed that Stirling was getting boastful, and he thought to himself that though arrogance may yet win the war through well-conceived and creative ways, drunkenness was a sin. He watched Stirling as he grew more and more tipsy from the wine.

With his extensive knowledge of all the many interwoven aspects of the war, Stirling had all the appearance of a proud man. Ogden was anxious to get inside and begin his sermon, but he was in the grips of Lord Stirling who took another sip of wine before returning to his talk about Matthias. "He'd be on the first line of defense in the Springfield area to protect us here at Morristown if those Brits came up from Staten Island and tried to attack our army as they remain encamped here in the Morristown area."

At that moment, Mrs. Phoebe Ogden approached the men, having returned from her time visiting with Mrs. Ford, the lady of the mansion.

Stirling took another sip as he tipped his hat to Mrs. Ogden. He bowed extravagantly as she approached. "Ma'am, how are you? And tell me, how are your endeavors in Sussex Country? I understand you are building a plantation, is that correct?"

"Yes. We call it Sparta,"[xx] she said.

"Interesting. And why such a name?"

Phoebe smiled. "In recognition of the strong, young men up there, and from what I can tell the mountains' likeness to those of

Greece with our readings of the classics."

"Very well, ma'am." Stirling tipped his hat and spun away. "I need to return to the mansion and to Mrs. Ford to find a refill of this fine wine."

"Of course," she said as her husband approached.

"Hello, darling," Judge Ogden said to his beloved wife.

"Shall we go inside, dear? They are waiting for your sermon."

He nodded, thoughtful. He wanted it to be just right. As the foundation for the new country had been sealed by the Declaration of Independence, they all found themselves fighting for such freedoms as promised in that sacred document. He wanted to convey both courage and strength upon those for whom the price might be high for such a return.

They walked inside the mansion, built for the late Jacob Ford Jr. and his wife Theodosia. Ogden thought of Mrs. Ford's generosity and courage in allowing General Washington, his wife Martha, Washington's five aides-de-camp, his seventeen servants, and any number of life guards wandering around to use the house as his headquarters. She and her four children, Ogden knew, had taken the rooms in the back. He shivered at the thought of her patriotism and bravery.

As the Judge Ogden and his handsome wife walked through the mansion, they were greeted with deference and bows. Reverend Ogden stood at the head of the great room, and others crowded round for his short sermon. The room was warm, stuffy. Ogden noticed Stirling sitting down now, clearly drunk. General Washington and his wife, however, looked stately and respectable. Ogden held such high regard for the general, for his insight and cleverness. He stood up and found the podium. He was a tall man, and his social abilities, aristocratic background, and scholarly training was in evidence by his stately stance and his manner of carrying himself.

"Good afternoon, my friends," Ogden began. "Just as in my favorite hymn from Isaac Watts, *Our God, Our Help in Ages Past,* this beautiful fugue depicts Psalm 90, where the poet says 'So teach us to number our days, that we may apply our hearts unto wisdom.'"

The crowd stood together solemnly, some of the women bowing their heads. They sang the cherished and solemn hymn, well selected during this tumultuous time:

O God, our help in ages past,
Our hope for years to come,
Our shelter from the stormy blast,
And our eternal home.

"This psalm, which Watts put to music, is known as St. Anne's hymn," said Reverend Ogden, "which is a name I know is dear to Lewis Morris. If given the chance, Morris may one day build a church to St Anne."

Those who knew that Morris was among the signers of the Declaration of Independence smiled to themselves, and indeed they all knew. Ogden saw even Stirling raise his glass in Morris' honor.

"For Morris and the other signers of the Declaration of Independence represented the foundation of the new nation for which they fought, a risky deed putting their lives on the line when they signed the world-changing document which guarantees our freedom, a freedom of infinitely more consequence than some imagine; for by this, it comes to pass that knowledge is more generally disseminated among all ranks of people, from the highest to the lowest; and thus they are rendered capable of knowing their native rights, of asserting, contending for, and maintaining their freedom. Yea, by this knowledge, they are rendered worthy of being free and of enjoying so inestimable a blessing as liberty. If any attempts should be made against the unalienable rights of men, by those in power, they will be much checked, if not rendered wholly abortive, by the unrestrained liberty of the press.

"So, we must carry on with our hearts strong and our faith in God, that he sees the righteousness of our deeds and actions and stays with us as we fight for these freedoms and liberties.

"May the favor[a] of the Lord our God rest on us, establish the work of our hands for us, and as our days go forward, may we gain wisdom and give that wisdom to others, for the benefit of human progress, for the love of our country and for our faith in one God. Amen."

The congregants within the walls of the stately mansion bowed their heads, and each one uttered, "Amen."

After a half hour of greeting the worshippers, Ogden began to feel tired, and he knew he and Phoebe had a ways to go before the end of the day. He leaned over to his wife and said, sotto voce, "My dear Phoebe, we should be off on our road west. The day is getting shorter. I provided a few words of wisdom here, we saw our son, and we should be on our way."

As the Ogdens left, a number of people congregated around the carriage and along the road. They politely and respectfully tipped their hats or curtsied to acknowledge the respect due to Judge Ogden and his wife. Just as the carriage was picking up speed, Matthias Ogden ran back across the roadway to provide his father with important news.

"Father," he said, out of breath from the run. "I have to warn you, that if you intend to go west, beware of the highway robbers. Men recently beat up one of our messengers and stole secret papers and valuables."

The judge nodded but said nothing as the carriage slowed to a stop for the message. He looked at his innocent wife. Phoebe appeared frightened.

"You should be wary of these men," said his son, "and don't be fooled. They may call themselves cowboys or skinners but they are all marauders."

"I heard they were trading secrets," said the judge.

"Don't be confused. They are also stealing and robbing innocent victims."

"Oh dear," said Phoebe, displaying a well-founded fear.

Aaron described the episode on the bridge with the messenger in further detail since he had heard it from the messenger. He described the men as well, their appearance and mannerisms.

"Trouble for all lurks in the countryside. There's a man named Moody who has been wreaking havoc. And beware of the one called Claudius Smith. He roams around with a gang and has no compunction."

"Maybe we should hurry along to the country home while it is still light," said the judge.

"Yes, please," said Phoebe.

Ogden bade his second son goodbye while Phoebe urged him to be careful, and they left Morristown and drove off toward the frontier lands to the west.

Chapter 5
Ogden Inspects His Country Home and Learns of Moody

"Home is where the heart is."
– Pliny the Elder

The carriage exited the village of Morristown, traveling along the busy routes where the commerce of northern New Jersey brought produce toward the city. The Ogden carriage approached the mountains that lay between Morristown and the Ogden's country home at Sparta, a place which was mainly heavily forested in the New Jersey highlands. The judge told his driver to pick up the pace as the daylight began to wane.

"These mountains ahead of us on the frontier of Sussex County are giving me concern," the judge said to his carriage driver. "Unlike Elizabethtown, the land seems to be filled with wild animals, Indians, and Tory bandits."

"Yes sir, Judge Ogden," replied the driver. He gave the two-horse team a holler and a slap of the reigns.

As the carriage rolled along the Morris-Sussex pike, the road became progressively bumpier. The carriage slid sideways as the ruts and potholes became more frequent and deeper. The rocks in the highlands appeared to be more abundant and larger in size than had been evident in the lowland, and the wheels would skid off the sides of the larger, embedded rocks and give the passengers a jolt as the carriage suddenly bounded sideways. Ogden had learned in his studies that most rocks were smoothly rounded by the sculpting of the Ice Age progression over millennia. Many of the stones appeared like nicely formed eggs from some giant bird, but others were squared off and sharp, as if they had been hewn with an ax and chopped off a block of wood. The carriage rocked back and forth with the judge and his wife receiving a physical beating as they were swaying and pounding.

"It is just like rough passage on a small ship, Phoebe. You need not to worry."

"I am frightened, Robert, about other, more surreptitious danger. The unknown out there has me scared. I've always worried that since there are fewer towns up there in Sussex County, we run the risk of meeting up with bandits and Indians. Constables out there are few and far between."

"I dare say," said her husband.

It was true that the Ogdens were cultured and educated and were used to the ways of a larger town, a place and a manner of living that their family had lived for several generations. Ogden realized that this meant they also were unprepared to live life in the more remote regions of the country, in an area where they would face hardship of country living without the finer luxuries available in the city. A short visit could be endured, but it would be quite a change of life to be there permanently.

Ogden knew that their comfortable home in Elizabethtown was becoming unsafe, though. British sympathizers had been growing in number and had been strenuously working against the Patriotic cause. The fact that Judge Ogden was such a highly visible leader in the New Jersey Provincial Assembly had been bringing focus on him personally.

"I do so wish we were going to the city," Phoebe said.

"It's a dangerous time. The Tories are more aggressive with their support of British troops, the same troops who are stationed in nearby Manhattan and Staten Island."

"But I so love our home in Elizabethtown. That is where generations of our family have lived. I'd like for our family to remain there. With the soldiers to back them up, our Loyalist friends find it easy to take the Tory viewpoint and to push their political leanings on us who find the Patriot way a saner choice for the course toward independence and freedom."

Sensing the judge's apprehension over the voyage into the country, Ogden's driver turned to advise the Ogdens of their travel.

"Judge, sir, I want to remain cautious, as your carriage driver, with the coming hills and the unfamiliar territory, so I can't get the team to go any faster," the driver said.

"Understood. Just do the best you can."

The driver's mention of the coming terrain brought the judge back to the moment. The judge looked about him and then back to the familiar Morris County. Journeying north and west would bring a more rustic landscape. The trip revealed frontier and wilderness in a land that was just becoming populated and occupied by mostly British and Dutch peoples from Europe. The natives of the land—the Lenni Lenape—were disappearing. But Ogden understood that the rural life to the west seemed to provide a more independent nature to the inhabitants than the more sophisticated ways nearer the city. A new and different life awaited the Ogdens as they saw the landscape unfold before them on the journey to the western corner of the colony.

"This journey to our country home may be a premonition of the changes we will need to make to be true Patriots as we head into a war."

After some strenuous travel, the Ogdens did make it to their country place. They found that the country home, although crude, was a suitable place to go if, in fact, they had to leave Elizabethtown due to the war. They stayed the night. In the morning, Ogden and Phoebe toured the grounds, as they did every time they went there. The plans were in the works to begin planting for the spring. All hands were on deck to begin the process. The horses had been fed and watered upon their arrival and were now saddled. The carriage was prepared, and Phoebe and Ogden packed their belongings and settled into the carriage. Ogden gazed at his wife and saw the worry in her eyes—for their boys, their two daughters, now married with sons in the army, the pending war, and the changes taking place at their beloved Elizabethtown home.

After a noneventful ride, they settled back into their family home. It was here where they felt most comfortable in their home of many years. They went back to work earnestly, acting as leaders in the community, trying to make Elizabethtown a safe and prosperous place for people to live. The judge had represented the people in the New Jersey Assembly nearby and now was a reputable and honored attorney. But early in the Revolutionary War, while sides were still being taken, the feelings of the populace of Elizabethtown simmered and rose in temper as the town became split between the Loyalists and the Patriots. Judge Ogden worried that with his role in local politics, he would become a target for anti-Patriot sentiment.

On the second evening of their return, Judge Ogden and Phoebe retired after dinner in the well-appointed sitting room with tea

Robert shared with his wife his concerns about the rumblings in town.

"You are a well-respected man, a leader of the community and in a broader sense the colony of New Jersey. It is good that you take a position," said Phoebe to her husband. "I am very proud of you."

"Thank you, dear," the judge said, blushing. He was bashful when praise was heaped on him, although he did take it to heart. Phoebe, however, did add some words that would come back to haunt him.

"But Robert, my dear, your prominent support of the Patriots may cause anger. I do want to ask you; What if a number of people here get angered by our siding with the patriots? What will happen to us and our living arrangements? You know well that many of them want to stay with Britain. Even the reverend at St John's Anglican Church would want you gone."

"I would never allow harm to come to you, my dear Phoebe. If we felt we were in danger, then we would move. It would be a forced change, and one that I would not want to endure. We would have to leave our beautiful homestead and move out to our place in Sussex County. That is precisely why I bought the land on the frontier some time ago. It provides a place for us to retreat from the danger of unruly mobs who might aggressively come after us."

Squeezed into a moral corner, Ogden kept to his conviction about the Patriots and their cause. But he had to decide on alternatives.

Phoebe began to cry. Ogden hated when his wife cried. If he could do anything else, then he would but he believed in the dreams and aspirations of the Patriots. He wanted nothing more than to be free from England.

"I am telling you now, Phoebe," said the judge, softening his voice, "we would certainly take our household items like dinnerware and a few other possessions. We started with barely anything to begin with, and we are still yet young. We can begin again. We will build the plantation up and produce and supply goods to others as well as ourselves. You will see, my dear. It is beautiful there, is it not?"

She nodded, wiping her eyes and smiling bravely.

At this point in the Revolutionary War, there were several deep and complex areas of disagreement. There was no simple answer.

The description in the Declaration of Independence said "all men are created equal," but there was a difference of interpretation for the status of enslaved people. This was true for most of those from the South, and also was true for many of those in the North.

Ogden had to ponder the difficulties and was aware that those looking for independence had to choose between two overarching principles. One was sticking with the "all equal" taken literally and lose some of the thirteen colonies in the movement and the fight for the independence, which would have diluted the message, the mission, and the force behind it, and probably end up with two nations if the Americans won the war. The other choice was having unanimity in the declaration and full strength in the fight against the world's greatest power. It was that course of action that inevitably was the consequence, though the issue, he knew, would not go away. As a compromise on a dilemma that many people took personally and emotionally, the situation would have to be settled ... later. Ogden wasn't sure if this was a mistake or not, and he had no crystal ball to read into the future and see what damage, if any, such a compromise might create.

As summer turned to autumn, life in the village continued on. Community was a strength for all.

The judge went outside of his house, along the neatly arranged wooden fence near the main street in Elizabethtown. Many of the neighbors out on an afternoon walk said hello when they saw him and soon many had gathered outside of the judge's gate.

"We have had a fierce fight so far against the British," said the judge. "I can only imagine how tough it would be if Charleston, South Carolina, and other points south were not with us in the fight and if the British forces were not so spread out as they now are."

One of the men, a tall, well-kept individual named Thornton, agreed. "It would be a much more difficult fight, that is for sure, and the interest and support of foreign nations, like France and Spain, would have been in jeopardy."

Another in the crowd, Jeremiah Strong, an active member in the Assembly, said, "It is a bone of contention, and yet have we met our moral responsibility."

Then, stern Mr. Wells, in a gruff voice, said, "In any event, this is the path we've chosen. That is what we have to live with at this point."

"We must fight for a *united* states," said the judge.

A few of the women, with children, tried to hasten their husbands home.

The judge noticed that while a few of the men nodded, most of the men, silently listening, stared down those who had nodded until all the men stood in a grim agreement. The judge walked back into his home after one of the wives said softly, "If we win the war, *when* we do, we will regret our decisions and leave a calamity for future generations to solve."

Her husband shushed her, and she took her daughter's hand and rushed off with her husband following behind.

Ogden ambled back inside and noticed Phoebe sitting at the table, lost in thought as she absentmindedly polished the silver. When she saw him, she gave him a weary smiled. "We face an imminent necessity of preparing foods for winter, canning the fruits and vegetable from the garden, and preparing jam and other canned goods should we need to leave."

Ogden nodded. "The sheaves from the grain harvest are in the barn," he said absently.

"I fear we may have to leave, Robert," she said.

He touched her gently on the shoulder and looked into her eyes. "It is my hope that we will be able to stay here. If not, then we will leave for Sussex County and make do at our country home."

He then noticed the silver sugar bowl. It was a handsome family heirloom. He told Phoebe that they should be sure to take it with them should they need to leave.

"Yes, Robert," she said. To Ogden, she seemed distracted and worried.

Chapter 6
Ogden Escapes From Elizabethtown, 1777 Summer

"Man's inhumanity to man makes countless thousands mourn!"
– Robert Burns

As the months rolled forward in the year 1777, the Continental Army began to create a powerful presence. The small village of Morristown was inundated with the young men in blue and white uniforms, moving about on their appointed duties. They were building defensive structures on the hill known as Fort Nonsense, gathering provisions to eat and clothe themselves, and looking around and foraging for animals to be used for transport or for riding or eating, and the hay to feed them. As the summer began to wane, Ogden—and others alike preparing for war—began to worry about the cold winter to come.

Some months after Ogden's visit to the Ford Mansion in Morristown, they returned. As the sound of their carriage racing down the lane neared the large, white edifice of the mansion, the life guards came out of their barracks to receive the Ogdens, a normal function in the protection of General Washington, but the air filled with the importance of a pressing visit. When the carriage came to a stop, Robert and Phoebe gathered their things and hurried into the house.

One of the first officers to come upon the carriage was Major Aaron Ogden. He had slowly emerged from the building and looked across the road to see the rush of wheels that approached. Aaron made his way past the horses while they were heaving and gasping for air and through the swelling dust cloud of road dirt as it continued forward before slowly settling. Aaron walked a step or two quicker, trying to catch up as he followed the two into the building.

Major Aaron stopped his father and mother in the main hall of the mansion.

"Father, is that you?" said the major, wiping the grains of the dust cloud from his eyes.

"Yes. Yes, my son. My dear boy," said Judge Ogden.

"Why are you and Mother here? This is an unexpected visit, and you appear disheveled and anxious. What has happened?"

They both looked at their son with wide eyes. The judge took a deep breath, and then exhaled as he looked ahead and said, "We have been run out of town."

"This cannot be true!"

"It is, my son. Our family was expelled from Elizabethtown," said the judge. The words seemed strange to say. He looked at Phoebe dejectedly.

"By the British sympathizers?" Aaron asked, clearly incredulous.

"Indeed, by the very people who were friends and fellow civic partners a few months ago. Those who were at our sides are now at our throats," said the judge, noticeably saddened.

"But, Father, we've been a community with common interests and values for so many years."

Ogden nodded, looking at his wife. "Alas, Now, with the onset of British rule getting stricter, it is like a vice turned too tight for comfort. Pain is now evident, and the citizens of Elizabethtown, as elsewhere, are diverging in their thoughts and acts."

Phoebe had sat down in one of the many chairs lining the entrance hallway as the judge went on.

"Oh no," Aaron said. "This can't be."

"Well, I have been very outspoken toward the Patriot cause," Ogden said. "Since I have been the Speaker of the New Jersey Provincial Assembly, I am highly visible. But as you know, son, we live in a Loyalist area nearby to Manhattan and the British occupation." The judge changed his disposition, just now realizing the grave seriousness of the situation. He was worried about the perils now raining upon him.

Major Aaron Ogden looked with great attention at his father, awaiting more information.

The judge appeared exasperated, perhaps from exhaustion. He looked at his son with helplessness as he explained.

"Recall that when I was the speaker of the Assembly, I was

called to be the New Jersey voice on the hated Stamp Act. When I differed to having the backing of the whole group, I was vilified, and they burned a likeness of me in effigy." Now the judge also had to sit down. "I am weak in the knees about this, but I need to tell you."

"Last night I was reading Aristotle. A wavering yellow light penetrated the shades on my study. The yellow light became brighter, and I could hear talking outside." The judge was uncomfortable in his seat.

"I went to the window to look and saw the crowd outside, in the street right next to my white picket fence. 'There he is! There's Judge Ogden!'" The judge's eyes widened. "I could see that the flicker of yellow was created by torches wavering in the breeze. The crowd seemed to raise their fists in unison to show me that they were angry with me."

"So sad this happened, Father."

"These were friends, people who lived nearby. These were people I grew up with, along with Phoebe. We had shared many memories and happy times. Now, last night, in the center of Elizabethtown, near our home, they began to be violent. At our ancestral home, no less. The Loyalist townspeople got all whipped up and then came by our property. They had turned on me. They were no longer my friends. They did not believe what I believed, that is, to be a Patriot. They showed a side that I had not seen before, one of animosity to me and my ways, my principles, my beliefs. They were burning my crops."

Aaron looked to his mother. Phoebe appeared to be in a mild state of shock.

"How do you fare, Mother?" Major Ogden asked.

She smiled wanly and said, "We knew we had to depart, and to do so as rapidly as we could. If they burned our crops what would be next, losing our lives to them in their whipped-up fury? Now we are weary and anxious having come west on Galloping Hill Road. We followed the path through the Watchung Mountains over Hobart's Gap, along the straight and flat road through the wetlands, and to here at Morristown. It's been a long journey with our necks craned behind us in fear of riders coming to get us."

"Didn't you have supporters? How about the church?" asked Aaron.

"Very little support. No, not even the church supported us," said the judge. He looked down and shook his head in disbelief. Being so deeply religious, this was a serious rebuff.

"My beloved church did not support me. Despite my earnest faithfulness, our Reverend Thomas Bradbury Chandler disavowed me. I had looked to him for spiritual guidance in my time of trial, and he showed me the door."

"This is the rector of our St. John's Anglican Church of Elizabethtown?" Aaron asked.

"Yes," said the judge. "He is an outspoken Loyalist nonetheless."

"This is terrible news," said Aaron looking between his mother and father. "You both look worn and in shock."

"Indeed, we are, son," said Phoebe.

"But at least, Father, you can retreat to the Sparta country home, can't you? With a distance of fifty miles, that places the estate beyond the reach of a quick British raid," Aaron said.

Ogden could see that his son wanted to relieve some of his father's obvious stress.

Aaron had a few minutes with his parents, but he was soon called away on pressing military matters. Over some roasted lamb the night before their departure and while still at the Ford Mansion, the judge said, "I have had the good fortune to rise to the top of respect among the people in Elizabethtown, but now I have fallen from grace to the depths of hostility from amongst many of my friends and neighbors. Once loved, now I am despised in my hometown. I would hate to ever see that happen again with me and my fellow citizens. I can't stand to see the loss of the respect that I work so hard for, over so many years, with my kinsmen and neighbors."

The next morning, the judge and his entourage started out slowly from the stately Ford Mansion. Even though they were very distraught, at least they felt the security of being farther away from the perils of the city and were behind the friendly lines of the Patriots and their Northern Army.

They continued through Morristown and toward the Morris pike to travel northwest on what would one day become a turnpike in the new nation. They made the day-long trip slowly up country to the remote Sussex County land that, though he didn't know it, he would now occupy for the duration of the war.

The Ogdens called for more of their household to come with them. This included several of their slaves to help with the care and upkeep of the land, farm, and dwelling. The household would also have to live more primitively, and they would have to work much harder now. They began to view their homestead in the country more like a plantation, and Ogden would be working hard himself to make the country homestead self-sufficient. He would have a house and outbuildings, a farm for food, and sheep and pigs for meat. Ogden had also come into the possession of a mining option; he owned an iron mine atop Sparta Mountain above his house in Sussex County and would have a forge along the Wallkill River so that he could turn the iron ore rock into usable tools and utensils, a livelihood that was something the British had prohibited and thus knowledge of its existence needed to be closely held.

There were many issues on the judge's mind as he journeyed to the remote area, not the least of which was his need to keep himself and his family safe from harm. This would include his wife, her sister, the children that would come with him, and the farm help and slaves who would follow him.

As the Ogden carriage arrived at the country property, the judge looked at Phoebe, and they both smiled with relief. They had safely arrived at the village that would one day bear their name—Ogdensburg—in the northwest region of the Province of New Jersey.

"Phoebe, my dear," he said. The relief he felt centered in the calm tone with which he spoke. "We are now safe. We are away from the enemy, away from those who would hurt us."

She sighed her relief, but also her anxiety and sadness for having to leave the town she loved.

A short time later, Ogden's slaves, Cuffee[xxi] and Joy[xxii] arrived, as well as six indentured servants who would all become members of the household. Just inside the house, they looked at Judge Ogden for his words on what would be happening now in the new frontier. It was frightening and a big change that they were all, now, on the frontier of New Jersey alone during the Revolutionary War.

The half dozen of his household outside were supplemented by about a dozen of the locals who had come to see the Ogdens move in. The judge rose to his feet and went outside where he surveyed the visitors and household members. After glancing at the wooden frame of his country home, he turned around and looked at the surprisingly large and growing group of people were surrounding their house.

The judge scanned the horizon. Down the Wallkill River Valley to the south lay the roadway from which they had just arrived. Several miles back was the hamlet of Sparta. Sparta was so named by Phoebe. She did so because of the solid standing of the citizens.

He then looked northward toward the few structures on some high ground in the valley that represented what would one day be called Ogdensburg. He looked to the west to see the Pimple Hills and the forerunner of the mine that Lord Stirling owned on Stirling Hill. The mine, if it could provide iron ore or zinc, would be a wonderful way to meet the needs of the Revolutionary War, as well as the Colonies, and in due time, would fatten his own financial holdings. Finally, the judge turned slowly to look toward the east, gazing upward at the long rise up Snufftown Mountain. It was just below the mountain that his own homestead lay. The wooden structure was on a gentle rise above the river and stood at the foot of the steep Sparta Mountain ridge line.

He knew he had to make some clear decisions and explain their situation to his extended family, and to those other people who had come to greet him at his country home. It was not surprising, the gathering crowd. Judge Ogden was well known throughout New Jersey, being a long-term political and religious leader and the leader of the Assembly during this time of great travail. The people here were dependent upon him, some for employment on his farm on the hillside or mine atop Sparta Mountain or at the iron forge along the Wallkill River. He used his voice, and tone, as he would have used it at the body of politics at the royal colony's Assembly. Looking to inform the populace of the area at those who had gathered round, he spoke clearly.

"My fellow citizens, I am comforted," said the judge to his family and the household they brought with them from Elizabethtown to the country.

He could tell every one of his own family that included servants and slaves was fatigued, with most of them having walked the distance of fifty miles. The menace of the Loyalist and British sympathizers in Elizabethtown was stressful; they'd had to leave in haste without most of their prized personal items.

The judge noticed that there were more people gathering. They all stood and waited. Judge Ogden collected his thoughts and constructed the talk that he wanted to have with his extended family and neighbors. They looked upon him with frightened, uncertain, and anxious apprehension and were eager to drink in some words of clarity and direction. The Revolutionary War had made for deadly mystery—there was no telling who was friend or foe. Perhaps, Judge Ogden thought, he could be a pillar of strength to his family and the community of Sparta. They noticed the judge momentarily pause during a long silence. Then he gazed at the now parked carriages that had pulled up to his plantation. Soon Robert was joined by his wife, and the Ogden couple were standing as a pair. Phoebe wore a full casual dress, and the judge was standing erect and polished and had donned his usual professional suit worthy of a respectable leader of the colony. It was a scene frozen in time, he thought, vowing to remember it: the beginning of a new life.

"Welcome all. At least, and at last, we are safe here," said Judge Ogden. "We are away from the dangers of the present age in New York City, where the British have gained a great stronghold and fortressed themselves across the Hudson River in Manhattan. They have a strong connection to their Loyalist sympathizers in Elizabethtown. Just like a nest of hornets. Those British camped on our property and were within a few yards of our home. They watched our every move there in Elizabethtown. The locals of the town were of mixed opinions and strong in that mixture. Thus, we couldn't tell friend from foe. Having had my image burned in effigy and my crops burned, I couldn't stay any longer. And the enemy is much less apt to come for us here. With this distance between us, we should also be safe from the violent opposition members of Elizabethtown.

"I am greatly demoralized, though, by the fact that I once was a leader among the people, a main player in New Jersey, thinking critically of the British presence, and maintaining a command of civic pattern and developed leadership for the colony. That was a short time ago, and now I am a fugitive. I've been run out of town."

***

Some of the women who came with their husbands stood near Mrs. Ogden as she spoke.

"We have a fine cabin. It has now become a safe house for us, just as we hoped when we built it. And we do indeed need it at this time. Where is our builder of the house? Michael Rorick[xxiii]?"

Young Michael Rorick, who lived on the river, had come up to see the Ogdens' arrival.

"I am here," he said.

"Mr. Rorick has done a most excellent job with our home," she said.

A smattering of women nodded, but some stood by with straight faces. Phoebe, as she was looking for Rorick's presence, said, "I see that you women are somewhat baffled by our home. I hope that you all can welcome us."

Mr. Rorick was a thoughtful and skilled builder whose vision for their home had been clearly realized. Rorick was a humble man, quiet and not very assertive. Phoebe said, "I remember hearing you talk to the judge about how you would build the house. You explained why the sawmill was advantageous, and that they would continue to need the ability to cut lumber and square logs for the outbuildings and other quarters for the people working on the plantation. You are a good man who has helped us get established."

The house was indeed a lovely place. It was a large house, with weather boards placed over square logs for the exterior. Phoebe looked around and said, "I love the interior with its elegant wainscoting, and a center hall that runs the length of the house. I am pleased to see that the rose bushes and lilacs are blooming. Behind the dense forest seems to overshadow all the rest of our home and barn. Yes, the dense forest has me fearful of such a dark and mysterious place."

The women who were attending stood still.

"I look forward to entertaining guests," Phoebe said. "I don't want to mention my worry about the rising tension and the deathly war with the British."

Phoebe watched as great activity occurred around the newly occupied homestead in the country. The two slaves removed items from the carriages and carted the food and housewares into the home. Soon, trailing behind them on the roadway, were a couple of farmhands from the city with the animals that they had from Elizabethtown. These men and women would tend to the oxen, sheep, and pigs during the family's time in the country.

Several horses used for work around the farm as draught animals arrived and needed to be stabled. The animals were moving about, uncertain of their new surroundings and anxious from their long journey up from the city along the rough roads to the emptiness of the country.

***

The people of the village, citizens who were mostly farmers, were also mixed in with some men who worked as miners at the Sterling Mine (named for Lord Stirling whose name was constantly spelled wrong) and whose ragged clothing reflected the work they did by chipping away the rock in search of iron and zinc. They locals came with their wives. The women also brought their children, and many carried their infants in their arms while other, older children tagged along by the hand or underfoot. Word traveled fast among the small community. They had come to see the Ogdens, whom they hardly knew. The town had previously been the site of secretive visits by Lord Stirling, who was serving as a general for the Continental Army and owned the one mine in area. Another noted Patriot, Lord Morris, from nearby, had also recently moved and retained his importance as a signatory to the Declaration of Independence. With the iron on the upward reaches of his acreage, Judge Ogden now possessed important resources to add to his own importance of being a fervent Patriot.

The crowd listened earnestly, though some in the back tended to hide shyly behind the folks in the front. Parents who appeared to hold onto every word Ogden said were pleased, and their young were encouraged by their parents to listen as Ogden spoke. Attention was drawn to the front of the crowd, toward the Ogdens, but most of the townspeople seemed to be keenly looking at and listening to the judge. The younger men seemed most interested, as they approached the age when they most needed role models, and they were most likely the first ones to be called into action with the enemy.

Most of the citizens of the Sparta area to the southward were Patriots. But there were others, men who were quieter and who sympathized with the British. Though Robert and Phoebe didn't know it, amongst them were two men, both of them secretly suspected as being sympathizers. It was men like these who were likely considering turning the Ogdens' whereabouts into the British authorities.

After they had finished greeting their neighbors, the Ogdens mingled with them while others in the small group gossiped amongst themselves.

"He is tall and alert, competent and confident, just like I thought he'd be," said one man with dried hay all over his rough outer garments, obviously a farmer.

"Yup," said another, a man who was covered in dirt, carrying a pickaxe and candle, traits of a miner. "I have heard about the man."

He shuffled from side to side with his dirty trousers and calloused hands gripping the pick. "He looks to be cultured and well-mannered. I can see why he has been a colony legislative leader. He is also very believable. And we do need our freedom from the British."

"Yes," said the farmer. "I would take his word at what he says."

"Right," said another man, standing immediately in front of the two, who owned the dry goods store. He was portly and a little better dressed than most of the others, with clean clothes and a close shave. "I would take what he said as true. He definitely is an honest man."

Then there was a group of folks at the back. They glared, arms folded across their chests. These were not Patriots.

Lieutenant Moody and Lowery hung in the back of this group of men, whispering.

What they said was heard by no one, but Ogden spotted them in the back and knew they were not sending good will. There were also what looked like other ne'er-do-wells. Ogden didn't know that one of them was a well-known bandit named Claudius Smith, but he suspected they might be skinners or something of equal bad will.

Ogden appeared to be alarmed when there were some in the back of the crowd who seemed to have spotted and kept their eye on the silver chalice that was being removed from one of the carriages that had rolled up near the dwelling containing the Ogden home goods. The judge looked at Phoebe, and they both appeared uncomfortable at this sighting.

Chapter 7
Passing by of Pastor Constant Hart

"Vice does not lose its character by becoming fashionable."
– John Wesley

The Ogden family settled in for the duration in the quieter and more remote countryside.

On one of the first days at the country home, Judge Ogden received company. He rose from his creaky rocking chair where he was warming up beside the fire. As he stepped forward, the rocker kept moving, swaying on its own for a while. He walked the short distance to the wooden frame door, responding to the sound of a tap on the wood. He lifted the latch and saw the light from the day enter in. There were two figures standing, looking at him. Though he didn't know them, Ogden believed they were friendly.

"May I help you?" he said.

The shorter figure was a man in a black coat and light gray hair. He stood erect and carried himself with the air of graciousness. He was impeccably dressed; the white collar that he wore beneath his finely woven white blouse revealed that he was a man of the cloth, a reverend.

By his side was a taller and well-proportioned young woman of about thirty years old. She was attractive with a good build and curly red hair that seemed tightly woven. She was carrying cheese.

The young woman grinned and then spoke. "My name is Molly[xxiv]. I work at Kelly's Tavern just to the north of here at Franklin Furnace Pond. I also work at Morrisvale, Mr. Morris' country home here. I bring greetings, Judge Ogden, with salutations from Lord Lewis Morris." She curtsied with the bundle in her arms. "Mr. Morris says that he welcomes you to the area here in Sussex County. I bring you this cheese from his farm."

"Ah, thank you for the delivery," said the judge graciously. He appreciatively smelled the cheese.

Molly smiled again.

"Indeed," said the judge, "you must thank him for me."

"Certainly, sir," she said. Molly then provided a curious addition. "Be wary of strangers, Judge, and those who might be in the taverns."

The judge was uncertain of what to make of this. He became suspicious of Molly.

The short man alongside her then stepped forward. He removed his hat and bowed slightly.

"Good afternoon, Judge. I am Pastor Constant Hart[xxv] of the Baptist Church here in Hardyston Township, wherein your property lies. I met the good Molly along the way from the Morrisvale farm and so of course came along with her to your house. I want to welcome you to the area myself."

"Thank you, Pastor Hart. As a fellow Christian, I am willing to help with preaching up here, to provide good examples of morality."

"And well we are all aware, Judge," said the pastor. "You are known far and wide as a devout man of faith and one who lives good Christian morals."

"Please," Ogden said, acting a bit humbly and lowering his head as he was opening the door wider, "come in."

"Just for a moment. I am passing by on my priestly rounds, as I am a traveling pastor, an itinerant minister serving as a circuit rider. I am trying to serve all of the countryside." He shook the judge's hand. "I want to thank you for helping out with the sermons that you may provide to the locals. I have heard about your stirring sermons. You have helped me in my job by your preaching. You are a good and righteous Christian from all that I have heard."

"Oh, thank you. Those are the kindest words that can be said to me. My faith in the Lord is my strongest attribute. But, with these times, I feel so much is lost at this point. Lost are the treasures of my home, my respect in the city, and my leadership in politics. I don't even feel safe, and more to the point, I have been accosted in my home city."

"Judge, always remember that despite earthly problems and threats, you are safe in the presence of God."

"Yes, of course. But it fills me with some fear as my home and my hay was burned in the city, and our reputation has been squandered. Townspeople have burned my representation in effigy for thoughtful decisions I have made that did not suit them."

"Despite all that, my suggestion is that above all, try to be sincere, and be honest." Pastor Hart gripped his cap with both hands a little harder. Though he provided comfort, he seemed upset about the hostilities Odgen was revealing.

"I try to be honest."

"Continue to do so. With honesty, I believe you will uphold the stature of a righteous man. By doing so, respect for you will be regained, and it will grow beyond yourself to others, and to the end that they may reflect the same honesty that you would consistently display."

"Yes, you are right," said Ogden piously.

"Be humble. Be gentle. And be patient, my dear Judge."

"Thank you, sir, for the comfort," said Ogden, his head slightly bowed in modesty.

Molly had been led to the kitchen to prepare some food and to present the fine fresh cheese from Morrisvale.

"Try, dear Judge, to live in a manner worthy of the call you have received—as judge and lay minister."

"I shall, and will do, to the best of my ability," said the judge. He knew that people called him Honest Ogden, but he didn't dare bring that up for fear of appearing boastful.

"By doing so, you will be comforted within, and you will be happy."

"I have just lost the respect of all those fellow citizens in Elizabethtown due to my Patriotic leanings. I don't hold out much for happiness as the war progresses and my faith."

"There are many evils in this world to pressure the people who dwell here."

Ogden looked harder at Pastor Hart.

"I agree with you, Pastor Hart. It is good to love one another. It is also bad to be tempted, to give in to evil."

"Things could always be worse. Do not be tempted. One could lose one's soul."

The judge had rarely heard so profound words as this.

***

On Sundays, the ever mindful and deeply religious Judge Ogden began to preach to his family and household who were present at the Sparta home. In town, Ogden invited neighbors to join his family. Since there were no churches in the area at the time, and because of Ogden's knowledgeable sermons and a display of his dedication to the Christian ethic, other neighbors began to hear about these evenings and decided to come as the months went on. Ogden's sermon would become an anticipated event, and his home became the meeting house for the faithful.

Steeped in the Gospel and passionate in his faith, Ogden read frequently about the various tales in the Bible. In his daily readings, Ogden seemed to favor the book of Daniel. He often opened to Chapter 5 and began preaching. A highlight of his church service was the Presbyterian distribution of the sacraments—the communion and the dedication of the Eucharist. For this purpose, Ogden used his cherished silverware, including his finely ornamented sterling silver chalice for the wine. The beautiful cup required no cleaning, as it didn't tarnish because zinc had been added to the copper and silver amalgam. The cup shined brightly, just as Judge Ogden's prestige shone with the luster of his ancestral heritage, and just as how his pride remained above the merits of the common man, unblemished or besmirched, containing the virtues of a good and moral life. The chalice exemplified the character of Robert Ogden II as The Honest Judge.

Although he normally felt refreshed and accomplished after the sermon, one Sunday after the faithful departed, the judge seemed disturbed.

"What's bothering you, dear?" said Phoebe.

"I noticed that one of the faithful spilled the sacramental wine today and left behind a stain."

"A clumsy neighbor," said Phoebe. "It should not be a problem. It will easily be cleaned out of the wood."

"Indeed, yet one should take care with the serious matter of taking the Eucharist."

"Of course, dear, but I wouldn't get worked up on it. People are prone to mistakes. Are you bothered by something else?"

"I worry that my God has found my own kingdom wanting, and

that He will number my kingdom and He will divide it, and He will put an end to it."

"Oh dear," said Phoebe. "Isn't that a little wild that in your reading of the Bible you are placing it on yourself personally?"

"We have seen this affecting us already in Elizabethtown. Our home is now gone, and we are left out here on the frontier. Even the rector in my home church has banished us for my leanings toward the Patriots."

"Oh, dear Judge Ogden," Phoebe said, using the name affectionately. "You are just tired from the sermon and fatigued from worry. We took a long trip just over a short month ago and we are still adjusting. Why don't you rest?"

"Phoebe, I just don't know. I sometimes feel as if I am frail and faltering. I feel like a failure having lost our home in the city, my positions of authority, and now in place of respect there is foment and disgust that many of those from Elizabethtown are exacting upon us."

Ogden looked over to the cabinet and saw the freshly polished silver chalice. He thought to himself, *We must take great care with that chalice. It is my link to our heritage.*

Chapter 8
Settling in at Ogdensburg

*"There is a pleasure in the pathless woods,
There is a rapture on the lonely shore,
There is society, where none intrudes"*
– Lord Byron

The distraught behavior of the judge continued for some time. "Phoebe, I am beside myself with grief about the loss of our home in Elizabethtown."

"I know, my dear, I know." Phoebe leaned his head onto her shoulders as he wrung his hands in desperation.

"I wonder if we will be able to settle down out here in Sussex County, far from the social life of the city, far from friends and family in our home area, far from the news of Europe and the civilized world."

Aware of the judge's association of life with the Bible, Phoebe said, "I think of Romans 13:10," as she leafed through the family Bible that they both cherished. She smiled as she found what she wanted to show him.

"This Bible verse may calm you, dear: You shall love your neighbor as yourself. Love does no evil to the neighbor; hence, love is the fulfillment of the law. Do you think so?"

"It is, it is," said the judge as he carefully sat himself in a nearby chair. "I find it hard to see the result of my diligent effort, my tireless work to help our land be free of British control, only to find that people have disagreed with me and in fact have thrown us out of our home and burned our crops. It demoralizes me."

"Surely this is God's work, and we do not know His plans for us yet," said Phoebe.

"That may be true. What makes it so much harder for me is to forgive those who have wronged us, and they continue to do so." He stood and put his hands on his hips. "I am a Christian with Christian values, but if I am wronged, can I forgive while it still continues?" He seemed perplexed.

Judge Odgen was at least grateful that he had built a warm country home and had purchased the land in the country years before, in 1777. As the war years progressed, the family became familiar with their new surroundings. The plantation was fully functioning and self-sufficient. The sheep grazed on the hillside, and the corn grew high. Phoebe became content with her broad garden, one of flowers and vegetables. Atop the steep hill, Ogden's workers were mining iron ore that was smelted and forged down slope along the Wallkill River. As the years went by, Judge Ogden took much comfort on the growing respect of his ways of right and of being honest. It had turned out that this was good preparation because they now needed the Sussex County home for their safety and well-being.

Along with the carriage driver, William Johnson[xxvi], the Ogdens were attended by their children and others who worked on the plantation.

Ogden often thought about his two sons who were not with them. Major Aaron was in the life guards, and Lieutenant Colonel Matthias Ogden was carrying on with other Patriotic duties near Morristown. He was also aware of the goodness of the earth in the northwestern fringes of the Province of New Jersey. The resources that lay beneath the forested slopes of the mountains and valleys contained very valuable ores. The hard rocks were in various forms of important and essential building blocks of society: iron and zinc. While some was difficult to mine and process, some of the ore was easily available; in fact, some could be obtained from outcrops visible on the surface and easily picked up by a passerby. These ores were also readily mined in shallow pits where the ore veins protruded from the land. The iron ore on Judge Ogden's land seemed to be endless, and he would like to take advantage of the economics associated with it as much as possible. Sale of the ore was complicated by the market conditions as they always affected sales. It was also at the mercy of the Tory sympathizers who would want to disrupt production. There were also labor shortages for the tough job of mining and smelting ore.

The difficulties with the mines reflected, in a similar way, the ebb and flow of life for the Ogdens. They had been successful and loved in the city, found hardship in the country, but overcame this by hard work and honesty. As a whole, Ogden began to see that the new life in the frontier and on the plantation was good.

One evening as they sat and had some tea by the fire, Phoebe said to her husband, "Judge, I feel that we are lucky people."

"Yes," he said, his spirits having begun to lift. "I can still help to carry on the right ways through my work as being a judge. I can also write. I feel that writers are the custodians of memory, and maybe I can carry on the ways of today through writing, through story."

"Greater than many of your thoughts is the fact that, my dear, it is by the grace of God that we are alive and well." She looked at her husband, somewhat concerned. "Isn't that worth so much to you, dear?"

"Though I worry about my legacy," said the judge, "my life, in summary, has been good. I would like to be remembered, when I am gone, as a good man."

"I believe you will," said Phoebe.

Chapter 9
Church Service

"Nothing sets a Christian so much out of the devil's reach than humility."
– Jonathan Edwards, American revivalist preacher during the Great Awakening

It was around dawn on a Sunday, the birds around the country home were awakening, and the land stirred with life. The judge was up early too. He was leafing through the Ogden family Bible trying to find the notes he'd written the night before for his morning sermon. The judge was preparing to open his home for church. Where a church building did not exist, the judge offered his home as a meeting house for Christians to grow in their faith.

Several members of the community surrounding Ogdensburg were coming in a group to the Ogden home. They were grateful for the judge, who they considered a just and wise man. They hoped for some direction, some way to understand and place meaning on their world, aggrieved as they were by war and division.

Ogden saw the men and women arriving to his home from down the lane for the morning service. The folks streamed into the home and sat on the chairs and benches that scattered about the room. Phoebe greeted everyone entering while the judge rehearsed what he was to say during the sermon. When the time came that morning, Judge Robert Ogden II addressed the gathering. He stood erect, and the faithful saw how tall he was, how his towering physical presence was reflected in his lofty and strong grasp of his faith.

"Greetings to all of the Christian church, and welcome to my humble home here on the frontier," said the judge.

There were twenty or so local souls who came to join in the religious service and talk with their neighbors. It was a friendly gathering.

Near the back, Ogden noticed two newcomers. He would have to remind Phoebe to help him in welcoming them. They looked the worse for wear, with dirty and time-worn clothing. They must have hard jobs, but their demeanor portrayed a surreptitious element to their ways. Although at a church service, their shifty eyes and anxious feet made one feel that perhaps they may have lived on the side of immorality. But the judge couldn't be sure and believed that, in the end, they would be converted to a new way of living, to prosperity in an honest day's work and to the lasting friendship that could be had among the faithful.

As the service began, the judge said, "The Lord be with all of you, my guests."

"And also with you," said the congregation in unison.

The judge recited a line from Matthew 23: "For they preach but they do not practice."

Later, when it was time, he said, "Let us share in communion." Phoebe passed the silver chalice that had been in their family for generations, and the worshippers were solemn and devout in their participation.

***

As the service was beginning, on a bench near the wall, an elderly local widow, hunched over as she was, looked up to see one of those scruffy men. A talkative woman, she asked a few questions, looking to create an atmosphere of friendliness and good neighbors. Exchanging pleasantries, a conversation that seemed to have been pried from him, the couple of audible sounds elicited from him were a weak staccato.

"The name's Claudius Smith[xxvii], ma'am." He wiggled a little and squirmed down the bench, which put some social distance between he and the widow. Without calling too much attention to himself, Smith clandestinely searched the room with an inquisitive eye. As the cup came around, his eyes lit up. He gazed at his friend beside him, and they both knew that a scheming idea had taken hold between them.

What Judge Ogden, busy in the front of the room with his religious service, didn't know was that Claudius Smith was growing famous—or should we say notorious, as an outlaw. Born in Brookhaven, New York, in 1736, Smith moved with his family to

Orange County, New York, in 1741. Thought to have fought with Mohawk leader Joseph Brandt[xxviii] as a Tory defender of the crown during the New York campaign of 1777, Smith earned the label "Cowboy of the Ramapos" for his use of guerrilla tactics against Patriot civilians. Smith and his cohorts stole livestock and ambushed travelers on the Orange Turnpike between Canada and New York from the cave now which would one day be memorialized as "Claudius Smith's Den" in Orange County's Harriman State Park.

The "cave" that was Smith's den for robbing was another unknown element to Ogden. The cave was nearby in the primitive rugged mountains and wilds to the north over the state line.

When the cup came to Claudius and his cohort, Richard Morgen[xxix], Claudius passed.

"No thanks," he said softly but decisively.

Smith was worried the judge had noticed, but he hadn't. The judge's voice in the distance up front broke the relative silence. "May our spirit for the cause of liberty and freedom be among us," said the judge.

"Yes," came the collective word from the enthusiastic crowd.

"There is a spirit of restlessness, of a freedom of will and ability with us here," said the judge, "and we need our liberty to enjoy this."

Again, the congregation enthusiastically supported the idea, and "ayes" were heard around the room. Neighbor looked to neighbor, as if a whispered secret was traveling around the room.

But in the back, though, Smith and Morgen were having none of this. Smith and Morgen were surreptitiously spying on the service, trying to figure out the layout of the house. Eyes scanned the room from the back. Smith spotted the pretty girl he'd met a few days before at Kelly's Tavern. She was the same girl who'd delivered the cheese to Ogden previously, and she also worked at Kelly's Tavern as a waitress. Smith knew from what she'd told him that she was an eager worker, being a recent Irish immigrant and indentured servant but required to pay off her passage to the New World. Smith was certain she'd remember him when he asked questions about the Patriots in the area and felt that they'd made a connection. They held their gazes for a moment until Molly turned away and listened to the judge's homily on equality and justice and the will of God. Smith felt that she recognized him but not enough so to make an impact. At least not at this time.

***

At the end of his sermon, before he closed the service, Judge Ogden asked if there were any question from the people who'd attended. The crowd had been very attentive. But shyness took over the room, and soon the congregants stood up to leave, following Smith and Morgen who both walked quickly to the door and led the congregation out of the house.

As the room emptied, the neighbors and guests went their own way to honor the Lord's Day, strolling along and chatting about the happenings in the hamlet, how harvest was going on the farms, and of current events in the war. Phoebe was busy as she helped prepare the Sunday dinner for the family.

"All seemed to go well," said the judge, coming into the kitchen carrying a book. "A couple of new neighbors were here, having moved into the hamlet, and are now helping with the mining operations. Strong mining men. But did you see those two fellows in the back?"

Distractedly, Phoebe nodded and said calmly, "Indeed, I thought they seemed a little strange. When I tried to introduce myself to them, and to bring them by to meet you, they rushed out."

"It's very strange," said Ogden.

Phoebe wiped her hands on her apron and said, "Well, we see many new people to the area. What book do you have in your hands now?"

"It is a book by Watts. It's called *Logic, or The Right Use of Reason in the Enquiry After Truth With a Variety of Rules to Guard Against Error in the Affairs of Religion and Human Life, as Well as in the Sciences.*"

"Well, that is quite a title, Robert."

"Indeed, it is," said the judge, smiling. He and his wife shared a small laugh. Then the judge said, "It sounds like 'reason in the enquiry after the truth' are right up my area of interest."

With that, the judge went into his study to read about the lessons of virtue.

Chapter 10
Attackers at the Door, Winter 1778

xxx

O whil'st I live, this grace me give,
I doing good may be,
Then death's arrest I shall count best,
because it's thy decree.
– Puritan Anne Bradstree, American Poet

    Winter crept in like a quiet and slow-moving shadow and brought a slowdown to the activities of the war. The chill and intimation of cold rain, ice, and snow had slipped to the forefront of mind, with the need to wear thick clothing, remain out of the wind, and generally hunker down for the season. As winter set in, the cold gripped the land, and the first frost fell upon the fallow farms and forest. As the change in weather took hold, the judge and his family had also begun to settle into their home in the country. The warmth of the fire and the balm of knowing they were surrounded by friends and family helped sooth the pain of the cold winter season.
    One day in the midst of winter, the judge peered out from the window looking downhill toward the road. He pondered the ways of nature, the way that seasons roll forward in a cycle through the year. People come into the world, grow up, and then leave the stage of life. Human seasons and those of nature repeat through the eons. As the winter sun lightly patted his brow with warmth, he noticed two men walk slowly by while looking toward his country home. They stopped and pointed his way. He realized these were the same two who had come to his recent Sunday service, dallying about on the road below. They were eyeing the Ogden home. The judge walked

outside to see if he could help.

Raising his hand in a wave, he said, "Did I not see you some time ago, at my worship meeting here?"

The men clearly had not expected the judge to see them.

"Oh, yes. That was I," said one.

Right away Ogden noticed that the man was rough around the edges. "What brings you to the area? We haven't met yet."

"Home," said the man. Ogden was aware of the man's strange, high-pitched voice. "I travel often between here and New York City."

"What is your name?" Ogden asked.

"I'm Smith, and this here is Morgen."

The judge nodded. "I am Judge Ogden."

The men seemed shifty to the judge. He knew there were many Loyalists in the area. He remembered the warning of the highway robbers. He wondered if these two men were there to bring danger.

"I am just passing through," said the man called Morgen. The other man, Smith, was turned totally in the other direction, watching a flock of geese fly overhead toward the zinc mine on the far mountain.

***

The fire burned in the fireplace sizzling with flame, producing a hot heat to the face and emanating the comfortable smell of wood smoke. The house smelled fragrant. It brought to mind the warmth of a stove and the coziness of a close friendly family on a cold winter's day. Basking in the glow of the hearth was the round iron kettle, blackened from extended use, hanging from the swinging iron hook that was crusted with soot. A stew of beef and carrots simmered in the pot. The scent was inviting, and as he came back into the house, Ogden could almost taste the broth on his tongue. The Ogden family were all looking forward to a late winter's evening and a hearty dinner. Phoebe, an excellent cook and even better baker, made a hearty broth with all kinds of filling, including turnips and onions soaking into the broth along with the dark tender chunks of lamb.

"I am growing to love it up here in Sussex County, and I take comfort that I am staying here in safety with you, my husband," said Phoebe as she rubbed gravy on her apron and waited for the stew to cook.

The judge knew she was referring to the neighbors and how they seemed of good intent. Referring to several youths who were prominent in the area, Phoebe offered compliments about them. "This is a healthy and happy land where our country home is located. We have such wholesome neighbors here in the valley."

"Yes, I think you are correct, Phoebe," the judge said.

"Why, think of those two youths Daniel Talmadge[xxxi] and Nathaniel Wade[xxxii]. They are both so kind and friendly, hard-working and industrious." She was speaking of two youth from down the road toward the hamlet of Sparta.

The judge considered the thought of Sparta and the Spartan spirit. These two boys, Daniel and Nathan, were hard workers in their own right. They worked breaking rocks at the Ogden iron mine atop the mountain, and for Lord Stirling at his zinc mine down the hill and on the western side of the Wallkill River. Ogden knew that the boys enjoyed their training with the militia, at the parade grounds up in Wallings, above the Sharpsboro forge, at the 2nd Regiment Sussex Militia barracks. He thought about how they represented the best of what could be found in the frontier land, handling themselves with physical strength and the honor of working diligently. They contained the industriousness of holding several jobs and exhibited what was to be known as the Yankee ingenuity with their novel ways of hauling timber down the hillside on wooden sleds.

The homey conversation continued between husband and wife, and Phoebe's sister, while out in the kitchen there was a rather large fire present in the fireplace, with yellow flames sprouting up from the wood as if reaching for the top. The stew continued to cook in the hot kettle in the hearth. The pot swung slightly back and forth as the flames beneath it brought the soup bubbling to a simmer while the contents continued to the cook. The home was nicely attired with neat horizontally positioned weather boards on the exterior.

The room seemed ornate as the walls were plastered and nicely adorned with wainscoted panels of woodwork which provided a textured appearance. To Phoebe and the judge, the house felt like a warm country castle. All around them, the dense woods went on for miles. Few people had ventured to move there yet. Phoebe oversaw the garden and the lawn. She worked hard to make the home comfortable and elegant.

The judge was a deeply religious Presbyterian and had worked hard to become an Elder in the church. This in addition to being a sociable man of society, he entertained frequently. One evening a clergyman, Reverend Jim Hawkins[xxxiii] had been to the home enjoying a warm dinner and good company. He was taken by the splendid ornamental shrubs. The clergyman noted, "Mrs. Ogden, you have made the wilderness to bloom as a rose."

***

Beyond this beautiful interlude in the dense forest was a land rising to meet the steep slope of Snufftown Mountain. The copse of trees uphill from the house ascended Snufftown Mountain, much like a blanket creeping uphill to cover the stony slopes. The cool, yellow sun crept over the sky, bringing behind it a chilly evening as the sun eased its way westward to settle down behind the distant mountain behind Lord Stirling's zinc mine. The snow still held to the ground in this early March, while higher sun during the day held the hint of the change of weather. Within the Ogdens home, the extended family sat down and enjoyed a warm fire and the savory, tasty lamb stew.

The dampness in the air seemed biting. There was a distinct sharpness in the surroundings as the breeze touched the skin. This was the edge of the cold that imbued the early spring. The stark environment was exaggerated by the spires of the evergreen trees that reached toward the blue sky, barely allowing the sun to penetrate. Winter ever so grudgingly began to turn and yield its authority. Ogden knew that this time of year you had to look for consolation from within and find gratitude in the surrounding love of family and friends.

The judge took a late afternoon stroll as a release from the stuffy hours. He walked around the immediate area of the home, just out by the nearby sheds with livestock and supplies. Ogden stood outside by the barn and paused for a moment. He thought he heard a sound coming from off across the open field and near the tree line. He leaned into the sound but then heard nothing, only the deep silence of the surrounding forest, the evergreens standing stiff like proper sentries surrounding a castle. When he was sure he heard nothing else, he returned to the house to warm up. A breeze had taken up, and now a winter wind blustered through the property from the west, sweeping the light snow cover around like it was a dusty patch.

Those evergreens wavered in the wind as if losing their concentration of being silent guardians. The sun was lower in the western sky and the waning light sharply defined the gray mountains and woods. As he approached the house, Ogden heard an unusual sound as if someone were chopping wood.

When he rounded the corner of the home, he saw the reason for this drumbeat. Three men were banging on the door of his home. The men were bundled against the cold, and they wore scarves around their faces, so he could not make out their features. The men didn't wait for anyone to answer the door. They pushed it together, and finally the weight of their bodies slamming against the door broke the lock apart. The door quickly swung open and rocked back and forth on the hinges.

The three men barged into the home. The judge rushed in and saw Phoebe and her sister sitting calmly by the fire. But by the time he could get to them, they had seen the intruders and were startled. Faces obscured by scarves revealed stern eyes which peered outward and pierced the home as if a sword slitting linen.

"What is going on here?" Robert shouted.

They turned to see him standing by the entrance of the room.

"Where's the money? We know you brought it up from Elizabethtown."

"What do you mean, sirs?" the judge said as calmly as he could. He knew not to rile them up any further.

"We overheard you in town talking about bringing your currency with you. We know you were given money for purchasing provisions for the Continental Army."

The eyes of the three men began roaming again, searching around the room. "We will have a look around for ourselves."

"Don't be ridiculous," Ogden said. "There is no currency here, and I am not funding the army."

Ogden felt that he knew of these men. Then he put it altogether. Smith, the one who had said his name prior. The same man who came to the service and with whom he'd spoken by the road. But now he knew. This was Claudius Smith, the Cowboy of the Ramapos. How had he not put it all together? And the other man ... was that Moody? Moody, the well-known and feared Loyalist who was often spotted in the area of Sussex County. Of course. He felt instantly the deep pain of his naïveté, thinking only good of all people during a time of rancorous war, rather than acting smart. He knew that Smith and his men had strong Tory leanings; that they took from the locals and kept whatever plunder they obtained for themselves. Now he stood by while his wife and her sister clung to each other in fear. He did not know the third man, but he would soon discover his name was Lowery.

"Hush, my dear," Ogden said to his wife as calmly as he could muster. "I will put a stop to this."

The two women stood up and gathered near each other. Ogden signaled toward the kitchen and the three of them slowly retreated into a corner of the kitchen near the fireplace, frightened and shaking. The burly men went down the hallway and into each of the four rooms on the main floor. At first somewhat careful, by the time robbers got to the last room, they were showing their anger in the way they thrust the personal items across each room. They would find no money. Ogden had been telling the truth. There was none to be had. But as they got to the dining room, they did see fine silverware. All three men recognized the sterling silver chalice, in normal use being a sugar bowl, used at the church services that took place in the Ogden home.

Two of the men arrived in the kitchen and grabbed the judge, clutching him by the collar. The family was aghast at the violence. One of the men—it was Moody, as the judge now knew the look of the man's eyes from behind the scarf—was about to shoot from a pistol, pouring in some gunpowder on the frizzen plate and pulling back the hammer with a click. The judge's eyes widened. Screams from the women arose with a deadly shriek.

A brief silence issued forth, then a moment later, a distant voice could be heard.

"Hey, come on down to the cellar," yelled one of the others. His loud, high-pitched voice was unmistakable. "I found the whiskey!"

Seemingly saved, the grip to his neck loosened, and the judge's heels again rested on the floorboards of the kitchen. The freebooters grabbed a candle for light in the growing darkness, and they dragged the judge around with them, this time by the scruff of hair on his head, under the observation of the barrel of the pistol. Determined, they then shoved the judge down to the cellar below. Hands on his shoulders, they pushed him onto a seat he had made himself from a log he'd found on the property. He sat, frightened for his life, while they looked at him with what seemed to be one common deadly eye.

The keg of whiskey that Ogden kept in the cellar was to serve guests. The barrel was nearly full as he, himself, drank very infrequently. The damp, dark room had been hand dug from the earth, with dirt walls; everything remaining unfinished but for a rudimentary floor of milled lumber that had been left from the building of his house. In the corner was Phoebe's impressive root cellar, with her bottled sauces and jams and jellies, and the potatoes, turnips, onions, and other rooted food stacked neatly along the shelves that he been roughly made.

The men sat down and helped themselves to some liquor. That's when Ogden learned the third man was named Lowery as Smith called him out. Moody grabbed Smith by the collar and hissed, "No names."

But it was too late. Now the judge knew the three men were Moody, Lowery, and Smith. They had tied Ogden up and secured him to one of the shelves his wife used to store goods for the winter. After a time, the bonds were gripping the judge painfully. Ogden listened as Smith, whose senses had been loosened by the liquor, began to detail his exploits for the Tories. He told of the number of cattle he'd stolen and handed over to the British, of the silver and coins he'd stolen and given to his Tory commanders. He spoke jauntily about how he had terrorized the Whig population of Orange County for the last several years. He told his two companions about the British who kept sending him out to do harm to the Patriots and destabilize any colonial strength and morale they could find. From these unlawful and heinous crimes, Ogden knew they were not respectable men, but thieves who had degenerated into a band of outlaws out for personal gain and the settling of personal animosities.

The judge kept his mouth shut. He was afraid for his life. He now remembered about James Moody, "that villain" as George Washington had once called him.

Ogden cursed himself for not putting it together earlier. In fact, he knew a lot about James Moody, as he was a thorn in the side of Washington's plans. He knew that Moody was a genius spy, and someone who personally took it upon himself to intercept important mail from and to General Washington.

He heard the story about Moody who had been living with his family on a five-hundred-acre farm owned in his father's name, but for his use. Ogden had been told that a Patriot militia came to Moody's family house to arrest him because he refused to give up his allegiance to Britain and swear loyalty to the United States. Shots were fired, but Moody managed to escape. In April 1777, he joined the New Jersey Volunteers [xxxiv], part of the group of Loyalists who wanted to remain part of the British Empire, under the command of General Cortlandt Skinner[xxxv]. So far, the revolutionary forces had failed to capture him.

Lowery said, "Are you still planning on kidnapping the new Patriot governor William Livingston from his home?"

Moody said, "Quiet man. What is wrong with you?"

Smith said, "You drink too much."

"I wouldn't talk," said Lowery to Smith. "You criticized too much. Moody here told me himself about his plans to kidnap the governor."

"Shut your face," Moody said.

Something about the tone of his voice must have frightened Lowery, because he did shut his mouth after that. But Ogden saw Moody eye him, and he felt afraid. This was no information he wanted to know, valuable information that could put his life more in danger because of inadvertently shared secrets.

Ogden tried to pretend not to listen. This information, he realized, could summon his death. Moody, he realized, must have been behind the interception of the messenger's notes to Washington. Ogden feared that Moody would do worse. Meanwhile, he worked at freeing his hands and feet, and began to feel the rope around his wrists coming lose. Soon enough, he knew he was able to slip out of them. But he needed to keep the ropes on and later surprise Moody and Smith with being free.

At one point, as the men all sat in front of the altar of their booze and poured, Ogden quickly cut the ropes around his feet, returned the knife to the pocket of his breeches, and left the ropes where they were so as not to alert the three thieves. During that time, the thieves who had gathered all the silver that Ogden used for his church services began to search for a bag or something to put them in. They found an old sack of potatoes, emptied the potatoes on the ground and put the silver in the sack.

"Drink to that," said one of them. They sat back down, and Smith continued on his monologue, which, after a while of listening, just confirmed for Ogden that Smith was an arrogant and cruel man who could think of no one but himself.

He said, "You find me indispensably shrewd and brilliant, don't you, Moody?"

The third man, Lowery, laughed, but Moody stood up. "Shut up, you drunken fool."

The other man looked somewhere in the middle distance, and Ogden could see how much he wanted to laugh.

"Did you know," Lowery said, "that Moody is planning to sneak into Philadelphia and steal the important documents written and signed by the Continental Congress?"

"I did not know," Smith said. "He may end the Revolutionary War by stealing all those signed documents. By stealing the very reason for the war itself."

The men, a little drunk, burst out in laughter. But Moody stood up.

"Damned fools," he said. "Shut your mouth, both of you."

Then, Moody looked at Ogden like he wanted to kill him. Ogden gazed back, realizing that he should not show the fear he felt.

"Now he knows," Moody said. "So, we have to kill him."

The men cursed. This, Ogden thought, was the problem with alcohol consumed with no care or thought to its effects. Now, their drunken mouths had put him in a desperate position. Ogden thought of his two sons, two strong, patriotic sons, and his daughters who had each married a worthy man. He thought of his grandchildren and of their happy lives. He pictured Phoebe huddled with her sister in terror in the kitchen. He would fight for his life if he had to. He would not die in vain.

Smith, who clearly needed a bath, walked over to Ogden, reeking of whiskey and sweat. He kicked Ogden, who didn't flinch. So, Smith kicked him harder.

"Kick me all you want, scoundrel," Ogden said, amazed by how strong, how unafraid he sounded. "They will send you to the gallows if you kill me."

"They will never catch me. Haven't yet." Claudius Smith beamed in defiance. He turned to his men, grinning and nodding while they laughed.

"Keep laughing. You think you're the Tory Cowboy of the Ramapos, but you're nothing but a rogue and a villain. Regardless of your capture and justice with the authorities, God will have you in the end."

Moody intervened. "They can throw me to the wolves. I don't care. There is no God, only England and my Tory compatriots. Your

Patriots stole my farm, you burned my house, you killed my father. My ghost will haunt you and your family for the rest of your known lives."

"They will never capture me," Smith boasted. "They haven't yet."

"One day, Smith, they will. And you will hang with the rest of your lot," Ogden said.

Smith laughed and mimicked Ogden in a baby voice.

Moody said, "Smith, I need you to shut your mouth now. I won't ask politely again. Understood?"

Smith nodded. He seemed to have understood at last.

Ogden realized he had the fact that they were drunk on his side. He could outwit them, and possibly get away from them. He was by then, totally free of his ropes. With the men's backs to him, he loosened his hands free, kicked off his ropes, and stood up. He was shorter and older than the three men, but he pushed Smith hard, and Smith fell over the beautiful carved chair Ogden had. The other men got up and chased Ogden up the stairs.

Ogden shouted to his wife, "Run. Get the constable. Hurry, Phoebe!"

Moody caught Ogden from behind, and as the women ran, screaming, Moody beat the old man within an inch of his life.

"I will kill you," Smith snarled.

"They will catch you. My wife has gone now to tell them who you are," Ogden said, his eyes already puffy from the beating, his lips bloodied.

Moody said, "Kill him, Smith."

Smith looked carefully at Ogden. "You're a religious man, yes?" Smith said softly, curiously.

"I am, sir," Ogden said.

"Then make an oath to God and to me, that you will not tell anyone who has plundered your house."

"I shall not."

"Or," Smith said, pulling out his knife, "I will kill you." Smith put the stolen knife, taken from Private Red Sullivan at the bridge, and jabbed it so strongly into Ogden's sensitive neck that both men knew it was only an ounce of pressure preventing a deadly stab thrust to cut through his throat. "Then your wife, and after that, your lovely daughters. I will hurt them before I kill them, and after that, I will go after your sons. Step by step, I will annihilate your family."

Odgen looked at Smith. Smith stared back. And in that moment, a pact was made. Whether it had been made with the devil or with God, Ogden was unsure. But he knew that dead, he'd be of no use to anyone. And the look on Smith's face told Ogden that he meant what he said.

"Okay," Ogden said. He felt faint.

"Say it. Say on God's honor, you will tell no one it was us," Smith hissed.

"I give you my word, before God and everyone, I will say nothing."

"Good," Moody said. "I am satisfied." Moody was the clever one, the one who was the notorious leader. He smiled as he knew that they had worked Judge Ogden's disciplined morality to leverage his obedience to their nefarious and evil intentions. "Hah! This may very well ensure that our deeds go forward and that the Patriot Rebels will be quelled and the British Army be the winners!"

Smith drunkenly nodded in agreement. He was rubbing his belly where he'd fallen, and sweating profusely, even though the basement had been cold. Lowery said, "He won't say a word. I can see it in his eyes. Let us run now. The wife has gone for the law."

Smith looked at Ogden and kicked him in the head one more time for good measure, knocking him out cold. Ogden did not see the three men make off with his silver heirlooms, his wife's silver service, and the silver candlesticks he'd carefully carried from his home in Elizabethtown to his new residence, here in Sussex County. And the judge remained unconscious for a long time.

ACT II
OGDEN'S DILEMMA

A sympathetic person is placed in the dilemma of a swimmer among drowning men, who all catch at him, and if he gives so much as a leg or a finger, they will drown him.
—Ralph Waldo Emerson

Chapter 11
Robbery Aftermath

"The roaring seas and many a dark range of mountains lie between us."
– Homer, The Illiad

    After the robbery, a cold winter night set down in the wetlands by the river. The dampness penetrated the air. Frost and snow created an eerie calm and silent night. There was no moon.
    The bursting and banging of the break-in had ceased. The rustle of the robbers and the screams and shouts from the home had died out. Down by the Wallkill River, nature remained settled and quiet. Just the gurgling of the river and the tinkling of the thin ice forming on the surface could be heard.
    When Phoebe and her sister ran from the house, they went straight to the two young militiamen on duty, both of whom Phoebe had only just been praising. Private Daniel Talmadge and Private Nathan Wade were slumbering in the early morning calm.
    "Nate, one of the boys, came here before but he was in such a tizzy that we didn't understand him as he ran by," said Nathanial.
    "Hurry, hurry," shouted Phoebe. "The judge is being held captive by three robbers."
    The two men, alarmed, stood up, loaded their muskets with dry powder from the powder horn they each wore on their belt, wadding from their satchel, and a deadly lead ball. All this was performed with the speed and efficiency of having practiced the loading many times. The men left the blockhouse and were moving their arms briskly with the ramrod removed from under the rifle barrel and then ramming the ammunition inside as they were taught during their weekly drills with Colonel Seward at the nearby Wallings regimental parade grounds.
    Daniel, always the leader of the two, sounded the iron triangle,

held by one hand on a string, and struck by the other hand with an iron rod. Then, both soldiers fired their muskets, one after the other. This loud sound, in a pair, would wake the locals so that they could respond quickly. The sound of the triangle rung into the cold, still air. The locals knew the alarmed sounded a troubling event like a fire, a shooting, or other disaster. The continued ringing of the triangle allowed locals to know from where the danger signal had originated.

The authorities were among those alerted. These included various townsmen and farmers on adjoining farms. These authorities furthered the alarm and mustered the militiamen.

The men gathered and clustered around the block house where they'd been found by Phoebe and her sister. Several curious women showed up and rushed back to their homes and returned to the two frightened women, lending out their warmest sweaters and scarves. Phoebe and her sister hadn't even stopped to wrap themselves in warmth before leaving the house, and were grateful. As the men decided their approach, the women, warmer now, told them to follow. They would show them the way to the Ogden home. They were followed by Privates Daniel and Nathan and then the rest of the men, locals, and militiamen. They stopped briefly at the Ogden home. The judge sat in a chair, speechless, staring at the wall and holding his neck.

"Judge, tell us what happened."

For the moment he took to gather his wits about him, Phoebe spoke up. "We've been robbed."

"Who was it?"

Phoebe shook her head and turned toward her husband, who remained silent. She pointed into the spruce trees, woods, and the mountain. "They went that way."

"What did they take?" asked Nathan.

"Silver. And other items, whiskey too. But the chalice and the sugar bowl are the most important to us," said Phoebe.

They looked at Ogden, who had recovered from the final blow and was being tended to by Phoebe and her sister.

"Who did this?" Nathan asked.

Ogden thought about it. If he told, they would kill him. "I don't know," Ogden said. "They didn't stop to introduce themselves." He was torn, and it almost felt painful. Because not telling them did no service at all to the troops fighting for America's freedom. But telling them would surely bring about his death and the death of the people he loved most in the world. This dilemma felt like a knife cutting him in half. He did not believe he owed something to the men, but he did take an oath, and he certainly believed in—and dreaded—the consequences. He knew not what to do and sat there quietly, ashamed of himself for what he considered is own fearful weakness.

The two men grimaced. "Well, when your memory returns, perhaps you can sit down with the authorities and go through the events with a little more clarity," said Nathan. Ogden heard, or thought he did, the sarcasm in the young man's voice. Nathan and Daniel, plus several other men who had saddled up, whistled and shouted, "Let's go." They all left to follow the tracks of the robbers in the snow.

The tracks in the shallow snow showed that the robbers had headed upslope from the home to the top of the hill. Beyond the trees, uphill toward where the spruces held to the steeper sections, beyond where the stones turned to boulders, and farther where the cliffs jutted out, the local militia tracked the freebooters to the top ridge that formed the spine of the highest points. They followed the footsteps of the robbers along the top and continued on, past the Ogden Mine on Sparta Mountain that provided the iron ore as raw materials and valuable resources needed by the Patriots. The tracks turned and headed from Sparta Mountain to the north along the Snufftown Mountain ridge line.

After the long climb uphill and hike along the same trail the robbers had taken, the posse of men came upon the place where the robbers had been encamped. The freebooters had apparently stayed overnight and then snuffed out the campfire a few hours before, as could be determined by the dead but still warm embers. One of the pursuers shouted, "Hey, over here."

Buried halfway beneath the snow was a silver sugar bowl.
"Must be the judge's silver bowl."
"If I may ask, where does this mountaintop go?" said Nathan, looking at one of the men in the posse who might know, having lived in the region for many years.

"The mountaintop runs northward, lad, and it continues up to New York colony. It is a wild region here along the heights. It is the area of wolves and bear. The timber is large and strong, and the coal job families eek out a dirty living making charcoal from the wood to serve the several iron forges we have down in the valley along the river. They have had a lot of trouble lately up there with the bandits, and a fella Claudius Smith who they say is 'The Cowboy of the Ramapos' is said to be up there in the cave."

"Is that so?" said Nathan.

"Yes, those bandits rob the mails for money. They also steal the messages that the Patriot Army sends, such as communications from General Washington to General Sullivan."

"Ramapos, eh?"

"Yes," said Nathan. "It is a wild area up there in the Ramapos. It is hard for our Army and our militiamen to monitor and protect the riders through the wild area. Also, many of the runaways go up there, like those British soldiers from New York City, and slaves."

After the men lost the trail, they went back down the mountain and home to Sparta. A formal inquest followed. Alerted, the Sussex County sheriff over in the county seat of Newton made plans to call upon the Ogden family to find out what happened and hopefully identify the culprits so that the lawmen could apprehend them.

Chapter 12
Jailbreak in Newton

*"If thou through this blind prison go'st.
Led by thy lofty genius and profound."*
– Dante Alligheri: The Divine Comedy, Canto X

News trickled down through the countryside quickly. Word of mouth from neighbor to farmer to teamster to merchant. From a dry goods business to a purveyor of hay for bedding of traveling horses.

The Patriots had their network of gaining the news of the day. And those who wanted to remain in allegiance to the British also had their networks. In addition, there were secret networks used by spies for both sides.

The locals recalled that it was said that back in 1775, when the British left Boston by boat for Concord to confiscate the military stores of the Patriots, the Patriots used covert methods to spread important messages. There was Paul Revere's ride, the use of lamps as signals, drumbeats and trumpets, and the use of a three-repeat shots of muskets across water. These methods allowed for a very rapid spread of alarm to the countryside, as far as twenty miles out. And it happened quicker than the time it took the British troops took to row across the harbor.

In the land of Sussex County, one piece of information that found its way out was about the Loyalists, also known as Tories. British sympathizers also learned about their men who were in jail in Sussex County. Those men had been apprehended, caught in the act of thievery and murder via information obtained from the Committee of Safety of Sussex County, including members such as Judge Ogden, Colonel Seward, and Lord Stirling.

Those with different sentiments than the Patriots did not sit idle. These men who supported the English may have joined the troops of Colonel Skinner, who went down toward the city to join regiments there.

Then there was Lieutenant Moody. He worked on his own mostly. He was shrewd, smarter than most, a brilliant spy. From time to time, he was compelled to gather men together to help him complete his well-known nefarious activities. Some of the information he'd interrupted had been an important dispatch from General Washington. But now that Washington was aware of the interceptions, it was always difficult to know whether the document was real or not. Nevertheless, he knew the declaration they had drafted and signed was authentic and his dream was to go to Pennsylvania and steal it. But there were more urgent matters to deal with.

Then disaster struck after Moody received instructions to abduct New Jersey Governor William Livingston[xxxvi]. Moody was happy to do so since Livingston's zeal for American independence translated for Moody to what he called actions that were "cruel and oppressive to the loyal inhabitants of New Jersey."

So, with four men, including his closest friend, Corporal Joseph Lowery, Moody returned to Morris County. But then he learned that Livingston had gone to meet the legislature, so Moody took his men to Sussex County. It was there that Lowery was captured by a Major Robert Hoops, a Continental officer, during a tryst with a local woman. Threatened with death, Lowery gave up details of the planned abduction, warning Livingston and raising the alarm[xxxvii].

A few days later, while he and several of his gang were gathered at the local cave, a few miles west of the Ogden home, Moody told them again about the raid on his family farm. Though the men had heard the story—frequently—they didn't begrudge Moody's retelling of it. They saw it as the moment he pledged himself as a lifelong Loyalist. Though his family had been Loyalists before, the loss of his farm, the burning of his home, the danger to his family hardened him. He would never forget such a loathsome ordeal. He had gathered the men and he needed to convince them to go on a certain mission. More to the point, he needed to get them focused after the debacle with Lowery.

"I know I've left you mates for a few days. I was considering blowing up the powder magazine at Succasunna[xxxviii], but they knew that I was hanging around and sent over a hundred men to fortify and guard the place."

His men grumbled.

"Aye, what a coup that would have been," said one of the men and part of the gang that had been in Burgoyne's army.

Moody said, "We need to go to Sussex County. Several of our compatriots are in jail there."

"Who?" asked one of his men.

"The Scotsman Robert Maxwell[xxxix] has been sentenced to death."

"What did the condemned fellow do?" said a couple of the ex-soldiers from the lost Saratoga campaign.

"He did some civil crime, nothing to speak of, and certainly nothing to execute him like some common criminal," said Moody, attempting to whip up anger toward the Patriots. Moody saw it was working. Some Hessians in his gang were still reluctant.

He smiled. "So, my soldier friends, how does that line go? The one about the outcome of the battle up at Saratoga that you fellows were in? You know, when you were fighting against the American General Horatio Gates[xl]?"

They looked at him with blank expression. The mention of the battle seemed to take their enthusiasm away.

Moody began to sing,
> "Burgoyne, unconscious of th' impending fates,
> Could cut his way thro' woods, but not thro' Gates."

All whoops and laughter blasted out from the other men's throats, but not those from the defeated Burgoyne army. The men were beside themselves in their frustration. It was like putting a sharp stick into a painful open wound. And Moody knew how to irk them. But despite the laughter, Moody and his comrades in arms also knew that the outcome of that battle made their lives even harder, as Loyalists, since Burgoyne's defeat led directly to the alliances between the United State, France, and The Netherlands. It also made Benedict Arnold[xli] a hero, at least for a little while, until one day he would betray the Americans and defect to the Loyalists.

"Let's move on out and get up to the Sussex jail and release the Loyalist prisoners," said Moody. "What do you say, brothers?"

They all agreed to go with him. Now, even those Hessians were fired up and ready to go.

Moody said, "I will gain much satisfaction in freeing members of the Loyalist persuasion who are in the county jail, this same Sussex County."

"We hear the jail is not far from your hidden cave, here in Muckshaw Swamp," said one of the new members of Moody's gang.

Moody said nothing, but there was a faint assent in his eyes. Then he said with a sinister growl, "It won't remain hidden if people talk. So keep it quiet!"

The man understood well what Moody was implying. He stopped smiling and closed his mouth, mindful of the warning in Moody's words.

The next morning, Lieutenant Moody set out with six men. They made it to Newton, home of the county courthouse and the county jail. They cased the building from a distance. As darkness began to fall, the activity of the village slowed and drifted toward a stop. The town calmed and stilled as night intruded, as if human activity was powered by the daylight and ceased with its withdrawal. Citizens retreated into the seclusion of their own homes. At an opportune time, the Loyalists emerged from hiding and walked to the entrance of the jail. The large, stone building was imposing. Constructed in 1765, it was a sight to behold out on the frontier of New Jersey, as it was one of the largest and most imposing buildings to be seen on the primitive frontier at that time.

The Loyalists approached the jail, and they started to plan out their attack. As the men spoke amongst themselves, the jailer suddenly shouted out of an upper floor window, "Hey you out there!"

Their faces turned from surveying the building and each placed their attention on the Jailer.

"State your business or be gone," the jailer shouted.

"I have brought a prisoner for you," said Moody, who had placed his round brimmed hat low on his head so that his face didn't show. He also leaned over and limped, as if nursing an old war wound.

"Put your hands behind you," said Moody quietly to one of his co-conspirators. "And act like a thief."

The men laughed. He *was* a thief, but that was beside the point. One of them said, "That shouldn't be hard."

"Enough," Moody said. "C'mon, hold him by the arm, as if his hands are tied behind him." The man—acting as thief—bowed his head. They held him, and he did look like a captured crook being held by the gang.

"This prisoner …" the jailer asked. "Is this one of Moody's men that you have retained?"

Moody turned to his gang and softly said, "I see my fame precedes me." He grinned.

"Well, what is your answer?" yelled the impatient jailer.

"Yes," shouted Moody. "We have one of Moody's men. Come on down and take him into the jail."

"No," said the jailer. "I am not to open any doors until daylight."

Realizing that the plan wouldn't work, Moody took another tack.

"Sirrah, the man who speaks to you now is Moody," said Lieutenant Moody. "I have a strong party of Loyalists with me. If you do not this moment deliver up your keys, I will instantly pull down your house about your ears!"

The jailer laughed, apparently haughty and stupid. Moody had been informed that the jailer was something of a weakling and one to be frightened, especially if he was alone, as he was this night. So Moody had his men, familiar with the Indian war whoop, began whooping, sending forth a variety of calls and yells so that not only the jailer but the residents of the small town began to panic, so sure were they that Indians were invading their hamlet.

The jailer began to make his way through the jail and retrieved a light that allowed him to make it to the doors of the jail, whereupon he allowed Moody into the jail and, fearing for his life and the well-being of all in the town, bolted down the stairs and ran out of the back of the jail, disappearing into the dark.

The Loyalist intruders searched the building. Moody went to the basement and rounded a corner. At that moment, in the dank, filthy room, Moody looked around under the flickering light of the flaming torch. In the corner, he found the condemned man. The prisoner squinted and raised his arm over his eyes. He was aroused in fear but said nothing. His eyes, which Moody would never forget, spoke of his terror and resignation.

"Are you the British soldier Robert Maxwell?" shouted Moody in earnest and in haste as he did not know when the break-in might be quashed.

"Yes, I am he," said the quivering Maxwell still seated on the cold and damp floor of the jail. "Is it my time already to go to the gallows?"

"Forget it, man!" said Moody. "I am not the executioner coming for you. I am here to free you, in the name of King George."

"Oh, sir! How thankful I am," said Maxwell. "I, a condemned man, owe you my life!"

"Come," said Lieutenant Moody. "Let us make our escape."

The band of thieves ran off, with a complement of prisoners from the jail who also became escapees.

The men ran off into the night. Many years later, it was proven that Maxwell had not committed the murder for which he was condemned to die. Nevertheless, what Moody could not know then was that Maxwell would one day be recaptured and later hanged in Newton.

***

"That villain Moody!" said the sheriff[xlii] later that night as he came down to the jail to see what all the excitement was about. He threw his alpine-style felt hat to the ground, with the quill falling out and gently wafting off into the bushes.

The sheriff was angry that the men had escaped during his watch. He passed the word along to the Committee of Safety. The sheriff was becoming very annoyed with Moody. He knew that man was a foe to the region. He had to answer to his superiors and the people of the county. And now, Moody and his Loyalists needed only to shout like Indians to fool the entire town. He was angry that on his watch, they let all but the civil violators free, including a condemned man.

With a snarling grunt, the sheriff vowed, "I will get that damn Moody."

With the sheriff's determined effort, the militia was formed, and a posse of men went to search for them. But Moody, his Loyalist New Jersey Volunteers, and the prisoners were not to be found. Only Moody and Judge Ogden knew where they were headed. The gang led by Lieutenant Moody stole away to a secret place, a place that only he knew, and that the judge knew: Muckshaw Pond, below the town of Newton. The sheriff and his men set out to search, secure in a dark and difficult area beyond the swamp, in a forbidding place of dense and tangled vegetation. But they could not pick up a trail and eventually gave up in defeat.

Chapter 13
Jailbreak Questioning

"Honesty is the best policy. If I lose mine honor, I lose myself."
– attributed to William Shakespeare, used by Benjamin Franklin in a letter to Robert Livingston

    It was early morning, dew sparkling from the cold night, and the world gave way to daylight. The calm new day saw the smoke slowly swirling up from the chimney of the stately Ogden home along the bottom of the slope of Snufftown Mountain.
    The judge, still recovering from his frightful experience, heard someone pounding on the door. He was not surprised to the see the sheriff.
    "Oh, Sheriff, hello again," said the judge.
    The sheriff said hello, peering around the judge to see if anyone else was around.
    What can I do for you? Some legal work for the county?" asked Ogden.
    "Well, uh, no." The sheriff removed his hat and bowed his head as if in prayer.
    The judge knew why the sheriff was there but didn't want to speak to him. He knew the sheriff would ask questions. He had gone over it all in his head.
    "I am busy on some papers, so if you were just passing by, I haven't the time to stop and chat. Mrs. Ogden can serve you some tea, if you wish." He seemingly loomed over the diminutive sheriff as he was almost bowing over.
    "I am here about Moody," said the sheriff. He gave off the impression that he was bumbling and not very smart, but underneath his acting, the sheriff was a very smart man indeed. In fact, his act—that is what it was, an act—was almost always convincing. But he knew that Ogden was a learned man and very erudite. Ogden

remained silent and poker faced. The sheriff had no idea what, if anything, Ogden would say.

The sheriff repeated the request.

It was as if the table had turned. The sheriff straightened up. The judge stepped slowly backward over the threshold.

"I would like to ask you about the men who did harm to you," insisted the sheriff.

The judge wavered on his feet. He was uneasy about a conversation on his robbery. A depressing feeling surged through him—a sense that he had let everyone in his family down, that he had put them all in danger. And with that came the other thought—that by not telling the sheriff about Moody's plans for kidnapping Livingston, or by not telling him where they went and that Smith was with Moody, he was betraying his country and the people who fought for its freedom.

"Sir, I understand that you may have work to do, but it is unseemly that you are dismissing the horrid event of the recent evening. Appearing that you do not want to discuss it," stated the sheriff.

"Oh, that event," said Ogden as he apparently recalled the robbery.

"Judge, we need your help." The sheriff seemed slightly impatient, but he also seemed to understand that Ogden had good reason for being reluctant.

"Okay. How can I help?"

"We have had problems at the county jail."

"Oh?"

"Our jailer ran off and there was a jailbreak and all the prisoners escaped." The sheriff looked puzzled, unsure of how this all happened and red-faced having to mention about the embarrassing event. The tone and volume of his voice was almost inaudible.

"I thought you said at one of our past meetings that the guard of the jailhouse was highly qualified," said the judge. "Trained by you personally, if I remember correctly?"

The sheriff looked toward some distant, non-existent object. He responded, but in a much quieter fashion. "I thought he was good. And yes, he was trained well by me and thought to be a true and loyal Patriot, and that he was reliable. But reality has shown me again that sometimes things are not what you thought they'd be." He looked at Ogden. He sounded somewhat remorseful.

"Yes, I do know what you mean," said Ogden, thinking how he'd prepared himself to fight off his captors and bravely help find them and testify in court against them. Now he felt he was just a coward. But, he reasoned, it was for the sake of those he loved, not for himself. And he tried to convince himself that such was an unselfish reason. "I suppose I shouldn't be so unabashedly proud as I have been." He looked at his feet but seemed to feel relieved of a burden.

The judge looked at him and thought of himself. Here he was, the sheriff, a well-liked and honest man, just as Ogden was. He had felt, until recently, that he was an impeccably unblemished person, but now he had doubts about his very own ideals.

"You know, judge, sometimes situations change. The way one looks at another person may be altered, the lens changes based on circumstance."

Ogden said nothing. He felt that he himself were being put on some kind of trial.

"We don't know if it was Moody and Indians attacking the county seat. It could be that maybe it was the Mohawk Chief Joseph Brant."

A chill went down the judge's spine. He knew that he could support a case against Moody, and maybe even tell at trial, all about Moody's strategy and the plans that Moody had in the works and had shared with him in his drunken boasting. Moody's disclosures included the planned jailbreak in Newton, the rescue of the former royal governor William Franklin, and the abduction of the first and current New Jersey Patriot governor, William Livingston, for ransom. And, heaven forbid, the scheme to steal the Declaration of Independence from Philadelphia. The judge knew of Moody and of Claudius Smith, who he sometimes partnered with to rob messengers of General Washington's messages and giving them to the British man, their general in charge in New York City, Sir Henry Clinton. He also now knew Lowry who had revealed Moody's plans.

The judge also knew that he agreed not to tell on his word of honor but, in fact, it was out of fear for himself and his family that he wouldn't tell. He felt no allegiance to the men other than the fact that they would kill his daughters, his wife, and his sons if he breathed a word. It was not God he feared, but men. The men had spared him his life and though he was a man of his word; he would never have been able to stand himself if he did not tell of Moody's plans. Not telling would put many lives of the Patriots in danger. He tried to imagine whether or not he would ever say anything. How would he act if Moody had never threatened his life and that of his family? He had to tell himself that what happened to him was in God's hands. He retreated to the idea that he'd made a promise, and he believed that, even if it might bring disaster or harm to others, he'd have to honor his word. But this was not true, and deep down, he knew he was only bluffing himself.

"Can you help me with the dilemma of who robbed you and who broke the men out of the Sussex County jail?"

The judge said, "I don't know who attacked the jail, sir."

"Well, then, how about any words of wisdom? A guess?"

The judge saw the convenience of the second alternative, avoiding the naming of Moody and Claudius, and indeed had words ready on his tongue.

"I would guess, perhaps, that the militia looked for the thieves in the wilds of Sparta Mountain and Snufftown Mountain. They might be found in some remote hideaway.

"Indeed," said the sheriff, "it is reputed that Moody has been hiding in a cave outside of Newton, in Muckshaw Swamp. The same rumor exists for that New Yorker, Claudius Smith, who they say has been hiding out with his band of thugs in the highland regions just beyond the Ramapos at Smith's Cave near Galloway's Grove."

He looked at the judge, whose face remained passive.

"Maybe one day," he continued, "we hope, that Smith may be pulled from Galloway's Grove and taken to the Gallows in Goshen."

The sheriff then bid Ogden goodbye. On the way out, he said, "A last comment Judge. If it's okay by you, I will take this feather here from your animal stockyard and use it for my quill."

"No problem," said the judge as the sheriff stuck the quill into his felt alpine cap.

Chapter 14
Blowing up Powder Stores at Suckasunny

"The gunpowder lay as harmless as sand, because no fire came near to explode it."
– Emily Brontë, **Wuthering Heights**

"Okay, men. Here's the plan," said Moody. The group of men leaned in over the candlelit table. Moody's hand swept over a simple map. His fingers touched onto a couple squares and lines, then he firmly pointed to a spot or two. Finally, he made a fist and hit the table, making his gang of men jump.

"We are going to blow up the gun powder magazine at Suckasunny!" said Moody, referring to an early name for today's Succasunna.

The men whom Moody had recruited, Loyalists from the surrounding area, looked at each other gravely. Their faces were barely visible in the dim, wavering light. Some of them were the men Moody had freed from jail, others came from the New Jersey Volunteers. This group also consisted of outlaws and escaped prisoners of war from Burgoyne's defeated army. The dirty bunch of scoundrels were laughing heartily, knowing that success in this venture would inflict severe wounds in their enemy—the American Patriot Army.

"All right, men," said Moody. "Let's get down to business."

"The enemy has a secret powder mill near the Ford Mansion in Morristown. They are making the extremely important and sensitive powder without which their muskets and cannons would be useless. So, this is our objective, to destroy the powder at Suckasunny."

"Why there? There's a mill closer in Morristown," asked one of his men.

"The mill in Morristown where they make the gun powder is too highly guarded for us to get at, it being right behind the Ford Mansion where the Patriot officers congregate. But they store it at Suckasunny, and that location is lightly guarded. We will strike there."

***

The group ventured out of their hideaway and made it on down the road to a grassy area near the site.

Moody's men were crouched down as they surveyed the property through the protection of numerous shrubs along the fence line. Squatting and kneeling, they cowered in the shadows of the stone wall as they remained hidden behind it. Lieutenant Moody's hands raised slowly as he pointed and motioned at several distant buildings of interest. In front of them was the important storage location for the Continental Army. Guards were walking sentry duty, with their muskets against their shoulders. Each guard's rifle was vertical, the butt stock held in their left palm with the barrel skyward. The bayonet topped each rifle.

Moody continued to discern ways to approach the storage sheds surreptitiously, describing an easy entry through the fence, and then he began talking of the means of escape. They all took a final overall view of the situation.

Many sheds were neatly arranged in an open area on a flat place among the many hillocks popping up around it like a hot, thick porridge bubbling on a stoked fire. Trees sprouted around the open plain like whiskers on a grizzly, old seafarer. Within the fenced compound there were surprisingly no more than a handful of Patriot soldiers guarding the massive magazines of gun powder that were stored in the location. The sheds had finely constructed roofs because of the sensitivity of the substance and the need to keep it ever so dry for proper storage and use.

Someone had once told Moody that the substance of gun powder was also known as black powder. It was a mix of sulfur, charcoal, and potassium nitrate. The last part of the mixture was known as saltpeter. A source of saltpeter came from bird droppings. Moody had a laugh when he learned that saltpeter has been obtained on islands where birds had been defecating for eons, and from caves where you could find plenty of the guano.

This saltpeter, mixed with sulfur and charcoal, when lit, exploded. Moody wanted the materials because they were a vital part of making the musket and cannon valuable for their lethality in modern warfare. Without the gun powder, the musket and cannon were just inert and pretty pieces useful only for a parade.

The powder was stored in casks. If even one of these dry, wooden containers were set on fire, the ensuing flames would quickly build up. Once the heat got into the contents, the whole place would blow up. This was Moody's plan.

As they waited behind the wall, one of the men said, "I think this will be an easy assault on the Americans."

Many of them laughed. They were quickly told to remain silent.

"We shall get revenge for our loss at Saratoga, that's what I'll say," pledged another.

"Quiet, men," said Moody, confident although cautious.

"We are going to blow up the powder stores at Suckasunny!" said Claudius Smith.

"Claudius, you talk too much," replied Moody. "You will get us all hanged." Lately, Moody began to think that Claudius might be more of a liability than an asset.

Lieutenant Moody was satisfied with the mission so far. He had whipped up his ragged bunch and had focused them on the job at hand. But he realized that they were too rambunctious and too inexperienced. He improved his plan.

"Men," he said as quietly as he could, "you stay here and make some noise in ten minutes. In the meantime, Claudius, you come with me."

"Why?" Smith asked.

"You and I will sneak up and make a fuse and light off a keg which will blow the whole place. We need you to divert attention, though. So, men, give us ten minutes. Then start making noise."

They all agreed to the plan. Moody and Claudius moved around to another side of the property and ran between some of the trees to creep up on a larger shed where they had seen two soldiers roll up another cask. They slowly moved forward from the trees, in the shadows that the maples made to the edge of the larger shed. They then slid around the wall of the shed to the door.

The two then opened the door and spotted a cask. They grabbed the cask and carefully dropped it down horizontally and placed it on its side and then popped the cork out the bung. The powder poured onto the dirt floor of the shed. Moody took a handful of powder and carefully ran a line of the powder from the keg through the doorway and around to the side of the building. It was just then that a guard was rounding the side of the same shed and about to discover the two men.

An instant before the guard was about to see Moody and Smith, the gang started hooting and hollering out by the stone fence. The guard halted, turned about, and then went toward the fence to investigate the noise.

"Whew," said Claudius, "that was close."

"Shut up and help me," said Moody as he continued to run the solid line of gunpowder around the shed. "I need to make this long enough that it will give us enough time to get away."

Claudius stood up and looked around. "You're going good, Lieutenant Moody." He grinned, crouching back down. "There's no guard around."

"Good," said Moody as he continued the line to a long enough distance, stood up, and slapped the remaining powder from his hands. He then pulled out a piece of steel and a piece of flint rock and started striking near the end of the powder line. One of the sparks from his striking landed on the powder and started the trail of powder on fire.

"Okay, let's go!" Moody said as he stood up and ran. His partner also scurried away from the line of lightning as it ran the trace around the shed and into the open door to the powder keg. The lanky frame of Claudius stood high, and his leather boots brushed against the ground as the sole of his foot landed on top of the line of powder, scraping it clear, breaking the course of the fuse.

As the two got back to the stone fence, they jumped over it and crouched down, plugged their ears with their fingers, and awaited the loud sound of explosion. Several anxious moments passed.

The sound didn't come. Lieutenant Moody waited and then took his fingers from his ears. He looked at the shed. He saw the smoke from the start of the fuse where he hit the line of powder with his flint spark. But he saw the remainder that went into the shed had not lit. Then he saw the scuff mark that broke the trail of the fuse.

"You idiot!" he sneered to Smith.

"Well, at least we made it away from there to the cover and

safety of these maple trees."

Moody felt a pinch something sharp in his side, and he turned around to see Claudius. He was slipping away, as if he couldn't take Moody's demeaning of his being slipshod with his feet. The pinch felt sharper, and more like a jab. Moody turned around as best he could with the pain to see that there was a Continental soldier jabbing a bayonet into his side. Another, taller soldier stood nearby, pointing his musket at Moody's head.

"You are coming with us!" the taller one said to Moody.

The soldiers took Moody away to the Morristown jail, where the iron door slammed shut behind him.

Chapter 15
Ogden Questioned on Gunpowder

"No legacy is so rich as honesty."
– Shakespeare, *All's Well that Ends Well*

Three well-bred and fed horses approached the Ogden plantation along the roadway from Sparta to Franklin Furnace. The horses were imposing, full in height, and of healthy disposition and bearing. They were striding at a proud gait. The three riders made an illustrious scene, riding in fine saddles and wearing splendidly colorful Continental soldier officer uniforms of buff and blue. They reached the area of the Ogden's home and turned from the roadway and onto the path leading up the hillside upon which the plantation rested. They galloped up to the house. As they dismounted, one walked forward and knocked on the door and they waited. Judge Ogden answered.

"Yes, sirs, may I help you?"

"Good afternoon, Judge," all three said in unison as they removed their headgear in respect to the judge.

The judge led them into the parlor where they sat down. He saw Phoebe out of the corner of his eye and gave her a look so that she turned away and scurried down the hallway.

The lead rider, a high-ranking man, said, "We are riders from General Washington's encampment at Morristown. We are inquiring about the robbery you sustained. There is talk of Loyalists with the intention of blowing up our magazine near Morristown, and such a thing would be perhaps a fatal blow to our ability to prosecute the war."

"I see," said Ogden.

"Well, sir, can you help us?"

"Certainly, gentlemen, certainly."

"So, then, who were the men that robbed you?" asked the officer in charge.

"I beg your pardon, sir?" replied Ogden.

"Judge, who robbed you?"

"I ... I—I really can't say," stuttered Ogden.

"Did you see them?"

"Yes."

"Did you recognize them?"

"Ah, oh. Not sure."

"So you *think* you know. Who do you *think* they were then?"

"Scoundrels, dregs of the earth."

"Can't you tell us anything more than that?" said an exasperated inquirer.

"Sir, I have thought about this at great length," said Ogden. "I have had much anxiety, sirs." He fiddled with his watch fob, hoping that time would pass quickly, maybe go faster if he jiggled and fidgeted with it, and then this inquisition would be behind him. "I saw their faces and spoke to them plainly." He took the fob into one hand and then used his other hand to scratch his ear lobe, pulling the lobe and twisting it back and forth and then tugging it down again. This energetic work and commotion did not seem to help the situation, as the three men continued to stare at him.

"And?" said the lead questioner. All three horsemen seemed to put their left leg forward, moving about on their feet as if standing there so long and becoming so anxious that movement was necessary to keep the blood flowing in their extremities.

"And then they left."

"But they put a knife to your throat, isn't that right?"

"Yes, yes they did."

"So, what made them not kill you, and to leave your house?"

"Do you know they took all my fine silverware? My precious sugar bowl and chalice?"

"Yes, so we've heard from the sheriff," said another officer. "And they recovered the sugar bowl."

"That they did," said Ogden, looking at it in its place in the glass cabinet.

"So, you are unable to tell us who these culprits where?"

"Correct," said the judge.

"You know, we captured a man who appeared to be ready to

blow up our powder. Nothing happened and he was alone, at least when we found him. If we could somehow tie him into your situation here, perhaps you overheard him say something about intentions on harming our cause?"

The judge knew that they had said something about the exploits like ruining the Continentals' stores. But ...

"So, Your Honor, can you provide any evidence about who it was? We have Moody, but surely there were others."

"Nothing that I can say, gentlemen."

One of the officers looked at Ogden with a kind expression.

"There is nothing wrong with being afraid ..."

"I, sir, am not afraid."

"We have fear for the health and well-being of your family, and after a trauma such as yours, I imagine, *they threatened you?* There is nothing wrong with wanting to protect your beloveds. But think also of your country, and your honor, sir."

"There is nothing to say." Ogden bristled. How dare the man call him a coward, and worse, imply that he was betraying his country by keeping silent to protect those he loved?

The officer smiled in a kindly way, but Ogden thought he saw contempt behind the man's smile. Maybe he only imagined it.

"Well, men, we must be on our way," the man said, looking at the other two officers.

The three officers mounted their steeds and turned them toward the road. One said out loud to another, with some frustration, "When we find who exactly has been marauding the locals, we will be able to arrest them. Then people like Moody will not be able to go about blowing up our powder magazines, stealing away the governor, and whatever else those scoundrels have up their sleeves. If only we would have a clear reason to arrest these men who are creating havoc to our new nation."

"Good day, Judge," said the lead officers while all three tipped their tricorns in acknowledgment, respect, and a gentlemanly goodbye to the judge.

"May our moral dilemmas resolve themselves into clear decisions," said the lead officer on departure, heard by Judge Ogden. "Officers, we will have to let the captured man go, as we have no corroborating evidence of his involvement."

Ogden went back inside his home, closed the latch, which remained slightly bent from the intrusion, and then stiffened against the back of the now closed door. There was a cold chill that surrounded his frame as he felt that his position was being recognized and understood.

The officers, as they rode away out of earshot, continued, "Yes, we ourselves must morally consider arresting people who are not yet confirmed criminals. We are speaking, among others, about Mohawk Chief Joseph Brant, and Indians of any nature or stature who might at this point be prejudicially taken in. It seems that just suspicion will not be enough to hold a man imprisoned."

So, in the aftermath of this investigation that involved Judge Ogden, James Moody was released and walked away from the jail in Morristown.

Chapter 16
Breakout Gov Franklin, 1778

"Expect nothing and you will always be surprised."
– Daniel Defoe, author of *Robinson Crusoe*

Lieutenant Moody had nothing nice to say of his captors. While leaving the village of Morristown where he was held, he looked back at the village, put his hands on his hips, and smiled, relieved to have been let loose due to lack of evidence.

While Moody was walking away a free man from the Morristown jail, another Loyalist continued to languish away in a Wallingford and Litchfield Connecticut prison—the jailed royal governor of New Jersey, William Franklin. Franklin had been the royal governor since 1763, appointed by the British. Then, near the beginning of the current conflict, Lord Stirling, along with several soldiers, arrested him and took him away to the prison. Franklin was the last governor representing the British in their colony. The Patriots had replaced him with another William: William Livingston, who was born in 1723 and had served as governor since 1776. He was an active politician who also had later signed the Constitution.

In the prison, Franklin demanded his rights. As an ex-governor, he felt that he was entitled to a different status than other prisoners. "I am the governor and deserve a larger cell," he said to the passing guard.

"Don't talk to me about it," said the guard. "You may have been the governor for the Brits, but you are now just a prisoner, a non-conforming prisoner of the Patriots."

The guard then sat on a low stool, took a bite of an apple, and tried not to pay attention as he awaited the end of the workday and some much-needed rest in the evening.

This was true. Franklin recalled the day of his arrest, how Lord Stirling had taken over the operation. Franklin was not surprised to see a well-dressed man and believed the rumors that Stirling even bought his own uniform for his service to the Patriots. He knew that Lord Stirling also acted in highly dangerous and important events, including the rear-guard action at the Battle of Long Island where he probably saved the Continental Army as they rowed away in the fog to Manhattan, Stirling sacrificing his own self and men so that Washington could safely cross to fight another day. Stirling did gain release. He was also known for his dramatic capture of a British ship *Blue Mountain Valley* off Sandy Hook early in the war.

"Lord Stirling may think himself a powerful man, but he is just a silly man who has clothed himself in fancy colored attire in order to better play the part of Patriot royalty." Franklin's comments seemed to fall on deaf ears of the guard. "He's just a whiskey swigging Rebel who sneaks in and snatches people—good people with a different opinion than he himself holds. And he locks us up in prisons and jails."

"Well, you made yourself well-known as being against our independency," said the guard as he gnawed at the apple from an orchard on the Rude farm nearby. "Mmm, this is a delicious Connecticut apple, extra tangy and tasty." The guard was consumed by the inviting tartness of his snack.

"Why doesn't my father provide me freedom?"

"Benjamin Franklin?" the guard said, laughing and taking another bit of his crisp apple.

"Yes, Benjamin Franklin," said the ex-governor.

"Because you and he don't have a good relationship; you are not close at all. You shouldn't have been so belligerent to your father," said the apple muncher as he put his palms on his knees, pressed, and stood up from his stool, took a few steps, and looked out the window of the jail. He was peering through the bars as the sunlight seeped in, separated into vertical patches, spreading across the stone floor like a golden rug. The light slightly warmed the cold that was ever present in the stone prison that firmly secured the ex-governor.

"My father can find the time and interest to be an inventor, author, statesman, and diplomat. But he can't find the time, nor the heart, to free me."

Finishing his apple, the guard slowly walked out of the confined area to spit the seeds out of the window, threw the core behind them, and returned to the stool.

A few minutes later, the guard got to his feet and went to speak to his supervisor, who then communicated the information from that exchange to the higher authorities. The security of William Franklin was a very important prize in the continuing Revolutionary War.

"That is very interesting," said the guard's superior officer. He had just come in from a meeting with his own superior. "Now, go back and let him out."

"What?" said the guard, surprised.

"You heard me, let William Franklin out, and be quick with it. The commanding British officer, Sir Henry Clinton[xliii], has arranged for him to go to Manhattan and be with the Loyalists there in exchange for our prisoners."

"Yes sir," said the guard.

He went to the cell to tell William Franklin the news.

"You're one lucky man," the guard said. "The British officer in charge in New York City has negotiated your release. You'll be going to New York."

The old governor picked up his clothes and departed under military escort, to be exchanged on the middle ground between the Patriots and the Loyalists.

While the guard, who had spotted a loaf of bread on a table, buttered it up, Franklin walked by him on the way to the outer door and grabbed the bread and quickly ate it with a laugh. In a last word, William Franklin stated that there was, "Justice due to the Merit of Mr. Moody's services."

He mentioned some important words about the man, from the British point of view. "That Moody, I heard, worked to get sixty recruits from Sussex County for the Loyalists, and Moody obtained much intelligence about the troop movements associated with Colonel Butler and General Sullivan[xliv] as he went through the county and out to the Delaware."

The guard was not amused and looked askance at his now former prisoner.

A contingent of British officers arrived, under a truce, to exchange prisoners. One of them overheard Livingston's praise of Moody.

"We have heard about Moody. He has a good name with us," said the British officer who was escorting the old governor back to Manhattan. "I hear he was well-rewarded too."

"Yes, he was. Lieutenant Moody got twenty-five guineas for Livingston, if he could capture him, and a hundred and two hundred for stealing mail."

The guard seemed impressed. William Franklin said, "Moody also got information on General Washington and destroyed a considerable magazine of stores near Black Point and took a number of prisoners, including officers. That Loyalist Moody worked hard and was very valuable to the British Brigadier General Cortland Skinner. You know, Skinner, who commands the Loyalists who are eager to keep the British in charge."

The British smiled to themselves, not letting on that they were listening, but listening all the same.

William Franklin mumbled to the British who secured him, "I wish that Moody would capture the Patriot governor Livingston[xlv]. That would serve those Rebels a good reply."

The British officer taking him in said in a low and guarded voice, "That might very well happen, sir."

Chapter 17
Sheriff Comes to Call

"Is it justice to make evil, and then punish for it?"
– James Fenimore Cooper, *The Last of the Mohicans*

The sheriff came to call on the judge. He knew the way, having been there before. He needed to get more information from Ogden. It just didn't seem right that the judge was robbed but knew nothing about it. And that Moody kept disrupting the peace. As the sheriff was responsible for enforcing the law, all this lawlessness was making him look bad.

He walked up the hill from the main roadway and approached the Ogden hillside plantation and the beautiful country estate. He stepped on the slate walkway and sauntered forward toward the home. He appeared to have a split professionalism. At times, the sheriff looked expert in his capabilities and in fulfilling his duties, and at other times appeared to look around pensively and baffled at simple things. One could not be sure if he gave the impression of a competent and intelligent investigator, or as a buffoon, though the people who knew him most intimately understood the man actually was a genius. He frequently tripped over the slate walkway as if too deep in thought and unaware of the world around him. The sheriff eventually got to the home and knocked on the door. The judge answered.

"Greetings to you, sir," said the sheriff.

"Do come in, Sheriff," said Ogden.

The men set down in the parlor and one of the servants arrived quickly with some refreshing tea.

The small talk had ceased, quickly dissipating with the men knowing there were pressing matters to follow. They were alone, and Ogden said, "And to what do I owe this pleasure?"

"As I mentioned before, on my last visit here right after the robbery, we at the county are very sorry to hear of your robbery, Judge."

"Sheriff, we remain in shock. My wife Phoebe cries without end. I don't know what to do," said the judge.

"Can you help me do my report, sir?"

The judge shook his head. "We are all struggling to recover. It was frightening."

"Oh yes, sir. I am sure you are very upset. On the way here, a townsman said that your wife Phoebe stated there were three?" mentioned the sheriff.

"Yes, there were three. I was surprised who they were, really," said the judge.

"Oh, then you knew them?"

This question stopped the judge in his tracks. He knew it was direct. He wished he could say something. But if the bandits discovered that it was him who revealed their names, he, his wife, and children would suffer greatly and die at their hands. He couldn't bear the thought of it and felt that it was all his fault. His feelings for the war were also confusing. How could he call himself a Patriot if he didn't tell the sheriff or any officers of Washington's army? The dilemma had begun to keep him up at night. He found himself thirsty all the time and forgetful. He was barely able to eat. Lately, he'd been into the whiskey a little too much. Even Phoebe cautioned him, saying that he was a brave man, and not to worry, that they would be safe.

"I mean, Sheriff ..." Ogden said. "I can't say."

"You didn't know them?"

There was a long pause.

"You did or you didn't know them?" said the sheriff. "Common sense would imply that if you knew them, you could tell me their names, especially with such a violent event at close range."

"I really can't say," said Ogden.

The sheriff fiddled with his pouch and then prepared some words.

"Is it that you *can't* say or you *won't?*"

Ogden looked at the sheriff but shook his head.

The sheriff said, "I take it that you didn't know them. I realize that this has been a traumatic event for you and that you all are in shock."

The judge affirmed this statement with a solid nod.

"Were you harmed, sir?"

"Well, yes. I mean no."

There was a long pause.

The sheriff looked ponderingly toward Ogden. The sheriff was wearing a Bavarian-style felt hat. He put his hand above his head. There was a goose feather stuck aloft at the highest point that he yanked out and brought down to his side. He pulled a little bottle and a piece of paper out of his small, leather satchel at his side and removed the cork. This was his traveling writing set—a quill and ink pot.

"I want to take notes on this conversation," he said. "I know that whatever information I get from you will be truthful due to your unquestioned honesty. You know, sir, that everyone in the county looks up to you. You, Judge, who are known as 'The Honest Lawyer,' and I say that with the utmost respect."

"Ah, yes, Sheriff, so I've heard," said the judge. "Thank you."

"So, you were unable to get a good glimpse of the robbers?" The sheriff looked at the judge, but the judge was looking in the other direction, apparently hoping to somehow avoid or sidestep the sheriff's inquiries.

The greeting and salutations—and questioning—had all taken place on the threshold of the front door. The same door that the robbers had breached, the same door that had been replaced due to the damage done by the robbers.

"The other door was shot." This was particularly true, since upon leaving, the robbers discharged a ball from their flintlock pistol which penetrated into the wood, although the judge didn't mention that part.

"Yes, we have had a rough winter, and a lot of buildings need repair this spring."

"Yes, a rough winter, indeed," said the sheriff.

Just then, Phoebe appeared. "Hello," she said to the sheriff. Her husband had kept most of the goings on from her, but she knew he was frightened and didn't want to speak to the law or reveal the names of the thieves. She tried to impress upon him that he must report them, but he could not be persuaded, only saying, "I gave the men my word." She was appalled that he would keep his word to a bunch of outlaws, but deep down she understood it had more to do with his fear that their family was in harm's way.

"Is everything all right?" she asked softly. She gazed with love at her husband and smiled for the sheriff, whom she did like.

"Yes," said the judge. "I have told the Sussex County sheriff my story, and I believe that the sheriff has what he needs from us."

The sheriff looked at the two Ogdens. The judge motioned for Phoebe to go back to her knitting and to leave the conversation to the men. With that observation, the sheriff smiled, tipped his felt Alpine hat, and stuck his quill back precisely into the hole on the top of his hat. The sheriff then put the cork back into his ink pot and placed it into his leather bag. He blew on the paper to dry the ink, then folded it and placed it in his pocket, near to his chest for safe keeping. A slight breeze kept the feathers on the quill flittering around, creating the image of the sheriff as if he were a court jester in some Medieval play, or a Swiss mountaineer about ready to yodel.

"Well, squire, sir, I will be on my way. I have another call up the road in Sharpsboro," stated the sheriff. "That is a strange situation. They have not paid their taxes to the county although they are making a lot of forged articles for sale." He smiled. "I mean forged as made from a forge, not forged as if for unlawful uses."

They both laughed. It was rumored that the British had been using the Sharpsboro forge to make weaponry for the British, and gold had been rumored to have been placed in the walls of the ironmaster's house.

The sheriff raised his hand to his head with his fingers reaching under the hat. He then squinted and scratched his head. "It's strange, too, that the old Quaker Joseph Sharp would not be savvy enough to realize that he's running at a loss. He'd better be careful with his finances or otherwise one of these days he'll see his busy iron forge at a sheriff's sale for its indebtedness." The lawman paused. "Well, this war is taking a lot of the old ways, and it is turning out to be a new day."

"Yes, much seems to be changing in our world today."

"Right, Judge Ogden. But let me tell you, I keep a tight ship up here in Sussex County. I consider myself to be a lawman's sheriff, one who keeps order in his territory."

"Yes, sir," said the judge, noting that the sheriff was only about half his height and quite small compared to most of the frontiersman build of the rough, robust frontier Sussex County community. "We greatly appreciate you and your men for keeping us safe."

"Yes, sir, you can tell that I am a man who can pull his own weight with most anyone who comes around these parts." The sheriff saw he had the judge's attention, what with no other place for the judge to go except back up into his own house. It would be rude for the judge to retire at this point, also since the door was almost closed because of the sheriff's examination of the condition. And, too, it seemed that the judge had drawn the door tight to the frame so that the sheriff could not look inside to ask more questions.

"Well, I best be on my way," said the sheriff as he knew that he had to check out the other problems in the county. "I feel that this robbery at your home is a key part to many of the difficulties preventing me from having an unblemished professional record."

"Yes, Sheriff. I hope that you can get to the bottom of this."

"I thank you for your input." He tipped his hat, walked a few steps down the path, then turned around. "You know, we have had some word that a Lieutenant James Moody has been roaming these parts. He is a Loyalist. But he has also been spoken of on his wild shenanigans throughout North Jersey so it might just be an unfounded rumor that he is here in Sussex County. In any event, he's been picking up sidekicks such as the runaway prisoners of war from General Burgoyne's army after they were marched through Wallings, right next to Sharpsboro, back in December of 1778. And he's rumored to be partnering with that scoundrel from up north of the colony border, that 'Cowboy of the Ramapos' Claudius Smith."

"Hmmm."

"Well, anyway, Judge. I am sure it is the shock of the heinous robbery that you endured. So good luck. And goodbye."

The sheriff tipped his hat a last time and left the two Ogdens at the threshold with the new door to the Ogden home and headed north to Franklin Furnace and Sharpsboro.

When Judge Ogden closed the door, his wife looked at him with such kindness and understanding that he had to sit down and collect himself.

She sat beside him, and they both faced the front and watched the sheriff go to the foot of the property and then mount his horse and trail off. The cold sun shone into the well-appointed room, and outside, the winter air seemed thin against a bold, blue sky.

"I know you are frightened," she said.

"I am not."

She interrupted him, "It's okay to say so. It is not the mark of courage to deny fear. Courage, of course, is doing the right thing despite the fear."

"I made an oath to them."

"But is an oath to a liar, a cheater, a scoundrel, and thief really an oath?"

He hung his head. Then he said, "They threatened to kill us all if I said a word."

She sighed. "I assumed it was something like that."

"I am afraid for my family, especially you and my daughters who are defenseless against brutes like them."

She stood up and came to stand beside him. Then she knelt and put her hands on his legs. She gazed up at him with her most beautiful blue eyes. It occurred to him that she was somehow even more beautiful than when they married. All these years of fidelity and love.

"Darling," she said. "You needn't be afraid. The more you can tell the sheriff, the more likely it is that they will be hounded until they are caught."

He nodded, swallowing hard.

"And you do not have a duty to them being criminals and Loyalists. Your duty is to your country."

"But what about the safety and ease of my family?"

"We shall all be aware of the dangers. We will take care and be mindful, eyes open, until these men are caught. And they *will* be caught. I know that evil does not last long in the world, and God will watch over us. I believe that assuredly."

Ogden fell back against the chair and sighed. "I will pray about it, my love," he said.

"Good," she said, standing up. "Now it is time for me to put the supper on."

Chapter 18
Stirling to Ogden on Governor

"Great deeds are usually wrought at great risks."
– Herodotus

There was a sound outside of the Ogden homestead, as it sat serenely beside the slope of Snufftown Mountain.

Phoebe heard the sound from outside, unnatural as it was. She was cleaning, busy as usual with the day's chores. She laid the broom down and ran from the parlor to the door to find what the cause might be.

Astonished, she looked up. At the hitching post, a regal-looking man was tying up his horse, a tall charcoal stallion, sixteen hands high, who sniffed and swung his head sideways as if eager to begin riding again. The horse was a bundle of energy, which seemed to be seeping out from his nostrils as they expanded, and from the muscles along his shoulders as they twitched and tensed.

The horseman had all the appearance of being a dapper gentleman. His attire was memorable, as he was dressed in a colorful Patriot uniform, blue coat, and a column of gold braid and buttons ornamentally covering a white blouse. He had white leggings and brass-fitted, leather shoes. The horseman, reflecting the attitude of his stallion, was also high in energy as he vaulted from the horse and jaunted about in haste. His movements were brisk and quick—as if he were in a sword fight with a leprechaun.

Quickly he tied the horse to the nearby post and wrapped the leather strap around it several times. He swiveled quickly toward the home and smartly secured his flamboyant hat to his well-accommodated hair and head. He was to the front door in no time flat.

"Yes, sir, may I help you, sir?" said Phoebe as she got to the door.

The well-dressed gentleman removed his broad, ruffled hat and bowed deeply to Phoebe.

"Hello, I am Lord Stirling calling upon Judge Ogden." He resecured the bonnet.

"Yes, sir," replied Phoebe as she mimicked the formality of the greetings. "Oh, yes, I am sorry, but you caught me off-guard so as not to recognize you."

When Phoebe turned around, the judge was already at the door. When he sighted Stirling, a broad grin came over his face.

"Lord Stirling!"

"Judge," said Stirling. "I am humbled, sir, to meet you again."

"Ah, my Lord Stirling, how very kind of you to say," said the judge.

"You are too kind," replied Stirling.

Joy, one of the enslaved girls, brought a snifter of whiskey for Lord Stirling. Phoebe had alerted her to the task that was certain to be expected.

The judge looked at the fine steed that the general had tied up, twitching and ready to ride.

"What, may I ask, is the reason of your visit? You must be so busy with important duties to perform during this war? Do you want to know the latest about my iron mine atop Sparta Mountain here, or for that matter, news about your zinc mine at the foot of my property?"

"A short roundup of events at our mineral resources here would be appreciated. But I have other duties too, Judge."

"Can you tell me, sir, how are my sons?"

"Lieutenant Aaron Ogden[xlvi] and Colonel Matthias Ogden[xlvii] are splendid soldiers and are acting in all good apportions. They are healthy and on duty. And they stand ready to protect us if the British were to try to advance upon Washington's headquarters in Morristown from Manhattan or Staten Island, ready to give their lives if needed."

The thought of such a thing troubled the judge, but he knew that war was a duty that cost lives. "Thank you, sir. Their mother, Phoebe, will be so comforted to hear about their good health."

"It is my pleasure to give you information on your sons."

"Might we give you supper, Lord Stirling?"

"No, I have an urgent matter to discuss with you, Judge."

Ogden looked serious. He had a premonition.

"Judge," began Stirling, "you know how I arrested Governor William Franklin and put him away in prison in Connecticut ..."

"Yes, and gratefully so. New Jersey started in the right proper direction. I am glad that Livingston will do well for us Patriots."

"Well, now there's a plot afoot that is to kidnap our current Governor Livingston—who, as you know, is my brother-in-law—and flee with him into parts unknown."

"This is terrible news, both for New Jersey and for our fight for freedom. And also, sir, I know that is bad news for you personally." The judge felt fear through his body as he thought about Moody and Lowery discussing just this event. How Smith had cackled when Moody told Lowery to shut up.

"Thank you for your concern, Your Honor."

"Certainly, Lord Stirling. I hope you catch those scoundrels who are trying to capture him."

"I am on a mission to do so," said Stirling. Being the forward person that he was, he had consumed the snifter's contents and ambled past Ogden to a seat in the nearby parlor.

"If I can be of any help, I am in your service," stated the judge, following his guest into the home.

"Yes, you can help me," said Stirling. Stirling laid eyes on a fine chair and sat himself comfortably in the parlor. While Ogden followed suit and slowly sat nearby, Stirling abruptly stood up and took his drink to the window. Outside, a thunderous rain poured down. He shuffled his tricorn back and forth, almost as if to scratch his head, and said, "I want to ask you if you know who might be doing this?"

Ogden remained seated, his body buzzing with anxiety.

"I wonder if it might have been one of those who robbed you some time ago?"

"I can't say who they are," said Ogden.

"Do you not have a duty to your country?"

"My duty," said Ogden, "is to God first."

"Yes, quite. I understand. But if you know of any of these scoundrels, it would be valuable information. I'd like to catch them before they make off with my sister's loving husband."

Ogden's happy state at the arrival of Stirling had slowly diminished. Ogden realized that he had been called out, that he had answers for his friend and fellow Patriot, a leader for the Continental Army, and Stirling was the man who sacrificed himself to hold the rear guard for Washington to save the army during the Battle of Long Island. He could help get the Loyalist who wanted to capture the New Jersey governor Livingston. But each time he considered telling someone, he saw the faces of his family members. He saw his own mortality.

Stirling knocked back his liquor as quickly as the servant poured it, and Ogden reached forward to collect the empty glass.

"Allow me to replenish this vessel," said the judge. His look toward Joy accomplished the refill.

"You can't remember even a glimpse of those robbers? Or do you have knowledge of their plans? I have to find out how to contain this contagion that is approaching the region."

"I, ah ... well ..."

"There are plots afoot that can seriously hinder our colony and the new nation that we are trying to build from this war." Stirling again removed and held his tricorn in two hands, gripping it in tension.

The judge said nothing.

"I think it must be Moody," Stirling said. Lord Stirling stood still as his hands curled the fine felt hat in his hands, obviously anxious for some answer, some solution to this puzzle that was unfolding and snagging the American Cause in the twists and turns of fortune, creating the ebbs and flows of the Revolutionary War.

"Yes," said Ogden. "This is probable." Then he looked at Stirling and quickly said, "But I wouldn't know, of course."

"As the primary aide-de-camp to General Washington, I am aware of much of the spying and the spilling of secrets that may undo this great nation." He looked at the judge.

Ogden felt that he was on the spot and that he had to answer.

"Well, I will say ..." The judge thought out his words, and began, "I only heard their voices ..." The judge cringed at his own lie.

He handed the refilled glass to Stirling, who drank it quickly down. Stirling looked at Ogden. The judge squirmed a bit in his chair. Stirling was still watching, gazing open eyed at his neighbor, his fellow Patriot, and leader of the local Committee of Safety. Ogden scratched the arm of the chair as if tidying up the wood finish. He looked up but Stirling was still staring.

Unable to restrain the ebullient energy within any longer, Stirling shrugged. Then with a huff, Stirling downed another shot of whiskey.

Ogden watched as his guest wiped his lips on his sleeve, between the brass buttons, lashed out for the door, then darted to the hitching post and untied and mounted his tall, charcoal stallion with a grunt.

"I'll take a fast look down the hill at the mine and see if they have found anything to offer for our troops and their needs for useful metal that has been difficult to recover."

"Yes, sir, Lord Stirling."

Ogden stood at the door, and he watched Stirling handle his horse. He waved once, and his horse started a trot. Stirling turned back and said, "Let me know if you can say anything to help our cause, Judge."

Lord Stirling gripped the reigns of the horse as he turned and trotted off down the hill to his mine of copper, iron, and zinc. He departed, leaving the judge standing in silence.

Chapter 19
Talk About Town in the Burg

"The Judge is before the door: he that cometh will come, and will not tarry: his reward is with him."
– George Whitefield, minister during the Great Awakening

It was another day on the farm, and not too long after Stirling's visit to Ogden about Governor Livingston.

Phoebe had gone into town to purchase some supplies and yarn for her sewing. She often grew lonely on the plantation, and without friends there, she found herself growing restless and perpetually sad. Her monthly trips to town, even if she didn't need anything, always lifted her spirits. She was accompanied by her sister and the driver of the wagon. At the last minute, the judge asked her if she would take the extra milk from the cows on the farm and perhaps barter for some dry goods. Phoebe didn't mind doing such labor as it allowed her some extra interaction, which she enjoyed. Unlike her husband, who enjoyed his privacy and silence, Phoebe was more boisterous, enjoying the company of others. As she reached the few buildings in the hamlet, she told the driver to stop in the dry goods store.

Walking into the store, the driver carried the milk and placed the pails on the floor. Then he returned to the carriage.

"Hello, Mrs. Beardslee," said Phoebe. Mrs. Charles Beardslee had been one of the earliest settlers in the area.

"Hello, Mrs. Ogden," said Mrs. Beardslee. "How are you?"

"I am doing fine," said Phoebe. "Can you use some milk, Mrs. Beardslee?"

"Yes, we could indeed. Can I offer you some yarn that we spun yesterday?"

"Why yes, thank you," said Phoebe. She watched as Mrs. Beardslee rolled the yarn. As she waited, she overheard a conversation behind her while doing so. Mrs. Wade and another woman were talking to each other about their homes and the war. Mrs. Wade noticed Phoebe and whispered to the other woman, "That's Mrs. Odgen."

Mrs. Wade didn't lower her voice enough, and Phoebe overheard her while she inspected some cloth for purchase.

"What's wrong with the judge?" said the other woman. "I hear he is acting strange lately."

"Not sure," said Mrs. Wade. "The judge seems to avoid conversation lately. He used to speak publicly, and he would clearly voice his wisdom to all who would hear. A very learned fellow, if I do say so." She continued, "My son Nathanial speaks of it in the field while working or training with the militia, and my husband the carpenter speaks of it when he works in the gun powder mill operations."

"I wonder about his mental health and bearing."

"He was robbed and acts very strangely when asked about the event."

Phoebe was set aback that they would gossip like that right in front of her. She and her sister exchanged glances. After she had finished her task, she nodded at the two women. Her sister did the same.

They stopped at the haberdashery for buttons, thread, and cloth, then for some tea and bread at the local café. They discussed the new development.

"I am distressed, dear sister, that my husband should be the focus of such intense scrutiny."

"But is it not true on some level, at least?" she asked. "He has been quiet, which is unlike him when it comes to spreading the word of God."

"This is true," Phoebe said thoughtfully.

When they arrived home, Mrs. Ogden immediately searched out the judge, who was reading by the fire.

"Judge, Robert dear," said Phoebe.

He looked up from his reading, straining his eyes as if from the shift in focus. "Always happy to see you, my Phoebe." He lowered the open-paged book to his lap. "Is there something I may help you with, dear?"

"We need to have a serious conversation," she said.

The judge closed the book carefully and placed it on the floor beside his chair as the fire glowed a light golden flicker against the leather-bound volume of classics.

Phoebe said, "I have heard some gossip about town."

"Have you?" Ogden said, not meeting her eyes.

"It was about you," she said and gave her husband a stern glance.

The judge thought, *This conversation is not going away, and it is not going to end well.*

"Phoebe, dear," he said. "I made a pledge, an oath, but it was to save my life. I had to pledge, on my life, and my family's life, that I would not reveal who they were."

"Yes, darling, as we have discussed. But ..."

"Then when questioned," the judge continued, "I did not know whether to be honest to my calling as a lawyer and judge, as a good Christian and family man, or whether out of necessity of me and my family's life or death situation that I should maintain a middle road of approach, not denying, but not answering questions posed to me that would reveal these men and thus endanger my family and myself."

"People are wondering why you haven't been to the village. Why you aren't preaching. You are usually so social, much more than I am, and they know that your faith in God is needed in these troubling times."

"Yes, yes, of course, dear Phoebe. And now, with them on the loose, they are robbing more people, trying to free the royal governor, trying to steal our new governor and more."

"And they are the ones who are trying to steal away the governor of New Jersey and even capture the Declaration of Independence," said Phoebe, well-aware of rumors of their shenanigans but not who or how or why.

"And poor Lord Stirling, asking about his brother-in-law whom I might be able to help."

"The choice, Robert, is between honesty and necessity. It is between loyalty to your country and aiding our enemies. Not toward thieves and loyalists, whose sole mission is to rob and maim and kill and destroy our mission to be free."

This was a clear and concise distinction by Phoebe.

"Yes," said the judge as he crumpled in place.

"Oh, Robert," said Phoebe, in words of comfort. "You shall make the right decision. I know you will."

Chapter 20
Kidnap Gov Livingston, May 10, 1780

"Why do you use short swords? So that we may get close to the enemy."
– Plutarch

Governor William Livingston walked through the central front door of his mansion, Liberty Hall, in the town of Union, New Jersey. He walked off the grounds of the mansion and out into the street. As the governor, he had several guards surrounding him, due to the proximity of the enemy. The large British presence was stationed in Manhattan. They also had troops—mainly Hessian solders—much nearer, on Staten Island.

"It will be a needed change of pace from this dreadful war to my country home," said Governor Livingston as he approached the well-appointed coach that was ready and waiting to take him away. He carried documents under one arm as he approached the ride. The four horses were anxious for the start, scraping their hooves along the cobblestone roadway and shaking their manes.

The governor got into the coach and left soldiers behind as the coachman mounted the front seat, shook the reigns loosely, and began to drive the horses to a modest gait. Seated with the governor was an aide from the Patriot government of New Jersey.

"Sir, may I help you with those papers you're carrying?" said the aide. He was always looking to ingratiate his employer.

"No, I have them here on my person, vital documents that they are."

"Yes, sir."

"We've been lucky that the enemy has not come to Liberty Hall," said Governor Livingston.

There had been close calls for the Patriots, with the strong British forces just miles away across the narrow waters of the Arthur Kill.

"Right, sir, we've been lucky. How about the time when they came out looking for George Washington and missing him there at your home."

The aide was describing the time that a beautiful wedding had taken place at the governor's home, with many guests, including the general of the army. Word got out that Washington was there, but by the time the British arrived, he was gone.

"Ah, yes. That was a beautiful wedding at my home," Livingston remembered. "The British were so angry at not finding General Washington that they barged into the house, took some furnishings out into the street, and burned them."

As if reading his mind, his aide said, "Yes, lucky. Imagine if they caught the general? Or the others like Lafayette or Alexander Hamilton? They would have hanged them as leading traitors."

"Well, I hope those Redcoats don't come again."

"Right, sir. Hopefully no word about of your movements is known. Those British spies are all over this area, though."

"Yes, my friend, the spies can also be executioners, scoundrels like Lieutenant Moody, or other Skinner Loyalists who would do us harm."

"Governor Livingston," shouted the coachman as he turned his head while still holding the reigns, "we shall be off this bouncing cobblestone roadway shortly."

"That will be fine," said the governor. "I am in need of peace and quiet in this never-ending war."

"Right, and we are still going to Morristown, Governor Livingston?"

"Correct, and then to my home in Parsippany along the meadows." He was anxious to arrive at his country home, where there would be solitude and he could gather his thoughts. Governor Livingston leaned back in his leather seat in the carriage, rubbing his large ears and scratching at his nose, which was noticeably red.

"I know that you like the spacious acreage and the beauty of the natural world," said the aide, hoping to help comfort the governor.

"Correct. Nature inspires me, and the warmth and friendliness of the country are a comfort." Livingston looked out the window of the carriage. The many small city dwellings of Elizabethtown passed from view and from memory, like the many details on a large tapestry being swept from view as it is folded.

"All that bickering and bargaining with the Assembly, and this damn war. I just need a restful break."

"That you do, sir, that you do," said the aide.

"It reminds me of my lifelong yearnings. Why, when I was a youth at Yale, in 1747, I wrote a long poem entitled *'The Choice of a Rural Life.'* I remember it, from rote and within my active mind."

"Oh, allow me to hear it then, sir."

Livingston hesitated, but his aide insisted.

> *"From noise remote, and ignorant of strife;*
> *Far from the painted Belle, and white-glov'd Beau,*
> *The lawless masquerade, and midnight show,*
> *From ladies, lap dogs, courtiers, garters, stars ..."*

Livingston went on reciting his entire poem, with enthusiasm, until he finished.

"Sir, I can tell that you loved this poem and that you are quite an orator," said the aide, always willing to curry favor with his superior.

Governor Livingston leaned over to the aide and laughed as he said, "So, my good man, what do you think of it?"

"Hmmm," said the aide.

The aide's eyes were closed, as if coming out of a reverie. Governor Livingston was becoming quite angered. "Is this such a boring poem that you've been lulled to sleep?" The governor's face reddened to the color of his nose.

The aide opened his eyes and slowly but unequivocally said, "It is brilliant."

The coach rolled forward, and the roadway did soften the sound of the journey. From hard cobblestone to hard pack dirt, the journey became a calming ride, something that could soothe a troubled heart, a ride to provide a time to console and create a peaceful mind.

Just beyond the houses of the city there were many trees beside the roadway. The country was appearing, with lush green trees and underbrush, filling one's eyes with the color of summer, the season of life.

Along this traveled way, with nary a horseman or pedestrian near, a rabbit jumped off the dirt road and into the brush. The carriage then came upon two fellows. These two men were standing there looking, waiting to cross the road as the coach came toward them and approached a small bridge. Governor Livingston and the driver of the coach did not notice them as the orator recited and the aide dutifully listened.

The short man stepped out in front of the coach, apparently unaware of the approaching carriage. The four-horse team slowed. As the team was nearing a halt, Livingston's aide noticed that one of the men was holding a hunting knife, and beside it was the clear outline of a flint lock pistol revealed under the overcoat of the tall one with leather boots.

"Driver, step on it! This is an ambush!" cried out the aide, aware of the risky situation and the indication of the men being outlaws. The coachman spanked the horses, who yelped and then rushed forward. The short man had no choice but to step aside. A loud blast retorted as the tall one quickly raised his arm, produced sparks of flint, and the smoke of black powder exploded. A lead musket ball whizzed by the governor and tinged as it hit the carriage structure.

The coach hurried forth, and with that, there was the safety of distance from the would-be captors.

The rushing energy of a fast escape shuddered along the roadway as the team of horses and frightened men recovered their senses. The horses slowed, and the men eventually regained their normal breathing while looking behind them.

"We're safe!" said Governor Livingston. "For now."

***

In the meantime, at another place in the Elizabethtown area, one of the Moody gang members was apprehended. Another gang member came to Moody's hiding place, where he and his raiders were on the lam and lying in wait.

"One of your men was captured," said the culprit, out of breath from his long, arduous, and risky journey.

"I've heard some rumors," said Moody.

The visitor filled Moody in. "Someone, a Patriot named Major Hoops, took him and slashed him with a small sword, and pointed a cocked pistol at his head. From what I heard, he extorted a confession from our compatriot, including about the orders coming from General Knyphausen[xlviii], and that you were going to meet him at the top of Jenny Jump Mountain." He was wary himself of this. "A rider left shortly after and alerted Livingston. It is now common knowledge of your plan, and the governor has changed his itinerary."

"Damn!" said Moody. "We must run and hide from those

Rebels."

At five-eleven, General Knyphausen's appearance was slender and perfectly straight. His features were cut at extreme angles, and he carried himself in a military manner. Surprisingly, he was very personable, and as a result, likable. He, like many Germans, was rational and logical, and he acted with concision, focused on mission success. But he also had a sense of humor.

Wilhelm von Knyphausen was a commander of German auxiliary troops. He had received from the British government, in 1776, the command of 12,000 Waldeckers and Hessians hired by Britain to suppress the American uprising. Knyphausen was highly confident in his abilities. He had defeated the Americans in every battle he fought. Knyphausen participated in the Battle of Long Island in August 1776, the Battle of White Plains in November of 1776, and Brandywine near Philadelphia in 1777.

His most notable battle was the Battle of Fort Washington in the fall of 1776. He led the most important of the four attack forces. Not one to stand back, he fought as a common soldier, removing barricades with his own hands. When Fort Washington was captured, it was renamed Fort Knyphausen in his honor.

He had a reputation for being aloof, but also for being a superior officer. He was admired and beloved by his soldiers, and when others spoke of him, they mentioned his ability and his fairness. On June 2, 1778, he received news that his wife had died. And he was not young. In his sixties, he began to develop cataracts. On the whole, he was smart and of a rational temperament.

***

As the four-horse team rounded a bend in the road north from Trenton, Livingston could almost taste that he was in the country.

Suddenly, the coachman yanked on the reigns, and the team reared back. Snorting and whinnying could be heard, and it jarred the governor off his seat.

"What is happening?" said Livingston. He opened the door and stepped out. In front of the carriage was an American patrol. Off in the distance, heading over a treeless knoll, were several men running away.

Livingston folded his arms as he watched, and the leader of the Patriot patrol approached him and suggested that they not go to the country but go toward Morristown and more suburban surroundings.

"Thank you for saving us from those cowboys," said Livingston. "We will put a reward of two hundred dollars of bills of credit, issued on the faith of this State, the governor's name. We may make it two hundred guineas true money."

"We must hurry," said the patrol.

"We will go to Morristown as you suggest, Captain," said Livingston. He was relieved that they were safe, but at the same time, he felt forlorn at the loss of a rest time. He nodded to the coachman in agreement but also despondently said, "*Mine be the pleasures of a rural life.*"

Chapter 21
Judge at the Fire

"Every man has his secret sorrows which the world knows not."
– Henry Wadsworth Longfellow

    For such a tiny hamlet as Sparta was, there seemed to be an inordinate buzz about it. People walked a little faster and motioned to neighbors to cross the street and chat for a minute. Townsmen had something to say, something to gossip about. Word wanted to get out, be expressed. The people were just conveyors of the word. Such was the rumor mill.
    The talk was about the freebooters, the robbers who took advantage of the Revolutionary War, who placed a roving foothold onto the land where law enforcement might be thin and wanting. In this hamlet, the talk was about Lieutenant Moody and Claudius Smith. They had raided the region for too long, they would show up here and there and steal, kill, and maim. One's house or barn might be burned. The more these dastardly deeds were accomplished, the more fearful the townspeople became. They were growing to be helpless. Moody and his escapades had become too alarming for the community at large. They all knew that these outlaw acts were going to hurt them, and between Moody and Claudius Smith, the raiders were keeping the farmers and merchants in fright, both day and night. The whole situation was wearing on the population.
    With each new heinous crime, some men came to ask Ogden how to deal with this and what they should do to protect themselves. They also asked him what he knew about his own trouble, and how he might resolve it. Among other neighbors, their consternation grew as they looked for any clues to the men responsible. The sheriff did his best to round up the scoundrels. Judge Ogden did what he could as one of the leaders of the county Committee of Safety.
    One day, Ogden heard some loud conversation from outside his

home. It seemed to be coming down by the road from town. He looked out and saw that a dozen or so of the townsmen were coming up the hill toward his home, speaking to each other, reassuring each other.

He went to the door to greet them as they arrived. Upon opening his door to them, they saw him there, and an informal spokesman for them took his hat off.

"Greetings, Judge Ogden."

Somewhat off guard, the judge recognized several and greeted them with his eyes.

"Good afternoon, gentlemen. A fine day it is."

"Yes, Judge, fine day it is, sir," said another, a stocky clerk.

All present, outside the home or in the threshold, seemed a little relieved that agreement and satisfaction radiated amongst them all. At least for the moment and on the talk about the state of the country day.

The apparent spokesman cleared his throat and spoke.

"Judge Ogden, sir." He went on, "We—our group here—had some questions."

"Yes, my good man, by all means," said Ogden to the informal spokesman.

"Well, sir, I mean Judge," he said rather hesitantly, "we have been fearful of those outlaws who have been prowling the land. Our families are frighted to go out from home, or to go to nearby towns—Sparta or Franklin Furnace—because they don't want to be approached by villains and robbed or harmed."

"That certainly makes sense," replied Ogden. "These are trying times," he stated slowly and clearly. Aware of the reverential nature that his presence was to them, the judge tried his best to convey his wisdom.

"Yes sir, well, the sheriff has not been of help in eradicating the threat," mentioned the stocky clerk. "I am concerned about my clientele, and about my inventory being stolen."

"No, no you are correct; the sheriff has not been productive in this regard," said a farmer.

"Right," said the clerk.

"The sheriff has not retained these culprits, nor has he enlightened us at all about how to handle this threat," retorted Ogden. He mused somewhat on the conversation, trying to add his wisdom to the group of townsmen's doubts of the current events.

A feeling of fulfilment seemed to ascend from the group. They perceived strength from the judge's words. They knew that the judge could help reassure the uncertainty of the times and provide them with some grounding of truth and firmness of faith.

The informal leader cleared his throat again and said, "We had thought, sir, that you might shed some light on the present situation. That you could tell us who it is that is casting a shadow of evil over our area."

"I would certainly like to help you," said the confident Ogden. "I have a lot of experience and have seen many things in my career. And in my zeal for church matters."

"Good then, Judge," stated a short man toward the back of the group. "Can you shed any light on who robbed you a while back? Can you provide us with information on this?"

The judge froze in place. Stationary. Statuesque.

"Judge?" asked the man from the back, the one with the hanging question that begged to be answered.

Nothing.

"Judge?" asked the clerk.

"I would like to answer your questions as I can," said the judge, finally regaining some composure.

"And ...?" asked the man in the back.

"I can't say." With that, the judge looked at the crowd of townsmen.

There was not an answer to be had on the serious question posed before the group. The judge had nothing to give to resolve the dilemma.

The feeling of opportunity dissipated from the group.

The group withered away shortly after.

Judge Ogden closed the front door slowly and retreated into his home. He could feel the pressure of the gossip to come and worried about his reputation.

Chapter 22
Plot to Steal America's Treasure

"Lay not up for yourselves treasures upon earth, where moth and rust doth corrupt, and where thieves break through and steal."
– Matthew 6:19

New York City was a hub of activity. Sail ships were plentiful and scattered across the waters. Most of the buildings were wooden and populated the southern end of the island. Smoke billowed out of chimneys on cold days. On warm days, there was a bustle of activity as people shopped and greeted one another in passing.

This was the Loyalist stronghold in America, a safe haven for those who supported the British. It was also the home of thousands of Redcoat soldiers and their officers. Green fields spread across the northern part of the island while horse drawn carriages moved in unison up and down the cobblestone streets of Lower Manhattan.

One of those horse-drawn carriages came to a stop outside of a well-kept building: Mr. Archibald Kennedy's house, Number One Broadway. The impressive building was guarded by a number of soldiers who were well-trained and drilled. The constant motion as the men shuffled to positions of defense in guarding the British leadership in New York City was evident. Many were standing at attention with their rifles and bayonets at the ready. This was the British headquarters in the western hemisphere.

The horse paused and whinnied once as the metal-rimmed, wooden wheels stopped after skidding a bit on the cobblestone. A short man scrambled out of the small carriage. It was James Moody who jumped out of the carriage and walked past the guards who did not stop him but saluted him with familiarity as he touched thumb and forefinger to his round hat and nodded at his entry to the building.

"Good morning, Lieutenant Moody," said the officer in charge of the guards.

"Good day," he said. Rank was not questioned as Moody was dressed as a spy. While military dress provided a daunting look, the much more dangerous spy clothing was subtle and unassuming.

"Go right in Lieutenant Moody. General Clinton awaits."

Bounding up the stairs, Moody walked past another stout guard at the open door through a carved, wooden frame of ionic design. He entered the plush room, decorated with the best accoutrements of the day. His eyes looked toward the ceiling and the paintings on the wall. As he admired the ornate decor, Moody's eyes spotted the man in charge. He was dressed in his military finest.

The general stood in the middle of the room, apparently walking about in it. A short salutation ensued, followed with bowing and snappy military salutes. They quickly got down to business while a servant brought them hot tea.

Clinton motioned with his hand, and Moody plopped down on a cushy lounge.

"Sir, General Henry Clinton, I have a plan," said Moody, eager to share.

"Yes, Lieutenant, go ahead," said Clinton, recognizing his guest's anxious need to share.

"There's a man named Addison."

"Go on."

"Well, this Addison fellow had been employed by Mr. Charles Thompson, born in Ireland, no less."

Clinton seemed mildly interested. Moody could hear the wooden-sounding rumble of other carriages arriving on the cobblestone outside, and he suspected it meant that other news was coming in. The headquarters of the British Army was a beehive of activity here in America with the war raging. It was evident that Clinton's attention was waning, and his mind seemed to be wandering to other thoughts and subjects. Clinton gently pulled aside the soft, white, linen window dressing and peered out the window and back at Moody, who had paused to fondle the miniature teacup. As Moody went on, Clinton was beginning to get perturbed.

Moody sipped the hot tea. He put it down on the table and said, "Mr. Charles Thompson is the American Secretary to the Congress."

"I have heard of Thompson," said Clinton. "They have called him 'The Samuel Adams of Philadelphia' and 'Prime Minister of the United States.'"

"That's correct, sir. Well, a Major George Beckwith, who is the aide de camp for our partner, Hessian General Knyphausen on Staten Island, has informed me that he has a prisoner named Addison."

At this point, Clinton dropped the window linen, pivoted quickly toward Moody, was all ears, and sat down on an overstuffed sofa right next to Moody in the luxurious salon of velvety reds and blacks.

"This Addison fellow has been searched completely, and the interrogation has been very thoroughly documented."

"That is standard practice. I am glad to hear our associates have been capturing and interrogating those Rebels."

"Yes, Sir Clinton. You see, the man works in Philadelphia in a small department. He is a small player in a minor role."

"Go on."

"Well, sir, it seems that Addison, who is thought to be a Patriot, is actually a Loyalist at heart. In addition, he has agreed to work for our side."

"Excellent, Moody!"

"The Patriots aren't aware of this, it seems. So that means he can get us access to the State House in Philadelphia. This is where the Americans conduct their meetings, devise their intentions for a new government, and draw up their documents."

"Hmm, very interesting," said Clinton, rubbing his chin.

"Right now, the Americans are back in Philadelphia. And I propose that we steal their Declaration of Independence!"

Clinton stood up and walked thoughtfully across the room. "Yes, we of course had left Philadelphia. People tell me it was a bad move to go there, leaving our Burgoyne to be defeated at upstate Saratoga. Then they said it was a bad move to come back to New York City, what with the Battle of Monmouth and all. At the top, there are many major decisions to be made, and no one can tell the future and what the many ramifications can hold from those major choices."

Moody was savoring both the delicious tea and his singular position in this conversation.

"There are many things to consider. Though it might turn the war in our favor, I should warn you, Moody, that you will provoke those Rebels. And if you get caught ..." He left the rest of his thought hanging in the air.

Moody tipped back the dainty teacup, English clay baked and shiny with enamel over fine, hand-painted, colorful, miniature blue flowers. With chin up, he finished the brew.

"I won't get caught," Moody said.

"I don't doubt your abilities at ... shall we say *liberating* our enemies of their burdens as have been many. Ahem ... but they will hang you if you are caught."

"Yes, but they won't catch me."

"I admire your confidence. I give you my blessings, but this conversation shall remain here, within these walls."

Chapter 23
Stealing the Declaration of Independence

"Success is determined not by the completion of some action, but by how one engages in all action with wisdom and intelligence."
– Plato

The Delaware River was placid on this dark and moonless night not long after Moody and Clinton had spoken. The slack tide showed no movement as the flat water gave it a smooth surface like a finely polished marble.

Then came a ripple, a small movement on the otherwise silent water. Out of the darkness came a wooden bow, separating the flat water into two parts, slicing through the calm. The skiff was dull gray in color, blending into the black of night, which made it appear shrouded in its mysterious journey. The skiff was headed in a westward direction, from the New Jersey shoreline to the luminous sheen of the City of Brotherly Love.

"Men, keep it quiet!" Moody whispered. The pace of the paddling continued, the squeak of the wooden paddle shafts as they struggled back and forth in the weary and worn oarlocks. But the splashing diminished. Lieutenant James Moody was positioned near the bow. Five nondescript bodies were seated behind him and were hunched over in the watercraft. Each man had both arms stationed over the gunwales, and ensconced in each of those pair of arms was a small ore. The men were paddling steadily, rhythmically.

Lieutenant Moody looked ahead, to the distant shore, a mile or so to the land before them, illuminated by the light of lanterns glowing in homes and businesses, and depicting the well-defined metropolis of Philadelphia. He had his mind set on his destination, and on hatching a mischievous and brilliant plan—stealing the Declaration of Independence from the Americans.

As the skiff slipped forward in the black night, one of the men looked up. It was John Moody, Lieutenant James Moody's brother. He caught the lieutenant's eye. Moody spoke softly to his brother.

"John, what is on your mind?"

The seated rower said in a hushed tone, "Are you sure we are heading in the right direction?"

"I have us on a dead aim for the Philadelphia ferry house, no problem. We need to keep moving as the slack water of this neap low tide will not last long."

"Okay," said John. "I was remembering the time when we were boys and we sneaked off the farm and went fishing all night. Those were good days, tender times before the war when we had no cares. Before they destroyed our house and our farm."

"John, my brother, there's been many battles and much strife lately. We have been on this battle against the Rebels for five years or so. But you have been my light, something to live for. Yes, if we can get those rebel Americans quashed, then we can return home again, back to our farmland, and you and I can live in happiness as we remain under British rule."

"You are the brother I have always looked up to, James. Yes, one day it would be great to get back to the shore, to the tidewater near the Atlantic Ocean."

The lieutenant's attention wafted off for a moment with his brother. "Ah, the salty air along the shore. Right, it would be so lovely to be down to the Jersey shore after this is all over. Or, I have heard that Nova Scotia has a similar draw to it, with a large tidal flow and good fishing." But soon his eye caught the lights of the city ahead of them, and he recentered his attention on their goal.

The two brothers carried the same thoughts, and they were similar in their ways. They also looked very much alike. They were close brothers, friends also who had common experience in their lives. The lieutenant regained his sense of mission, ended the conversation, and looked ahead to see how their progress was going.

The others all looked up to Lieutenant Moody. Amongst the five rowers, including John Moody, were a local Loyalist named

Addison, a man named Laurence Marr, and Claudius. They kept rowing on a steady course.

"Okay, men, silence henceforth," said Lieutenant Moody. They went forward for a few more minutes, then Moody raised his hand and in a hushed voice said, "Stop rowing." The oars were carefully pulled from the water and brought into the skiff, and the men anxiously looked up. The skiff glided softly onto the shore.

The ferry house was an imposing sight in the quiet darkness. From where the skiff was grounded, there were tall piers reaching skyward, looming before the skiff as if giant trees in a forest. At the top of the pier was the ferry house, a shack that could receive larger boats and passengers when the tide was higher.

The rowers got out and pulled the skiff farther ashore. The dank smell of the sea was in their nostrils, and the muck of the mud pulled their feet down like suction. They all went up the embankment, one of them carrying a large satchel for the lieutenant. They gathered near the planked dock head that led to the ferry house at street level.

Since it was the middle of the night, the streets were vacant and quiet. The only sound heard was that of pulleys and canvas gently tapping against the wooden masts of the ships berthed along the shore as they modestly jockeyed about on their ship to shorelines.

One man, though, stood in the shadows of a building across the street from the ferry house. He stood stiffly and motionless.

Lieutenant Moody looked over toward the man and signaled to him. The fellow removed his cap and came slowly across the roadway to Moody. Moody tapped him on the shoulder and said to the group, "Our new partner, Addison, will be on his way to the statehouse."

The men looked at Addison. A couple smiled, and another grimaced.

Be on your way, Addison, you know your task," said Moody.

"Yes sir, Lieutenant Moody." Addison put on his cap and started on his way.

"Don't forget to bring the Declaration of Independence back with you!"

"Right, Lieutenant Moody." He laughed.

Addison looked proudly at his comrades. Nary another person was nearby when he walked onto the cobblestone city street, damp with dew. There was a slight glimmer coming from the pavers due to the reflection of the few flickering streetlamps that had been lit at dusk by the lamplighter. As he moved away past the last streetlight that led from the ferry, Addison faded away into the darkness and then disappeared around the corner of a building.

"What is he going to do?" asked one of the men.

Moody looked back and forth to see that the group was alone. He then said softly, "Addison is on his way to break in to where his day job is at the statehouse and steal important documents that the Patriots have stored there. He is known as one of our Loyalist comrades, but he was freed by the Hessian/British General Knyphausen. His freedom is dependent upon him living up to the terms of this act."

"Lieutenant Moody, what will we do while he goes to the statehouse?"

"We will wait here for his return."

As Addison disappeared from view, the rest of the crew turned to walk onto the ferry house to await Addison's return with the treasured documents. Walking ahead, Moody saw, at the edge of the dock head, a frail, elderly woman sleeping in a sitting position. Claudius quietly motioned this to the rest of the group who were coming behind him. The crew slipped by her until Claudius scuffed his leather boots on a plank board. One eye opened on the old woman's face, and she spotted Lieutenant Moody alone as he was trailing behind his squad of men. He stopped, as he knew he would be questioned as to why he was here so late at night with no ferry scheduled.

"Hello, ma'am," he said. He tipped his round derby and evinced a grin, with his silver tooth showing between his red lips. Hoping to shape the conversation, he said, "Well, I see you are the lady of the ferry house. We—I mean, I—am here awaiting arrival of a dear one from New Jersey tomorrow morning." He thought that would do it, but not fully. She continued to view him using the one eye.

"Where do you come from?" she said, her voice barely audible.

"I am a simple man from the Jersey Brigade."

"Name?" she said, still half asleep but gaining interest in his presence. He felt that she wouldn't even remember the conversation come morning because she seemed to be in and out of sleep.

"I am Moody. From the Jersey Brigade," he chimed in, lying through his silver tooth enough to make the devil himself proud.

The old lady thought for a minute and mentioned the schedule to the talkative fellow in front of her. "Sure, the next boat is expected mid-morning." And the eye shut as she returned to slumber. The sleep didn't seem to hold, though, as she began to move about and eventually got up to leave, apparently disappointed by the loss of her quiet corner in the otherwise still and sheltered ferry house and with the gang shuffling and mumbling and one snoring rhythmically.

Meanwhile, the crew was in the back of the ferry house, sitting and waiting. Moody tried to encourage them.

"Men, your actions here will turn the tide of the war against the Rebels and to the benefit of the British." The gang of men smiled smugly and with a great sense of determination.

The Loyalist Maar said, "You are quite the great man."

They all agreed, and Claudius chuckled. John looked on at his brother with a sense of gratitude for his accomplishments, eyes filled with tears at what they were about to conclude successfully.

Moody pulled back the string that gathered the top of the dirty, white satchel, the one that they had brought by the rowboat filled with coins, cash, and gold doubloons.

"Men, let's award the return of Addison and settle back with cigars and whiskey!"

There was total agreement.

For the next hour or so that night, the men waited, smoking, sometimes taking a sip of the whiskey they'd brought, and dozing intermittently. Just before dawn, after the long day of preparation, the anxiety that it would turn out well, the tiring row across the Delaware River, and several of the crew fell asleep in the ferry house as they continued to wait for Addison's return.

Lieutenant Moody said to Claudius, "This is too much for me. I am going to the far corner of the ferry house to get some shuteye." He went around the corner. Following close behind was Claudius, wanting to keep some distance from the others, what with the doubloons in the satchel.

Moody sat down in the far corner. He finally dozed off. Unsettling dreams crept into the lieutenant's head.

***

Suddenly, the slumber was shaken. Loud sounds pierced the ears of the sleeping lieutenant. He shook with a start. Claudius started to put on his tall, leather boots and get up, but the lieutenant put out his arm and held him down by the shoulder.

"Shhh!" he hissed with a finger to his mouth.

Through a knot hole in the partition that separated this small cove from the main ferry house, the lieutenant was able to make out what was happening. That frail, elderly lady, short as she was in the chair the night before, stood ramrod straight as she stormed into the door of the ferry house. Behind her was a squad of Patriot soldiers, muskets drawn and pointing them at the three men in the front of the ferry house as they were scattered across the floor and then pausing with hands up.

"Here are those slovenly men, soldiers; take them away," she said dryly.

The leader of the soldiers said, "They wanted to steal important documents from the statehouse, but Addison would have none of it. He got free from the British and put an end to this dastardly plot." The soldiers looked on, waiting for confirmations.

The woman looked at the motley bunch and said, "Where's Moody?"

Moody remained silent, but he knew his luck had run out. But then to his surprise, the old lady pointed to his brother, John.

"That's him!" said the old lady. "That's Moody! That is the one you are all after!" She glanced at John. "Yes, that's the one I saw last night!" Sadly for John, he had been mistaken for, and confirmed, as his notorious brother Lieutenant James Moody.

The Patriot squad of soldiers pointed their bayonets into the chest of John and dragged him out of the ferry house, along with the other two.

Without a moment to think, Claudius grabbed the satchel of money and ran to the one window at the end of the ferry house and jumped out of it. Lieutenant Moody followed behind and jumped. He suddenly worried that the tide was out and that they would break their legs as they would land in the muck and rock.

The next thing that Lieutenant Moody knew, he was gasping for air, underwater and struggling to breathe. He was flailing away with his arms, yearning to reach the surface. He finally did so and exhaled and then began coughing. Coming up beside him were a pair of leather boot soles, turned upside down. The two boots began splashing back and forth, as if they were walking in reverse. They then disappeared, followed quickly by the familiar face of Claudius spitting out water.

"Phew," said Claudius. "I am alive!" He then looked around. "but the satchel, the valuable satchel, I had to let go. It is gone to the bottom!"

"You and I are lucky to get away," said Lieutenant Moody. They both swam to shore, and Claudius skedaddled toward Northern Liberties, where the Lawrence family—Morris's in-laws—lived. The lieutenant hid in a small stream, a ditch that came from the Old City as a sewer. Several patrols of Patriot soldiers passed within yards of him. He then made a long walk when night came and hid in Indian corn fodder haystack. A passing patrol bayoneted the stack. So much for the sheaves being cut down. But they missed stabbing Moody, remaining unaware that he was inches from the bayonets.

Days later, having escaped, and now across the Delaware River and in New Jersey, Lieutenant Moody met up again with Claudius Smith. They walked by Moody's old farmstead. There was not much left, having met destruction at the hands of the Patriots.

"Claudius, you made it!" said Moody, thankful for one compatriot escaping. "Where's the money satchel?"

"When I jumped from the window, I hit the water, along with you. I was gasping for my life and to stay on top of the water. Without knowing it, I dropped the satchel and my boots. By the time I gained my breath, the boots popped up beside me, so at least I have those."

"Urggh!" exclaimed Moody.

Claudius looked skyward, following some noisy ducks heading toward the shore.

"One of these days we will beat these damn Rebels," said Moody in disgust.

"There'll be a lot more work to be done," said Claudius, "and a lot more reward money coming our way if we play our cards right."

"Well, we blew this last one," said Moody.

"That's for sure," groaned Claudius. "First we get double-crossed by that Addison fellow," he said while grimacing, "followed by that seemingly frail, old woman getting the soldiers. And then finally losing that satchel in my hands, the one with all that doubloon reward money."

"A shame," said Moody.

"Now, Lieutenant, what are you going to do about your brother?"

"I don't know."

"I heard some rumors," said Claudius.

"And they are?" asked Moody.

"He has been captured while we slept behind the barrier where they didn't find us. And they thought he was you. They may kill him as they continue to think that your brother was really you."

"Claudius, that is a dilemma for me. A tremendous problem. Me or my brother, what can I do?"

On November 14th, 1781, John Moody was executed, and Laurence Marr later was hanged as well. The world thought it was Lieutenant James Moody.

Lieutenant Moody understood that the notoriety James attained, and that his brother admired, would pain him for the rest of his life.

"Oh, my dear brother John, only wanting to retire and fish in the tidewaters," said Moody, thinking of the last conversation with his now dead brother.

Chapter 24
Judge in His Library

"A room without books is like a body without a soul."
– Cicero

A hundred or so miles away from Philadelphia, the town of Sparta was far from the cobblestones that Moody saw reflecting the lamplit glimmer in the city of Philadelphia. While some of the Moody gang were hanged, including his brother, Lieutenant James Moody escaped back into New Jersey. And this did not comfort the judge when he heard about it.

Judge Robert Ogden II felt that harm may come again to visit he and his family. When all else failed, he retreated to his ornate study in Sparta. The moral matter that he was enduring had been troubling his mind for too long. He sat in his chair beside his work desk. He rubbed his brow with his fingers as if he were in pain.

Phoebe happened by, on her way to the kitchen. She looked at him with concern. "Robert, dear, are you in pain?" Not hearing a reply, she walked in. She stood in front of his desk as he finally looked up.

"Hello, dear Phoebe, what is it?"

"I am worried about you."

He felt he needed to level with his wife. "You know all the various people who have been coming up to the door and asking for me?"

"Yes, of course."

"Well, I've been avoiding, time and again, to divulge the names of those detestable thieves." He stood up and grabbed a book from the shelf, a classic tome from the ancient Greek world. He laid it open on his desk and ironed flat some creases on the pages with a slow sweep of the palm of his hand. He spoke to Phoebe.

"I have had a good life and have done the right things. I live comfortably, as did my grandfather and my father who were respected men in the lawyer trade. I received a liberal education and have taken up a prominent position in my county and my colony. I have become judge and speaker of the Assembly for our royal colony of New Jersey."

Robert was, at this point, preoccupied with thought and continued to press the creases of the pages, one after the other, in the many pages of the classic, a work by Aristotle.

"Too many thoughts, even the logic doesn't make sense with my problem, my predicament."

He kept looking down and tried to see if there was anything in his books and his library that would have a suitable answer for his dilemma.

His wife remained in front of his desk, listening. "Many take comfort in my expressions. They do so knowing that in my views, there are assumptions of assuredness, that my remarks are held as without doubt, to be without stain of bias or selfishness. What I say, both in the courtroom as judge or in the parlor with social interaction or as a disciplined Christian, is taken to be dignified and the truth. Many have considered me an honest man."

"Yes, that is true. You are known to many as the honest lawyer."

"Those haughty days as a youth with carefree abandon were light; small issues at hand with little responsibility. On balance minor deeds done with little need to make account. Then as a young man, the leverage of social standing and aristocratic influence tended to help me rise to high levels of society, to be a power in politics and an enabler of calls for freedom and independence."

The judge did not say what else he'd been thinking. Having been chased out of his home in the city, having been chastised for some decisions, his likeness tarnished in effigy and his crops burned, and then robbed shortly after at his country home, he felt that he was violated.

Robert Ogden looked around the room at the volumes of law books and classical literature crammed into his shelves. These books had acted like brushes that were used to color a painting that represented the world he knew. The volumes described the stories that built western civilization and shaped the ways of living life in the Western world. This was also his accepted way of life.

"And now I am at a pinnacle of my career, and my life, and I can direct the thought of great masses of people, but I do so not by the sword or strong muscle, I do it by a simple word or two. From my hearkening, from my public discourse, this colony has become split. Many have heeded my words and taken to the Patriot calling. Others have been drawn closer to the British side. Their anger and their zeal have led them to soil my reputation."

His hand quivered as he pressed down harder at the creases in the pages, lines that were visible on the page but lines that would not go away.

"And now I find myself distressed and agonizing over my current situation. There are bad men who have performed bad acts. And now they are lurking to do more and may do such devious plots to quash the Patriot cause, and masses, treating the colonists like my hand is pressing down on these pages from long ago. What am I to do?"

He placed his full weight upon his palms.

Chapter 25
Imprisoned at West Point, Battle Stony Point July 16, 1779

"There is nothing so confining as the prisons of our own perceptions."
–William Shakespeare

July 21ˢᵗ, 1780 saw Lieutenant Moody walking down a road which was somewhere north of New Jersey. Much of the state considered itself part of the new American nation. But the British considered the colonies to be under their authority. Moody crossed over the border into New York—a place some called a colony and others deemed a state.

Moody whistled out loud, happy with the day. He happened upon another person, a young man, who stated his preference for the Loyalist side. He questioned why Moody was so joyous.

"Well," said Moody, "while some of the skirmishes up North here have not gone quite our way, our British strategist Sir Henry Clinton has correctly decided to move against the Rebels down in Charleston, South Carolina. He will be sending 8,700 troops by the British Navy under Arbuthnot on December 29ᵗʰ to besiege Charleston." He continued to whistle and then said, "Yes, by May of this year, the Rebels, under Benjamin Lincoln, had surrendered the largest number of American Rebels thus far in this was. 5,500 men!"

"I feel that I am safe up here in New York, and I like to put on airs of how fancy it is to be here."

Moody expressed himself so, in a visual manner. He was dressed in his favorite clothing, the fancy dress of the British soldier. His pants were clean and white, no rips or tears and great weaving and sewing evident from competent mills and industries in Britain. A fine and shiny gorget[xlix] was hanging from his neck, an ornamental reminder of the times past when knights wore armor about their breast. His wore a blood red coat. The trim on the inner opening was deep black, emblazoned with gold buttons streaming down in fine order. His belt was made of leather and festooned about his waist where he carried the necessities of war—a knife and a supply of gun powder, wadding, and deadly musket balls. The uniform, replete with ornaments and military hardware, made him feel respectable, though some might think him pompous. He walked with a stagger of prominence, and a swelling feeling of superiority. As he glided along the roadway, his uniform produced the contempt of some of those he met along the way; they eyed him with sneers and jeers. Still, he kept and wore upon his head, whether in street clothes or these clothes of a royal trooper, his beloved, round, black derby. Worn daily, it was one of his most treasured possessions. Moody believed that sporting such a stylish uniform meant he was in good stead with the greatest army in the world.

Also, as is the case in the Revolutionary War, wearing his uniform could have a decisive effect on his life. He knew if one was found in their uniform and caught by the enemy, they would be considered a prisoner of war. In this war, prisoners were treated with some degree of responsibility by the other side. They would be fed and housed, although sometimes poorly as in the case of the Patriots housed on the prison ship Jersey holed up in New York Harbor in Wallabout Bay. Many were traded for a soldier captured on the other side, and some were "paroled" or "pensioned" and thus freed from being a prisoner. But if the active fighter did not have the uniform of his sworn country with whom he had allegiance, he would be considered a spy and would likely be hanged. Spying could have an enormously deleterious effect to either army; they could leverage their hidden strength to make the others lose the war as a result. And spying was believed to be a dirty and contemptuous profession. Moody was known as a master spy, among the ranks of others, like George Washington himself.

As Moody trotted through town, imperious and confident, he stopped to gaze at his reflection in a shop window. What he didn't know was that after taking part in a battle in New York Colony along the Hudson, his life would drastically change.

***

"Moody, keep it moving," said a well-dressed American Continental soldier. Moody turned to see the soldier prompting him with a long rifle: a musket with a French bayonet shining at the tip. The soldier had taken his weapon and pushed the point into Moody's back, just hard enough to make him keep walking down the dirt path at the same pace. Moody gasped a little as the point of the bayonet penetrated his clothing. He then winced. But he kept his stride as it was now a compulsory march to a stockade.

Moody was one of several hundred Loyalists captured at the Battle of Stony Point. The column of solemn soldiers trudged along. Up from the rear of the column came a horse and rider trotting beside the forlorn British sympathizers with their heads bowed as they shuffled slowly along. The horse was reined in by the rider so that it slowed down and walked alongside Moody.

"Well, well," said the rider. "Looks like we finally nabbed Lieutenant Moody!" The rider was American General Anthony Wayne. He looked on the Loyalists with derision. "You tend to take my attention away from womanizing." The general had white hair and a red, Irish drinker's face.

Moody slowed a bit and looked up. This provoked the soldier to once again prod him with his bayonet. Several Americans laughed as Moody hastened his speed for a step or two after each prod. Not one to be outdone, Moody began singing out a poem.

> *"And now I've closed my epic strain,*
> *I tremble as I show it,*
> *lest this same warrior-drover, Wayne,*
> *should ever catch the poet."*

One of the guards said, "I'd advise you not to tempt the general with the writings of the British Major André. He gets so mad at deviant behavior, swears and spits out, that they have called him 'Mad Anthony Wayne' due to the blusterous, Irish temper."

Coming back near Moody on his mount, the general looked contemptuously at his prisoner.

"So, that Major André of yours thinks he's artsy, eh?" said General Wayne. "Maybe, if we do catch him, he will hang from a noose. And maybe I will be present for the hanging."

The soldier placed his bayonet on the back of Moody's head and plucked off his beloved round, black derby. It bounced along the dirt roadway. Moody scurried to pick it up.

"Be that as it may," said the general. "You seem pretty cheerful. Maybe you should get some lashes with the whip, eh? Yes, some lashes, well laid on."

Moody then became quiet and marched along as instructed. General Wayne said, "You remind me of the spy Jemmy the Rover, my old neighbor who was always absent-without-leave from his post in the Patriot army. But for you, Moody, we will send you to a place you could never escape—the lock up in our great fortress West Point." Spitting on the ground in disgust, the general used his heels to pinch the horse's belly and he trotted up the ranks and out of sight of the column of men.

***

Moody sat dejected on the cold slab of cement in the jail cell. He had been caught once more and was now in the custody of the American Army again. But this time, he felt he had no way of escaping from this large stone prison in the fortress at West Point. He looked out the bars in the window and onto the sights outside. The view of the cliffs far below was magnificent, and the mighty Hudson River flowed by, majestically blue, wide, and serpentine as it wound its way through the trees of green that reached skyward. The light from the sunrise crept into the room, brightening the cell with a pale yellow on this mid-August day.

Outside of his cell of confinement, the guard announced, with all the discipline of a well-trained soldier, the following statement that was well within earshot of Moody, in fact, pointedly to Moody. "August 10, 1780, prisoner Lieutenant James Moody is accounted for, in this West Point prison. And that he certainly was placed in the dungeon in leg irons and handcuffed, with two guards inside and two guards outside. Situation confirmed and approved." He saluted the officer who was making his rounds. The loud report of the guard and the stern manner of verbal delivery were ways of assuring that the prisoner would not be able to escape.

I don't see any way that I can make it out of here, Moody thought.

His head drooped. The garrison was well fortified as it commanded the Hudson River and its approaches, and the Patriot fighters were commanded to keep it secure from invaders. It wasn't even worth the time to think about escaping. There was not much else to do but sleep, to rest as best he could if an opportunity to flee came up, despite the pain and the hardship. He was hungry and needed a bath, but ample food and bath were luxuries that he was not afforded as a prisoner. In fact, he was forced to wear leg irons and was handcuffed. Water poured into his cell when it rained, and he ate from a filthy bowl a disgusting mash of rotten flour and meat. From the irons, his wrists and ankles became lacerated, and the jailer tormented him, making sure he knew he was to be hanged, and pointing out the various indignities of such a death sentences.

One night Moody was awakened by the scuffle of feet and the commotion of busy tasks taking place outside his cell. He heard the scratch and clunk of hallway door locks being opened and the shuffle of shoes, the familiar sound of feet drawing close together as soldiers would prepare and stiffen to attention for a salute to a senior officer. The scramble of words and the clamber and bustle against grit on the stone floor were unmistakable predictors that something was happening. All the guards in his view came to attention and held their rifles at parallel to their vertical and ramrod straight bodies and held closely with two hands to their neatly attired uniforms.

Suddenly from a distance in the echoing hallway came the voice, "All rise and attention! The commanding general is approaching!"

Shortly after, in the sudden quiet after the call, sure-placed footsteps grew in intensity and then flowed around the corner in the dungeon. Several well-attired officers in a group were following a man who was the obvious leader. He was of a general's rank, and he was followed by his staff as he rounded several of the small cells adjacent to Moody's and then stopped in front of Moody's bleak abode.

"Open the cell door," said the general. A guard snapped toward his key ring and bent toward Moody's cell door lock.

Once the door was opened, the general walked into Moody's cell.

The general had a broad forehead and neatly coifed hair. He had very black hair, dark like fully decomposed pine tar, and olive skin that resembled that of a light-colored deer. His eyes were black dots that stared at Moody coldly and without a sign of empathy. He wore a white neckerchief adorning the golden epaulets with spine, buttons, and golden fringed braids hanging down, all confirming signs and signifying the rank of a general.

"Moody, I presume?"

"Yes, sir," said Moody.

"I see you are enjoying your lunch."

"I can't consume it. This is not food but an obscenity."

"Your loss," said the general. Then he looked at Moody like he was contemplating a cow for sale. "So, you are the fellow whose name is a terror to every good man?"

"That's what I hear, General. To all the Rebel men, that is."

"Well, you've got yourself into a pretty situation," the general said and then went to the other end of his small cell where there was a window in the thick, gray stone. The window was only a small slit in the very thick, rough-hewn rock face of the wall, and the view, otherwise beautiful, was interrupted by the presence of the iron bars of the prison cell. The general saw the mighty Hudson River flowing slowly toward New York City and then the sea.

The general stepped to the side of the window slightly so that he could see the nearby grounds and yard in front of the prison. "If you look out this window, Moody, you can see the gallows that has just been built. You have long merited to be hanged from such gallows. Perhaps you should prepare for eternity."

As he realized what the general was saying, Moody lost all feeling in his legs. The irritation that he was suffering from the iron chains was suddenly out of mind as it had been displaced by a cold chill overtaking his body. This was the end of his life, and there was no way out.

Terrified, he said nothing.

The general laughed. It was only then that Moody realized he was speaking[l] to General Benedict Arnold[li], and immediately he blamed this horrible man who had taken over the fortress. What Moody didn't know was that even while Arnold held him captive, Arnold was plotting to run from West Point, turn Loyalist, and hand the garrison over to the British.

Nevertheless, Moody relaxed. Surely Arnold, who Moody had no reason to believe was of help to him, would not deign to walk him to the gallows. Moody tried to calm himself. While he didn't know when his last day would be, he prayed it wasn't today. He felt some relief.

The general turned to him. "In this atmosphere of shifting loyalties, in the midst of partisan raids and internecine warfare, you have thrived, Mr. Moody. But no more. You shall be taken to the gallows soon enough. Your trial is set for September 1st. You might someday recall that I told you that."

The general smiled cruelly and left the cell.

Moody was left to think of his life. How he had come to be facing his death when he was in his prime. He recalled the day he refused to sign a loyalty oath to the Patriot government of William Livingston. How after that he had suffered verbal harassment and threats each day that he remained. He remembered how once the Rebels waved tomahawks over his head. And that time one of the Patriots had attempted to kill him while he walked the grounds of his own property with a Loyalist friend. How they had burned his family's crops and tried to murder his parents.

After he left, he happily joined the New Jersey Volunteers, and he recalled how, the first day, he had made acquaintances with people who agreed with him. He was not someone who made friends easily, but he enjoyed not having threats of death hanging over his head. It was Skinner, he recalled, who recognized his nascent talents as a spy and his skill at guerilla warfare, and through the last Royalist Attorney General Cortlandt Skinner, Moody was proud to say that he had become one of Britain's best and more productive agents.

He tried to tell himself that he would die proudly for the cause. But his stomach ached from hunger, and his body roiled painfully from the wounds of his arrest. He wondered if it had all been worth it, and though he knew on some level it had proved good for his beloved Britain, he was not sure if the risk, now as he faced his painful and humiliating death, was worth it.

If he had only returned to Bull's Ferry one day later or one day earlier, instead of on July 21st, just as General "Mad Anthony" Wayne's men attacked the fort. He recalled the words as they echoed in his brain, that the captain had shouted, "You will be hanged for a spy."

On September 1st, he was at first hopeful when he was moved out of the treacherous and disgusting cell at West Point and into a hut at Washington's encampment. He'd been placed in a dank cell—which he decided was much more comfortable—but he noted how close it was to the camp's liberty pole and felt his head throbbing and his stomach burning. Hunger was his primary concern, and he hoped the food would be better there. Moody thought of how wonderful it would be to live to a ripe age and fish in solitude in Nova Scotia.

"We have been ordered to remove your leg irons, by orders from the general himself."

Moody was relieved, but he tried not to show any emotion. He assumed, "by the general himself" they referred to Washington whose many correspondences he had interrupted and given to his Loyalist faction heads. Inwardly he was shamed by this humanitarian gesture. But he also began to craft, immediately, a way to escape.

"The trial has been moved to September 16th," said one of the men. "But rest assured, we will get rid of you no matter what. You have clearly enlisted men to fight against this state for the British. There is evidence practically falling from the sky."

The man laughed. Then he said, "You have done so in the service of the king, and you know our laws; the penalty is death."

"And," said another jailer, "the governor will personally prosecute you and handpick the members of the court to ensure you will receive a verdict of guilt."

The men turned around, laughing snidely, and walked out. When they locked him up, the keys jangling as they walked away, Moody spit on the ground and then crumpled into a heap. But he would not give up. Without the leg restraints, he was halfway to freedom, and one cold night he begged for a watchcoat off the sentinel outside his door and covered his hands as he used what he could—a post and a hole in the dirt floor—to bend and finally break the wrist cuffs. Then he waited, and when the sentinel was distracted, he burst from the room, out the door, whereupon he grabbed a musket from a guard and then marched with a purposeful gate as though he were one of Washington's men, while the word had been sounded of his escape. Keeping calm, Moody cut through the lines of men, crawling sometimes, undetected, then spent the next fifty-six hours eating birch leaves until he reached British lines at Paulus Hook on the 21st, five days after his scheduled trial. The men were amazed. They took him in and fed him, many admiring Moody's sheer guts and stamina. His would be a name, they all knew, that would go down in the annals of history.

Chapter 26
Sir Henry Clinton

*"The firmer as the Rebels pressed, the loyal heroes stand,
Virtue had nerved each honest breast and industry each hand."*
– British Major John André, from his poem *The Cow Chase*

One day, being summoned to report, Moody made his way to the British commander's dwelling on Broadway in the southern half of the island.

The door opened, and the British officer looked him up and down as he entered the exquisitely furnished room in the aristocratic mansion in Manhattan. An aide moved forward to take his round derby, but Moody refused, clutching it tightly. He spotted Sir Henry Clinton and walked forward to shake hands. Moody was extremely appreciative of meeting the most important British person in North America.

"Come in, Lieutenant Moody. Make yourself comfortable. I hear you have some information for us."

Moody started to put his precious hat on the entry table but changed his mind and kept it firmly in his hands, clutched at this point as if for dear life.

"Thank you, sir," said Moody.

"We can't be too cautious, Lieutenant," Clinton said with a frown and a depressed tone.

Moody took the tea that was offered to him by an aide-de-camp and sipped.

Clinton said in a low voice, "Caution is so necessary. The other day our beloved Major John André[lii] was hanged as a spy by the Americans."

"Oh. Yes, sir. What a terrible loss."

"He was such a personable young man. He was an artist, singer, soldier, and gentleman with great social skills. He was a prolific writer. He had composed many of my dispatches handled by spies. He was so close to me. Did you hear that he did a self-portrait on the night before his execution?"

"Yes, sir, word of that kind travels quickly."

"Oh my," said Clinton "Even General Washington had said of Major André that 'he was more unfortunate than criminal.'"

"Yes, sir, I heard that Washington also said that he was an accomplished man and gallant officer."

"Poor fellow. I had many good times in his company. He lived in Benjamin Franklin's house when we were in Philadelphia. He went with me on our campaign in Charleston, South Carolina. Many good times in his company."

Clinton got up from his seat and walked about and looked toward the window for a moment of thought. He pulled the white doily window shade aside with his hand.

Sir Henry Clinton was in charge of New York City's British Army. He was also a major general. Among his many badges of honor was his Knight of the Bath. He commanded with distinction at Bunker Hill, Long Island, and the storming of Fort Washington and Fort Clinton. He was also involved in episodes along the Bronx River and Westchester County—home of that American Patriot Lewis Morris III, who was a signer of the Declaration of Independence and who, unknown to the British, was living nearby to Judge Ogden in Sussex County. He was proud of his many accomplishments, and Moody, watching him, could see that in the way the man carried himself, with distinction and honor.

"This war is not going the way that I wanted," said Clinton. "This lovely view from my window is no balm for me." Clinton dropped the window shade and gazed at Moody.

"Well, Moody, what do you have for me?"

Moody went over to the table at the entrance to retrieve his hat where he'd hid a letter he'd intercepted from General Washington. In walked a man who Moody was too surprised and stunned to greet. Moody was motionless for a long moment. At last, while Clinton smiled, Moody exclaimed, "General Benedict Arnold!"

Immediately, Moody made as if to run, thinking that somehow the Americans were just outside the door, having taken over Clinton's apartments.

"Calm down, Lieutenant Moody," said General Arnold.

Moody looked at Clinton, who did not seem at all worried. He was confused. "What is going on here?" he asked. He recalled those moments, speaking to Arnold in the prison at West Point. What a horrible, little man he'd seemed.

"I am now with the British," Arnold said calmly. "Come to make my peace with you. I knew at the time, I'd soon defect to the British side of things, but I could not well reveal that to you. I had hoped to find a way to set you free, but the guards were everywhere, and I couldn't arouse any suspicion."

"Oh my." Moody thought about the recent events. He wasn't sure whether to be angry or relieved.

"Yes, and I see you also brought the letter that I requested you to." Arnold clutched the letter. "Do you know of Major André?"

"Of course," said Moody.

"Major André was hanged a short time later," said Clinton, still by the window. "The hangman was a Tory, and he was released to go back home to Smith's Clove."

"Smith's Clove where Claudius Smith is?"

Both men nodded. "I find that you, Moody, are a faithful British spy."

Clinton walked anxiously around the room. "We are ready to move out and into the Jerseys to take Washington. He is a short distance from Staten Island, and if we send the Hessians from there, they could be in Morristown in short order and take Washington out, kill him, and be done with this war. We could then follow with troops from Manhattan here or Staten Island and wipe out the northern American Army."

All three men considered this in contemplation.

"We need you to give us some information, Moody."

"Yes, Sir Henry Clinton," said Moody "I am at your command. I will be unknown in the parts I need to go to get information."

Arnold said, "You freed our sympathizers from the Sussex County jail, escaped the Morristown jail, got out of West Point prison, broke free from being chained on a liberty pole at Washington's camp on September 17th, 1780, and made it here, so certainly you have the wherewithal to help in the future."

Both men smiled, though Moody could not ignore the worry lines around Clinton's eyes and mouth. "Right then, Lieutenant Moody. You are to help us seize the mails of Washington, and thus get his secrets of the American military strategy and plans. It may be our only chance to win this war."

Two men were suddenly at the doorway, looking in. One was an admiral, and the other was fancifully clad.

"Good afternoon, gentlemen," the fancy dresser said.

Both Sir Henry Clinton and General Benedict Arnold remained completely silent while bending gracefully, in fact reverently, before the two new guests.

Arnold leaned over and softly said in Moody's ear, "That is Admiral Digby who is chief of the fleet, and he is escorting Prince William Henry."

The startled Moody turned to Arnold and asked, "Prince William Henry? You mean from England? You mean the prince who is in line for the royal throne of Britain?"

Arnold nodded.

"Oh, my!" said Lieutenant Moody, and he too removed his round derby hat and bent as low as he could in respect to the crown.

Admiral Digby remained at attention at the doorway entrance to the room. He was of reserved stature, as would be fitting of a man who'd be a baron. He was known as Admiral of the Red and outranking other admirals and commanded the North American Station. He had a powdery white face with short, jet-black hair and the calm demeanor which is fitting for a man who would help to move the United Empire Loyalists out of New York City if, heaven forbid, the British were to lose the Revolutionary War.

To his side was a rather rambunctious young man in gaudy and colorful dress. He could be no more than sixteen years old, a restless child it would seem with a baby-face and a plump belly. It appeared that he had taken a drink or two, held his hand to his hip, and looked skyward.

"Hmm, reminds me of Claudius," Moody mumbled to himself.

Benedict Arnold heard this, though. "Watch yourself, Moody. I know of Claudius Smith. His luck will run out one of these days, I do predict."

"This room looks too stuffy for me," said the boy who could one day be the future king, King George IV, if he did. "You men can stay here and play cards or whatnot. I think I will roam the streets of Manhattan and look for fun!"

The three other men swiveled their eyes to each other, telegraphing a thought to the effect of, "Whose turn is it to watch the prince now?"

"Don't fence me here, gentlemen," said Prince William Henry as he giggled like a child. "Although it wouldn't be that bad, like in the West Indies plantations where the slaves are in a state of humble happiness." The prince then pranced down the hallway and out the front door to the streets of Manhattan.

Admiral Digby finally spoke. "I am jealous of your positions, gentlemen." The admiral then turned and ran off behind the lad, shouting, "Can someone help me follow the prince? He is on a course to drunkenness, womanizing, and he will undoubtedly create an opportunity for harm by those damn Patriots!"

Chapter 27
Ogden to Reveal June 23, 1780

"Ready to ride and spread the alarm, through every Middlesex village and farm, for the country folk to be up and to arm."
– Henry Wadsworth Longfellow, *Paul Revere's Ride*

Warm tea and a cozy seat.
That's when it began.
Sitting closely with his beloved wife Phoebe, Judge Ogden chatted calmly about maintaining the home. It was a pleasant conversation, the type that comes easily to a couple who had been married many years. Such conversation helped shape the day, informed partners of their loved one's health, and brought soothing to the troubled soul.

The judge had a feeling that there was some commotion about. Phoebe's knitting was certainly consoling to hear; the little "knock-knock-knock" of the wooden knitting needles as they slowly spread out a nicely laid knitted pattern.

Slowly, coming to his ears, was another repeating sound—a high-pitched tinkling. It came not from the house but from outside.

The judge got up from the table, carrying his tea with him as he opened the side door. The early morning revealed a brilliant day's beginning. It was a warm June day in 1780, with a cloudless light blue sky and no wind at all, a very charming country sight. From the southerly direction, he heard the sound of church bells near the graveyard in Sparta; a place where he and his beloved Phoebe may one day lay beneath a marker. They were handheld bells since the church, with the judge's significant contributions, was not yet built, and homespun meeting houses served the purpose currently. But it was Friday, not Sunday, so why the call to church?

To hear better, the judge walked around the house to the downhill slope, which overlooked the valley. As he came around the house, he could see the vast expanse to the west, where Stirling's mine lay with Mucksaw Pond nearby and the Wallkill River flowing from south to north.

The smooth vista was marred by a black column of smoke, thin but distinctly in contrast to the pastel blue sky. It was far in the distance to the north, up near Goshen, so only appeared as thin as an ink stroke from a liquid laden quill pen, but it was black and sure and trailed off high into the still morning sky.

The judge realized that this was the call, the hail to rise up. This was the alarm for the militia to muster.

As he came upon the front of his home, he noticed the normally sparsely trafficked road was full. There were many travelers by foot, several wagons and carts as well. There were many young men carrying the family muskets, and they were all heading south along the road.

As the judge came to the roadway, he was greeted by most of the young men who were passing by with a tip of the hat in recognition of his esteemed position of honor among the citizens of the village. He could see, though, that behind the pleasantry of greeting, there was a bold brashness of youthful enthusiasm, the solid feeling amongst the young men of being able to make a difference in the fight for freedom. There was also in the air the feeling of fear, fear of the unknown and possible death as the boys and men marched to the south. A rider on a tall horse slowly made his way north, speaking to the travelers.

As he came upon Ogden, the horseman stopped and said, "Good morning, Judge. The call is out for the militia to gather and go to Morristown. I am Sergeant Thomas Talmadge, of Woodbourne, an express rider for the Sussex County Militia. Word has come down that the British and their Hessian mercenaries are coming from Staten Island with 6,000 men with arms and want to make their way through Hobart's Gap and seize Morristown, kill General Washington, and defeat our army."

"Oh my," said the judge. He was now at the road in the bustle of movement. He saw the men heading south. As more men passed by, he was looking southward and could see Sergeant Talmadge picking up speed as he reassured the younger ones. He also saw the immense plume of thick, black smoke spiraling skyward from the fire beacon atop Sparta Mountain[liii] as it repeated the urgent signal that was seen in the distance at Goshen, and Beacon, New York colony.

"Yes sir, Judge, it is serious. The enemy came out earlier in the month along the same route and burned a number of homesteads in a nearby town—Connecticut Farms—but were turned back. This time they are coming out in large force and determined to make it through Hobart's Gap."

Later, this would be called the Battle of Springfield. But for now, the judge hurried back inside and told Phoebe, who now was standing near the door in anticipation. She was stunned and then started to cry.

"Our sons are in harm's way!" She fell into the chair which moments ago was a place of solitude and comfort. She leaned over, weeping and holding her handkerchief. "Our Matthias and our Aaron Ogden are both probably going to fight the enemy, and I have fear for their lives. They could be killed in defense of our freedom."

As the Battle of Springfield raged on and was entering its most grave phase for the Patriots, the judge became more and more anxious. He could not sit in his comfortable and quiet solitude and in the safety of the remote Sussex County plantation. He needed to help the cause; the Patriotic Spirit could be lost.

He realized, grimly, that his sons could be caught up in the battle and might lose their lives. The judge could take it no longer. "Phoebe, I must do what I can, the life and survival of this family to next generations may depend on it. There is too much at stake."

Phoebe nodded. She was stoic and grim-faced.

With great resolve, the judge made his decision. "I must go tell who those culprits are. I will tell the names of those whom I had sworn to keep secret."

Chapter 28
Judge Goes to Morristown

"By failing to prepare, you are preparing to fail."
– Benjamin Franklin

Ogden had his driver get ready to ride, go to the barn and prepare the horses, and rush his carriage with him on board down the hill to the roadway to Sparta, and then along the path of the future Union Turnpike and Morris Turnpike routes, squeezing by the road that was crammed with soldiers who were joining the others along the busy roadway. All these boys and men from Sussex County and Morris County were heeding and responding to Washington's urgent call.

The judge was swept along in the tide of Patriots heading toward Morristown. There were those militia who were part of the citizen's army who would be alerted and would get ready and then make it to the battle in a short time period. There were others, usually young and new in the militia, who trained frequently and were to be called to action very quickly. These rapid responders needed to take their muskets to work—in the corn field or the shop—so that they who could be called out to service immediately were ready to respond in sheer minutes. They were quite literally Minutemen. They heard very quickly of the need for men by way of the beacon system, an ingenious idea spawned by Lord Stirling and General Alexander, who owned the property at the foot of the hill where his homestead of Ogdensburg stood[liv][lv][lvi].

As he worked his way down the Union Turnpike, Judge Ogden blended in with the flow of men. Members of the militia, individual volunteers, soldiers of all shapes and sizes were gathering and journeying with a common purpose. The number of Patriot soldiers along the way grew in strength and enthusiasm. They were all eager to help, eager for battle, eager to defend their homes.

After a time, Ogden entered the village of Morristown. His carriage made its way to the small hill upon which sat a large mansion. The immense Ford Mansion with its bright white appearance appeared as if it were itself a lighted beacon, as a symbol of the brightness of what the future nation could be. All three fireplaces were hard at work warming the house and heating water for coffee and tea for the officers running to and fro. Cooking was underway at full steam for the many people inside and around the building preparing, serving, eating, and participating in the build up to defending the area from an assault by the oncoming enemy.

As the judge got down from the carriage, he walked toward the Ford Mansion. He had never seen such a bustle as was happening now. There was an urgency of preparation for war. He worked his way through the house. Quite noticeable were the many officers in their fancy uniforms. Messengers scurrying about, bringing in papers with information about enemy movements and also who then were departing to take orders to aid in improving defenses. Women were handing out food for the troops and officers who kept coming and going. The large Ford Mansion was humming. The judge walked into the front of the house and then out the back door down the central hallway, then out the back door.

In front of him he could see the large, white canvas tent, Washington's tent. Washington's headquarters were mobile and constantly moving to the locations of new battles as they cropped up.

He stepped onto a gray slate or two that kept the mud away on rainy days. He then walked onto the matting of lush grass where the yard was green with the summer's natural life; the birds chirped, and the lawn was soft. A reminder of an early summer day in Ogden's own youth. But now was not the time for dreaming. Now was the time for action, to keep thought together and with purpose, because one's freedom of choice might be torn away from these people here present by the strength of one of the greatest of world powers—the British. Ogden moved forward in earnest as he went to find out about his two sons and also to provide important information.

A few feet farther brought the judge to the great tent that served as General Washington's headquarters. The tent reminded him of some large cloth structure where a Medieval jousting event might take place on the plains overlooking cliffs near the windswept coast of Wales. It wouldn't be surprising to see a knight in armor shuffle by on a cloth draped horse with a shield and his large spear ready for tilting another knight for the love of a lady, perhaps a yellow shaft with red spirals painted on it. But enough of Medieval musings.

He reached the open flap of the tent, and his attention came back to the current serious situation. The judge took a deep breath before going in.

Many soldiers of different rank scurried about, each with their own focused mission. A dozen officers ran to the ranks that were forming outside of the mansion along the Vauxhall Road. They brushed the cloak of the judge as he strained his neck to orient himself inside General Washington's white tent. He held his hand to his throat subconsciously, a kind of reminiscence of the knife forced there, and of his oath. One of the life guards spotted him and walked him into the other end of the tent where the leader was. Huddled around the general were scores of officers.

Just then, Lord Stirling walked over to greet the judge.

"Well, hello Judge, my good man," said Stirling as he put one foot in front, removed his tricorn hat, and leaned slowly forward in a gentlemanly bow.

"Neighbor Lord Stirling," said the judge in a perfunctory fashion, preoccupied by his grave reason for coming near the battlefront.

"What troubles you, Judge?"

"I must finally relieve my weary heart."

"Ah, I know you carry many reservations with you, devout churchman that you are."

"But ..."

"And you have used your Christian and judicial and legislative skills in the most conservative ways."

"I need to unload my conscience and give you notice ..."

"Notice?"

"Yes, I know who my attackers were."

Stirling looked kindly upon his friend. "Your honor is your name. I realize that a man must follow the voice of his own conscience, and he must, at all costs, protect his family. I may well have done the same that my people are always kept safe."

"Thank you," said Ogden. "But I have a duty to my country."

The judge was interrupted by Stirling. "We know well, by now, who attacked and robbed you."

The judge stood motionless. He felt, for his good name, as a man of courage and stout Patriot, he should utter their names. "They are British Lieutenant Moody and the cowboy Claudius Smith."

Stirling said, "I admire your courage, sir. We have just been informed of the same through our own spies."

As he stood quietly, he was relieved for the first time in months. Yes, the burden was removed, but no, he didn't make the commitment—it was handed to him. Such is life; it is never what you would expect.

The rest of the men in the tent were moving at a fever pitch. The judge knew that telling or not telling, he would never have been protected. If he had never said anything, how would they know it was he who said something? He understood then his foolishness and felt, at the same time, his honor return. The judge was comforted that they were aware of Smith and Moody and that they were on the case to capture and punish them.

His mind was cleared. The judge felt he wanted to thank Stirling for this. "Lord Stirling, I am so grateful."

Before he could say anything more, Lord Stirling's name was voiced loudly and urgently as he was called by several officers of the Continental Army. He did turn to say some parting words as he was pulled away.

"Your sons, as you may be wondering, are alive and well and serving as good Patriots, sir."

"Oh, thank you for that news," said the judge. In spite of the tenor of the day and the solemnness of war at its heightened state, the judge silently rejoiced and knew Phoebe would be calmed by the news.

The grin disappeared from Lord Stirling's face, though. Several Patriot officers came up right behind him and faced Stirling. "General, the British have a massive force, some 6,000 men. We are putting our efforts in defending at the river, a last barrier to them coming to Morristown. They are breaching our defenses at the Galloping Hill Bridge," said one of the men.

The war might be lost.

Stirling showed a look that he wanted to say more, but the great preparations for the impending battle would not allow.

ACT III
HONESTY &
TABLES TURN

"There is a tide in the affairs of men.
Which, taken at the flood, leads on to fortune;
Omitted, all the voyage of their life
Is bound in shallows and in miseries.
On such a full sea are we now afloat,
And we must take the current when it serves,
Or lose our ventures."
– Shakespeare, Julius Ceasar Act 4, Scene 3

Chapter 29
Washington's Tent for the Battle of Springfield, June 23, 1780

"He will win who knows when to fight and when not to fight."
– Sun Tzu, Chinese philosopher (~500BC)

"The boats are ready to take our men across the water," said the aide-de-camp Major George Beckwith. He snapped a brisk salute.

"Ah, yes," said Lieutenant General Baron William von Knyphausen. He bowed slightly and then offered a proper and quick military salute. "Proceed," were his words, with a strong German accent.

General von Knyphausen was deftly dressed and splendidly fit, wearing a colorful German uniform with medals jangling from his chest.

Now new animosity had been brewing, and as this heated up, it would erupt in this clash to be the Battle of Springfield. By June 1780, General Knypausen could exercise some of his leadership, since normally the man in charge, Sir Henry Clinton, had been away traveling to the South, and was set to besiege and then capture Charleston, South Carolina. The Hessian general took it upon himself to go to New Jersey with this massive and irrepressible force of troops to attack the Americans and punish them once again for rebelling against the Crown. He would then have an easy and short march to crush General Washington in Morristown, New Jersey. The village of Morristown was only a handful of miles to the west.

After speaking with Knypausen, both men looked at each other and took a deep breath. What would follow could change world history.

Major Beckwith ran off and shouted, "Load the transport craft!" Six thousand men in British and German uniforms hurried their way toward the shore. Some British seamen stood near the various watercraft and helped to methodically place the many landlubber soldiers into small boats. Paddles and oars were distributed. A shove off from the shore placed the boats into open water.

"Proceed to the Jersey shore," came a shout, and the rowers began stroking the oars for the short journey across the Arthur Kill and the Kill Van Kull rivers and estuaries, departing from the British bastion of Staten Island. The whole episode was an astounding display of military might and action. Six thousand men took some time to load up and row off. Six thousand men was an extremely impressive sight, and they were such a strong force that it was certainly believable that they could alter the course of the war in the western hemisphere.

The boats were starting on their way with the leading troops. Several officers were standing with great interest around Major Beckwith as they studied the tactical plans for the attack. They all had great enthusiasm as they were about to hit the Patriots again, and now with full force of an army.

Major Beckwith and his officers then got into boats and began their way. Watching it all from the rear was the Hessian commander, along with his senior staff. Knyphausen produced a slight smile, wearing his usual calm and confident expression.

Lafayette had conjectured, based on stories from some British officers, about the long voyage that Knyphausen had taken from England to New York City.

Knypausen had instructed his senior staff and encouraged them as a good leader would do. A smaller contingent of troops had come out two weeks prior but had not gained the full distance they had wanted to. They had marched through a small village known as Connecticut Farms. They were turned back, but not before torching the town and burning the buildings.

His senior leaders had now gathered around Knyphausen. They looked on as he planned his foray in force from Staten Island to thrust toward Washington in Morristown.

"The setback from a few days before will now succeed," he said at one point to Major Beckwith in his thick German accent. While they were observing Knypausen's map, he grabbed some bread and, with his thumb, started spreading the butter on it. "We will push our sword westward, cutting the Jerseys in half and slicing into Washington's heart in Morristown."

This was a critical time for the Americans. The plans had it that as the British were approaching Morristown, the entire American Army would be exposed and then attacked. Extreme danger was building. There was only ten or so miles distance from the Hessian soldiers' column after they had gone through the burnt and smoldering remains of Connecticut Farms and then to Springfield, up through Hobart Gap, and then to General Washington's headquarters. No real impediment stood in the way of General Knypausen's approach to Washington's homey quarters after the town of Springfield had been captured. The Redcoats and Hessians would burn the town and then follow the road up the mountain and through the passageway known as Hobart's Gap. From there, they would have a scenic view of Washington's headquarters in the distance and a short march before them. The last part of their march would be easy and quick, as it was a straight and flat road then led only ten miles through an indefensible swampland leading to the heart of the Americans' army.

General Knyphausen went over the strategic plan again. To get to Springfield, the plan was to take two roads, both leading westward—Galloping Hill Road to the south and Vauxhall Road to the north. On the map it looked like a simple "Y" that was rotated from its top to clockwise to the right. The well-traveled roads enabled a fast and easy transit of men, material, and cannon. On a straight line to the west, Washington's troops were at camp, resting. The tender headquarters of the whole American Army lay like a delicate flower, positioned in a home that had no defensive position to protect it. Once Springfield was breeched, there would only be Washington's one hundred or less life guards—troops trained to protect him, but just a few men in reality.

General von Knypausen smiled with anticipation of the victory over the Americans. "I shall accomplish the success that has eluded Sir Henry Clinton," he said to Major Beckwith, "and will do so without him while he is down in the South."

The great open area of water upon which the vast armada of little boats carried the troops was an amazing sight. This sight was viewed by Patriot eyes. Word would spread early and quickly, far and wide.

***

In Morristown, General Washington was concerned and

beleaguered. Knowing full well of the strength of the British, he was not confident. He was very worried. He had been provided the alarm of the enemy's advance. He realized that only a handful of miles separated him from the thousands in the force that were marching straight at him, along the established roads. Riders were coming to him with the urgent news. Washington knew that the opposing force would consist of the dominant contemporary military knowhow, bearing and precision that was time-tested in the Old World of Europe. He stretched his arms across the planning table and agonized at what word would be coming in next from the front. With the Southern Army being suppressed at Charleston, South Carolina, and with the whole Northern Army of the Continental Troops present around Morristown, General Washington knew that fate might come to play her final hand at the card game of the American Revolution. And the results did not look promising for the Patriots.

Rider after rider kept approaching the main flap of Washington's tent with news of the British assault. The advance of six thousand men from the enemy's fortress-like enclaves along the Hudson River seemed to be building toward an inevitable curtain on the play known as the fight for liberty.

One rider shuffled in and spoke. "General Washington, there are thousands of the enemy gathering and mustering on the Jersey shore, on the west side of Newark Bay. And they have lugged with them over fifteen or twenty pieces of heavy artillery."

General Washington was surprised at the assault, not that he did not expect it; he did. It was just that it was happening; now, at present, and not just in a dream. And that there was such a massive military onslaught about to occur. The enemy men, and now the many pieces of heavy artillery that could be decisive in battle. It was a frightening spectacle to behold and to oppose. The preparation was in Washington's hands.

Another rider came in shortly thereafter and said, "General Washington, sir, many enemy men are marching. They are going through Elizabethtown, and all of them are buoyant and in good spirits, singing as they march. They have proceeded past the Ogden home, the Boudinot residence, and then Saint John's Anglican Church and cemetery."

"Seventeen miles to Morristown," murmured the general. He knew many of the people who occupied the homes and businesses along the road to Morristown. Many had homes in Elizabethtown along the route. Dwellers included the Ogdens. Judge Ogden played there as a child, grew up and married there, and raised a family in Elizabethtown. And now the British were marching through.

Standing quietly in the background of the tent was Judge Ogden. His ears perked up when he heard his home being mentioned. He wanted to know all he could about his precious dwelling in Elizabethtown; the British had burned down homes for lesser reasons than Judge Ogden's known Patriotic leadership. But even more important matters were now urgent in the new United States that was struggling to survive its birth.

"Word is coming in that they are passing Liberty House, where the governor resides, Governor Livingston," shouted a man from the edge of the tent, vocally describing rumors that were coming in from the east.

Washington bowed his head as he sat at the table in front of several rolls of Erskine's maps as an aide helped spread additional ones across the table. "Fourteen miles to the Ford Mansion just feet away from here, and they are swiftly marching toward us," he said. "We appear doomed."

***

As activity increased in Washington's tent, Judge Ogden sensed that even his small seat in the corner was becoming an important one. The area was growing as it became occupied by officers and aides, alarm riders coming in, and messenger riders leaving for the front. He knew that now was not the time to ask the general any questions.

He saw Lord Stirling laugh and point one officer toward his direction. It was his son, Major Aaron Ogden!

"Oh, my Aaron," the judge said. Aaron spotted his father and ran over. They embraced as only father and son could.

"Father, my brother Lieutenant Colonel Matthias Ogden is called forth to engage the enemy in battle. He is in command of the 1st New Jersey Regiment, Continental Line, Jersey Blues, and is instructed to guard and be a bulwark against the impending force of the British. Those Redcoats keep coming west. Brother Matthias and his men are now at the Springfield bridge along Vauxhall Road."

"We must pray for him," said Ogden, looking at his son as if he'd never see him again.

"I must go, Father. Our men are gathering outside, and we will leave soon. I will let you know what I can, when I can."

"God's speed, son," said Ogden, grateful that Phoebe was not here to see this travesty and to fear for the lives her sons.

Another rider came in, out of breath, sweating from the heat and the hasty ride and leaning with exhaustion against Washington's strategy table.

"Sorry sir, but I ... I have news that there are, in fact, two armies approaching us. One from the east along Galloping Hill Road to the south of Springfield and one from the east along Vauxhall Road north of Springfield. We only have limited troops, and the enemy has a tremendous number of men—stretching down each roadway as far as the eye can see."

"So, they have separated their forces, soldier?"

"Yes, General Washington, they are now two contingents of very strong columns of men who are overtaking us, sir."

"Twelve miles," said Washington. "From the bridges at the Rahway River to our humble headquarters here." He took a sip of tea and thought for a long moment. "And if they breech our defenses on those two roads, Vauxhall and Galloping Hill, then they will join up in Springfield and be a massive force heading west to this table here."

General Washington took his glasses off and rubbed his eyes.

"We must tell our General Nathaniel Greene that they will have to hold the line." The general looked around and asked an aide to get a new rider.

An officer turned around from the general's table and shouted a command. "We need a rider to go to the battle!"

A messenger rider jumped up and stood at attention in front of the table. Lord Stirling was writing out some orders. Stirling was interpreting the command of Washington's orders, scribbling as fast as he could.

"Now take this and tell General Greene to use the code cipher to understand this," said Stirling as he blew on the ink and then stuffed the now dry paper into the shirt pocket of the rider.

Another rider had come into the tent sometime later. He had bad news. Dirty and sweaty, he stammered, "General Washington, the British and Hessian enemies that have approached Springfield from the south along Galloping Hill Road from Elizabethtown are very powerful. We have met them at the bridge, First Bridge, and in steamy fighting we held them off. Our troops have fought long and valiantly. But the enemy kept coming, and they had cannon—fifteen or twenty pieces—and then some of them went around First Bridge, wading through the river itself to the south of First Bridge. Then came bitter, close fighting in the trees, forcing our men to retreat."

The constant high-pitched sound and motion in the tent had quieted and paused as everyone was fervently listening to the disconcerting news. Concern had replaced the action as men heard and thought about the worst that could come. Eyes stared at eyes. A pause, momentarily. After a common, unspoken thought, the activity continued.

***

Aides and officers quickly stepped away to duties, solemnly and now with greater motivation. As one bevy of soldiers swept past Washington, the judge noticed him seemingly alone. Although there were many officers working around him, and the knowledge by all that he was the center of attention, Washington remained alone. He had the weight of choice, a final decision, life and death burdened heavily on his shoulders, and his only. Everyone else was a player, an actor on the stage. It was Washington, though, who led the stage show, who directed the orchestra, the players, and play. It was he who made the strategic moves that would send the Patriot army in one direction or another, at times baffling and flustering the enemy, and at other times looking frighteningly like defeat was before them. Washington was now agonizing over this new situation that he found himself, and his army, in. That German von Knyphausen was about to pierce the American front with a vibrant sword of strength and might, and then as a result rush into Morristown like a juggernaut.

One aide offered some water to the judge, which he took while he sat on the stool at the edge of the tent, out of the way of the officers working to keep alive the fragile freedom won and lost at such a cost. Lord Stirling came next to speak. The judge stood up in anticipation of the news that Stirling would bring.

"Judge, here's the latest news on your son," said Stirling, without a wasted word during this time of immense gravity.

"We've been speaking to the battle commander, General Nathaniel Greene." Stirling grabbed the ladle and dunked it into the bucket of water that the judge had just drawn from. This was a sobering time, and water would do well to quench Stirling's thirst.

"Colonel Ogden's men are holding the defenses although falling back on the west side of the branches of the river. They are being attacked by Lieutenant Colonel Joseph Barton—the Loyalist from Sussex County," said Stirling. "I knew from Colonel Seward that I should have arrested him, and here he is attacking us, and perhaps we might suffer the worst."

Ogden said nothing. He prayed silently for his sons and all the men who were fighting.

Ever the optimist, though, Stirling said, "We shall see, we shall see."

"May the Lord be with us," said Ogden, ever evoking the deep Christian faith he possessed.

"I recall many of your calming and stirring sermons," said Stirling. I must tell you that Reverend Caldwell was ingenious. Caldwell, you may recall, lost his wife in the preceding skirmish."

Ogden nodded. He shuddered to think of his own dear wife Phoebe in such a circumstance.

"Reverend Caldwell came up to the front where the troops were firing at the British with their muskets. The Patriot men were using up their supplies and were soon going to be unable to shoot. As the firing and gunpowder were flying to and fro in the haze and confusion of battle, the men said to him, "Reverend, we are running way low on our wadding, and without it we can't continue to shoot. We will have to cut and run!

"Caldwell looked around and in his Presbyterian Church for paper for the needed wadding. Where to find paper? He realized that there were song books, the same that you spoke of when you gave a sermon here some time ago. The reverend handed out the song books to the troops so that they could rip out the pages, many of which were songs by the composer Isaac Watts. Screaming above the booms and blasts of war, the reverend stood amongst the Continental soldiers and the militia men around him. He yelled 'Give 'em Watts, boys!' as the Patriots defended their homes with their guns blasting musket balls powered by our Christian hymns at the enemy."

Ogden marveled at the power of God and the ideas of men.

Ever-exuberant Lord Stirling exclaimed, "That might be the encouragement we need to get on the offensive and win the Battle of Springfield. Good faith and great Yankee spirit! Remember this date, sir, Friday of June 23rd, 1780."

Ogden nodded but knew that Springfield was tearing apart, amidst the sound of battle, with flames rising from burning buildings, the hail of gunfire, the boom of the British cannon, and the puffs of many muskets pointed at deadly aim.

***

There was also the lesser noticed thick smoke of the signal beacons. There was the signal smoke as it rose aloft atop Newark Mountain in the Watchungs and Hobart's Gap. Each fire was to give the warning and make the call along the alarm system of the region from here all the way up to Beacon, New York along the Hudson River and near the headquarters in Newburgh. The trail of smoke to the heavens represented the cry of the troops as they were begging urgently for more help. Men near the battle looked at the sky.

"Remarkable!" came a response from one officer in Springfield. "The bravery exhibited is astounding gallantry. What to do now? What if the smoke from the beacons yields no result?"

"It sounds like a disaster is beginning to take hold for our American force," said another officer. The other men leading the troops at the bridges all looked at him, grimaced, and nodded slowly.

***

Back at Washington's tent, there was a summary elicited from the commander, a summation of the battlefield reports that had been streaming in, a thoughtful murmur for help. "Men, we now have to get word to the last bridgehead between them and us. Now that First Bridge has fallen, we must keep it together at Littel's Bridge." He rubbed his head. "We must get word to hold the line out to Major Light Horse Lee at the southern approach at First Bridge and Major Matthias Ogden at the northern approach to town."

The general raised his hand and signaled an officer to get another rider.

The officer swung around and yelled, "Another messenger rider come forward!"

Eager to respond, up jumped a lively young man, ready to ride into the battle to deliver orders to the front. The officer was Aaron Ogden.

The judge was proud of his son. But a bolt of fear raced through him when Aaron was handed the message and he heard General Washington mutter, "It is not looking good."

***

Lord Stirling leaned over near the general again, jotting cryptic words on paper as quickly as the ink on the quill would allow. Finishing with a broad stroke of his hand, he then blew on the wet ink and folded the paper. Stirling shuffled his feet to see the next messenger rider who would carry the mail. He saw the officer coming toward the strategy table, and Stirling walked forward to stuff the message into the rider's shirt pocket.

"Ogden!" said a surprised Stirling at the site of the officer.

"Yes, sir!" said Major Ogden as he snapped to attention.

"Take this message to ... to your brother."

"Yes, sir," said Aaron as he briskly spun around and headed for the open flap of the general's tent. A steed could be heard nearby, sensing the excitement of the occasion and whinnying and twitching in anticipation.

On his way out, the judge grabbed his shoulder.

"Godspeed, son, and safe return," was all that the judge could muster. There was only time for a glance at each other.

"Hey, Major Ogden," yelled Stirling, "keep in mind that I hope those beacons atop Hobart Gap and Newark Mountain are still blazing."

Washington was approvingly attentive as he turned toward the conversation. "We need that warning to gather militia! And we can use all the militia that can come at a moment's notice as it is."

Lord Stirling then walked toward Major Ogden to impress upon him the importance of his verbal message.

"Now more than ever, we need those beacon fires to be burning so that we can provide and alert around the countryside. It is of utmost importance that we get those militia men from the surrounding countryside to come and gather in for our defense against the enemy!"

Washington nodded in agreement. Major Ogden swiveled his head and extended a puzzled look toward his father.

Outside the Ford Mansion, the boys and men of the militia were streaming in from all points west. They were gathering and clustering together. They were finding their units and mustering.

Their numbers were increasing. They were also collecting in desire, and enthusiasm, and in strength. They were making a fighting force to be reckoned with.

The beacons were extremely important during the war. The design, generally attributed to Lord Stirling, was used at strategic communications points, atop mountains visible for a long distance. It was the sight of the smoke that alerted militia to muster and come together for the common cause of protection and of liberty. The call went out through the beacons as they burned and as each spread their respective column of smoke skyward, ultimately reaching across the region. Ogden was alerted to this battle by the one on Sparta Mountain and by the chime of the bells and the sound of the firing of the guns. Many from Sussex County were alerted by the one to the north, just south of Goshen, New York atop Fort Hill Mountain. The word was also conveyed by Sergeant Thomas Talmadge of Woodbourne who was riding the main roads and spreading the alarm to local farms by horseback.

"Your ride is ready, sir," came a shout from the yard, and the judge watched as his son, Major Ogden, rushed forward, out of Washington's tent. He quickly mounted the horse and set his course for the Battle of Springfield and the Vauxhall Bridge just twelve miles away.

The judge bowed his head and said a prayer.

Chapter 30
Battle of Springfield With Ogdens

"Victory comes from finding opportunities in problems."
– Sun Tzu

Traveling upon a fast horse and with single-minded purpose, Major Aaron Ogden sped from Morristown through Chatham and then across the flat, wet meadows of the Central Valley wetland. He needed to get the message to his brother and the troops at the Vauxhall Bridge, just twelve miles away. They had to hold the line, or the vitality of the northern Continental Army would be in jeopardy and the American Revolutionary War might be lost.

The galloping horse slowed down as messenger Major Aaron Ogden reached the point where the roadway started uphill the grade to go up the Watchung Mountains. It was fortunate that the steep, tall mountain range had a lower point to it where this roadway went. The gap in the range allowed for a much easier transit. This low passage in the mountains was known as Hobart's Gap.

As the messenger's horse trotted forward and they came to the peak of the mountain, they came across some soldiers, a surprisingly few number of men, who were stoking the fire of the signal beacon. The smoke produced by this pyre was billowing to the sky.

One of them shouted, "Are you here to help? We need extra men."

"No sir, I am on a mission to the front," said Aaron.

"We are down to a handful of helpers here. We need to keep putting wood on the fire and keep the flame going and the smoke at an optimal hazy hue. We could sure use help. Many of the others were rushed to the front to help with the battle. We hear that the British are moving ahead and coming in this direction." He sounded scared. The others with him were also fearful of the loss of their lives and new country. They dropped the wood they were carrying to the fire and shook their heads in disbelief.

"No, you must keep the fire going. It is imperative that you continue signaling. Our hopes hang on the signal being seen throughout the countryside and the militia then come to support us." Ogden looked behind the saddle toward the fragile village of Morristown.

"Yes, sir, we will keep at it," said the Patriot soldier as he turned back to the handful of others. They all then picked up their wood that they had been carrying and took extra short logs to stoke the fire and keep the towering column of smoke alive. Black tar was being added, which made the fire burn black, making a better smoke signal for those in the west to become alerted.

Major Aaron then started down the other slope of Hobart's Gap toward the East. The towns below stretched before him as he rode ahead. He had a clear view of the great metropolis of New York City and the many suburbs surrounding it. This vista was representative of the early American landscape. It was a view to the east that included Manhattan with the comfortable homes of the leaders of the British military, the Hudson River with hundreds of sail ships of the mighty British navy bobbing at anchor in the harbor, and the many Loyalists safely distant just beyond the Hudson River. Staten Island was closer and easier to note. This was where the legions of Hessians were housed, soldiers of fortune that they were, some impressed into service of the King of England from their native German regions. Nearer on the New Jersey shore was Elizabethtown where the Ogden family home had been for generations. Aaron Ogden knew that it was along the roadway from Elizabethtown that the enemy troops had been marching, in force and with artillery. It was along this roadway that the enemy had to be halted.

He could hear thunder-like explosions in the distance. This was the reports of the cannon shots coming from the battle ahead, echoing along the mountainside as if it were a hollow chamber. Above the distant towns, on Newark Mountain, he could see another beacon as he just did at Hobart's Gap. The other plume of smoke was rising skyward in an anxious attempt to alert the local Patriots and bring forth the militia. These signals sent the word of the enemy's approach, and the call for help of a desperate attempt to defeat the large force of enemy.

Major Ogden saw several wounded men staggering up the road to go west. They looked up at him wearily.

"Sir, the battle ahead is horrendous. The British are hitting us with many cannon shots. They consist of well-trained troops who have inflicted heavy casualties on us. They are advancing, and we need more support." Their report also consisted of groans and shrieks from painful injuries.

Aaron Ogden rode onward to the east, where he could also see smoke billowing up from the town of Springfield. The British and Hessian troops had broken through the Patriot removal of planking and their proud resistance on First Bridge, over the Rahway River, as the messengers had reported. The Galloping Hill Road, to his righthand view, was the approach to Springfield that had fallen. And now the result of this could be seen with the homes that were on fire.

***

Major Ogden continued his ride, picking up the pace as he realized the battle was still underway. As he was distant, he could hear the British cannon thunder. As he approached, the small arms gunfire could be heard. He continued his ride and heard the yelling of men as they notified others of their desperate plights; the screams of those in an impossible position, and the screams of those with painful wounds of war as they lay helpless on the battle fields.

As Major Ogden closed on into the western approach to Littel's Bridge, he could see the white smoke rising from the gunshots fired and drifting across the land like a silent purveyor of death on a chaotic scene. He could see men running everywhere frantically as they tried to hold off the British. It was then that he spotted his brother, Colonel Matthias Ogden.

"Fall back," was the word from the colonel.

The colonel's aides saw the major's approach and alerted him. Aaron dismounted and ran to his brother. They embraced as brothers would, and Aaron handed Matthias the message. Matthias quickly read the communique.

"Reinforcements?" said Matthias. He uttered a disbelief of this. "We are in a critical situation, brother Aaron. We need many men to help."

While Aaron impatiently awaited description, Matthias spoke of the grave situation.

"I am somewhat in shock. My horse was shot out from under me."

"I am so sorry to hear, brother Matthias. At least you are still with us and in command."

Matthias though, was caught in the moment and realized he needed to stay focused. "Patriots had blocked Littel's Bridge, and we have been holding the enemy back. We are surviving by a thread. And we've been removing planking from the roadway so they can't pass. But the British had waded and forded the Rahway River to the north of the bridge and are about to out flank us. We need to withdraw back to the final bridge, that of Edgeson's Bridge just below the signal beacon atop the hill of Newark Mountain."

"Yes, you know that the Galloping Hill Road bridge has been captured and the enemy is pouring over it to the south of here," said Aaron, with the news from Washington's tent. "They are in Springfield and burning the place."

"So, this is a final stand, here in Short Hills," said Matthias with a deep and despairing breath. "I long for an end to this conflict."

***

Reinforcements were now streaming in from the west. As the men regrouped, it took some time. But then word came back from the scouts near the bridge. They were running quickly. Normally they were hunched over to avoid gunfire and sniper attack. But now they were standing upright. The constant gunfire to the east had changed its sound somehow; there was a difference in the pitch of the battle.

Several men ran up to their commander.

"Colonel Ogden," said one, out of breath. "The British have retreated."

The Ogdens looked at each other. Another scout came from the rear. He had news from behind the front as well.

"Colonel, this is word from General Greene. The militia has arrived!"

All men smiled and were relieved.

"There are many. Thousands of militia have answered the call of the smoky signal beacons. They have come in response to the alarm riders, like Sergeant Thomas Talmadge as far away as Sussex County. As you can note, the British have seen this, and they realize how useless it is to advance farther. The militia have arrived in strength. Along with their numbers, they have military weaponry in the form of thousands bringing their own muskets, and with locally produced ammunition such as that from the powder factory behind the Ford Mansion and from the stores at Succassunny. The men have arrived and saved the day, with regiment after regiment now positioned just below Short Hills and the signal beacon atop Newark Mountain. The enemy are on their way back to Staten Island."

Colonel Ogden said, "I doubt that they will come back, knowing that a short call to arms will end their intrusion into the affairs of America."

Chapter 31
Newburgh GW & R Weathersfield, CT, June 22, 1781

"We intend for the present to keep the Matter as much a Secret as possible, and I would Advise you to do the same."
– General George Washington 1777

North of Manhattan, about sixty miles away up the river, was a beautiful home that served as one of Washington's headquarters. A soldier sprinted around the side of the stone house and ran onto the front lawn. The grassy green rolled down over the edge of a fabulous vista that overlooked the mighty Hudson River Valley.

"General Washington, there's a messenger rider here, having been urgently called by you!" declared an aide. The heretofore sprinting soldier snapped to attention near the military leader.

The general was deep in concentration as he was scanning the vast expanse of the Hudson River that lay in front of him. His elbows were outspread, and he had both hands gripping his long, brass spyglass. A stiff breeze from the east cooled his face, and it was turning his powdered white skin to a wind-burned red. The edges of his tricorn hat flapped and buzzed in the wind. Washington took into account this splendid stretch of the river. The Hudson River came from the north, to his left, on its long sojourn from the Adirondacks, passing where the Battle of Saratoga had been, through Albany and the Dutch influence, and now at Newburgh and in front of his view. It then wandered down toward the magnificent Storm King Mountain. Just beyond the mountain, a few short miles away, was the fortress of West Point and its strategic position. The Hudson drifted to the south and Manhattan—home of the British Army. For him, it was another day of war, standing in front of the Hasbrouck House. This was the location of General Washington's Newburgh headquarters.

"Sir," said the aide who was standing near the general, "I must tell you that the rider is very worried that he will fall into the hands of the cowboys who will rob him of his mail and also take his personal purse and may harm his body. He is well aware that the route of the riders from here through Ramapo Valley, Galloways Grove, and Smith's Clove is well worn but that it is also well-known by the enemy."

"Yes, I have heard of the complaints of our messenger riders. I am also aware of the difficult conditions that they may encounter. Let him come near," said Washington, still scoping the various puffy, white sails skimming across the water of the river in the distance below through the lens of his spyglass.

Having been given permission, the aide motioned for the rider to approach, and stood behind the commander. The rider drew himself to a slow, deeply respectful attention. He had the traditional buff trousers and blue coat with tail, but also had long and braided blond hair that came partway down his broad back. While he appeared timid at first, the rider loudly addressed Washington with his fear. "General, I'll shall surely be taken if I go through the Clove!"

The general slowly dropped the telescoping looking glass and turned around to see the soldier. He studied the man for a moment and said, "Your duty is not to talk, but to obey!"

The general turned back and raised the monocular again to check out a larger vessel tacking briskly north with the use of the wind and tidal rush.

As the rider departed, the general twisted around and gave him a last glance. He saw the blond pigtail bouncing sideways on the rider's broad back as it was sharply outlined by the blue cloth. Washington thought about the situation. He knew that he might send the rider, who probably had a young wife and small children, to his death. But on a larger, more strategic level, he realized the shadowy but extremely important outcomes that could be obtained through communications, spying, and deception.

He also saw Lord Stirling, who was coming across the yard from the house. Washington was concerned. "We need to take another route. The criminals and robberies are getting too much to handle."

Stirling said, "I know of a route that is more remote. It is to go in a westerly direction, one that would take the rider past property I own in New York colony and then also past Colonel Seward's fortified log home, and then past Ogden's iron and my zinc mine in the Jerseys as he goes to Easton. A messenger can take the mails by this route, and then other riders can carry the mail to points south."

Washington took a deep breath of the brisk, swelling breeze as he looked back upon the Hudson River and more sailboat traffic coursing along.

"Speaking of Ogden, we finally know who robbed him. We know that Claudius Smith was in on it, as well as James Moody. They will both hang when caught. Moody escaped West Point, just below us here." Stirling then pointed to his right where a large schooner sailed the blue waters around the corner and was then shielded by the stone shoulder of Storm King Mountain.

"The two men have stolen our mail a number of times, and I know they give the information to Sir Henry Clinton who can foil the best of our plans."

"Right, General Washington," said Stirling. "Moody's very resourceful and faithful to the Tories. If he were to intercept our mail, he would have word of the same to the British, and done quickly and accurately."

It was then that a thought came to the general. The wind was continuing to whip up from the east. The east, where beyond the shores of New England lay the Atlantic Ocean and thence the British Empire. The east, from where the invisible wind blew, shaking the leaves on the trees and filling the sails to speed the wooden ships plying the Hudson River in front and below him. Harkening from the east, the wind represented a force to be reckoned with, although the wind was impossible to grasp and catch.

Both Washington and Stirling had to brace against the strong wind.

"I have an idea," said Washington.

"You are thinking about the mails, sir?"

"Yes," said Washington. "The highway bandits in this region are so aggressive. And our ability to keep the riders safe is so difficult with the long lines of communication between mountains and forests. We know from experience that attaining a successful transfer of correspondence is questionable and risky."

"You are correct, sir."

"So, maybe we can take advantage of this leaky system," said Washington.

"Ah, I know what you are thinking, sir," said Lord Stirling.

"Such a plan could work," said the general.
"Such a plan could win the war!" exclaimed Stirling.

***

On May 18, 1781, Moody and four men went about twenty-five miles from New York City. Here, they lay in wait. They stayed in their spot quietly and in anticipation. There was a predictability with these Rebels, so they waited and stayed still.

Up to the north on this remote dirt roadway, Moody could hear the pounding of the earth by a traveler making a good pace on a journey.

The rider came by with his horse at a brisk trot.

Moody and his men stepped out and drew the horse and rider to a halt. The rider didn't move because one of Moody's men had a musket pointed at his head.

"Give us all your mail," said Moody.

"Please don't shoot," said the rider "I have a wife and child."

"Claudius, put the rifle down," said Lieutenant Moody as he rummaged through the mails. "How many times have I told you that you will have us both hanged if you keep up your brutality where none is required?"

Moody smiled widely as he saw some pieces of mail that he liked. He finished his business with the correspondence. Seeing this, Claudius slapped the horse and told the rider to leave.

One of the men alerted Moody that an American patrol was marching up the road from the south, just beyond some trees that, for now, provided a leafy cover for them. These troops were sharp and orderly, with clean and operational muskets at their shoulders. They were ready to fight and protect the mails. There were at least twenty healthy and disciplined men.

Moody said, "Men, we are no match for these lads. And there's no place to run."

He checked the road ahead and saw the rider they had just robbed riding away at a fast clip. Moody knew if they stayed put, they'd be sitting ducks and would likely be shot. To the west side, the landscape away from the road presented itself as a steep and vertical uphill cliff with no question about getting even a few feet away before the need to climb up in direct view of the advancing soldiers. The only viable escape was to the east. Here, the hill was a steep drop down, and then there was a ledge as well, and perhaps just as steep of a cliff. With no time left, and no way to tell where they were going to land, Moody leapt over the edge. His men followed him.

The Patriot troops arrived at the scene and noticed Moody and his men sliding down the slope. The troops fired on the retreating gang of robbers. Bullets flew like a storm of hail, but the men dropped off the ledge. The fall from the ledge was only about five feet, and the Patriots watched as the Loyalists got to their feet and ran off into the distance and were swallowed by the trees and the undergrowth beneath. Moody had given the Patriots the slip once again.

Chapter 32
Chain of Express and Deception, around June 1781

"Few men have virtue to withstand the highest bidder."
– General George Washington

The dirt which made up the traveled way wound circuitously through the upper reaches of the ridge line of Snufftown Mountain. The road was higher in elevation than most of the surrounding countryside of northwestern New Jersey. This area was, at the time, in the backwoods of the nation, a part of the outer fringes of colonial America. The road was just beyond the reaches of the British Army, but its remoteness allowed for the lawless escapades of highwaymen and criminals. It was a middle ground for the actions of strong-willed men; the wild lands of the expansion of civilization infringing upon the primitive wilderness of America.

It was here, on the colonial frontier, that robberies would take place; mostly the mails were targeted, and information that went back and forth between the Patriots was stolen frequently.

About forty miles away, in New York City, Sir Henry Clinton made plans that would be carried out by spies and Loyalists. And for the Americans, Washington was in Morristown or Newburgh much of the time, and his decisions would be carried out by spies and troops of the Patriot cause. An important segment of decision and execution of orders was the delivery of the information to the parties. Communication from commanders to the warfighters. The mail system provided the means for the correspondence between these parties. There were troubles for the Patriots taking mail near the New York City region, especially if it went by roads near where the British resided in Manhattan. So, the Americans had to carry their message farther to the outlying countryside. It was here to the west and toward the Delaware River, where messenger riders were now to journey.

***

The roadway through Vernon and Snufftown was primitive, with a rough dirt surface. It was dusty in dry weather, and in wet times muddy with frequent holes punched in the brown hard pack surface by the various horses who plodded back and forth. Long furrows that showed where carts and wagon wheels had gone began to develop. The riders despaired of the road, even if they felt safer.

It was around one of the many bends in this road that a rider and horse sauntered forth, moving at a moderate gait. In working the mail system, there was a change of horses every twenty miles or so, and the messenger would continue on with a different horse. There were various stops where horses were kept, fed, and rested. This rider, coming forth, happened to be at a midway point, an area where a rider might feel comfortable during a ride with the mails in his leather saddle bags and his mind drifting off onto days long ago fishing in a favorite spot.

The rider liked the horse. It was pretty and fresh, having been switched out up the road near Goshen, New York. The dull gray quarter horse was a common breed, and it seemed fitting to watch the pair move along as they were bordered with light brown shafts of straw that arose from beside the traveled way. The road stretched through the high country on Snufftown Mountain and wandered through the highlands sinuously like a river meandering through a flat region on its way to the sea. The road went where it could, wavering back and forth in a difficult land of crags, outcrops, and cliffs. The path went beside wetlands, on the bottom of the slope of steep grades, and around large boulders and erratics—those huge rocks that the glaciers had moved eons ago and seem today to have been misplaced among pastures and fields by some giant hand that had dropped them in the wrong place. The early morning was still dewy, and a slight breeze wafted through the many green leaves that embraced the road on each side, as if sheltering it from the sharper features of the land beyond.

The rider on the gray quarter horse looked like he wanted to be anywhere but there, perhaps sleeping under a tree or having warm tea or maybe fishing at a tranquil pond.

"Keep on track, Nelly," he said to the horse as she seemed to wander off the beaten path for some fresh hay. He leaned forward and patted her shoulder with his open hand to reassure her. The rider was a young man who left behind his two young sons, a wife, and a fledgling farm. He patted her on the neck and provided slight pressure to help convince her to move toward the center of the road. Nellie's saddlebags twisted and bounced slightly with the movement of her legs and hips. The horse might have heard the sound of the stream trickling down the rocks from the steep grade of the mountain off to the right as she lumbered southward. The water glistened in the sunlight as the horse and rider stepped through it, Nellie splashing her hooves. They continued on the road and began to round the easy corner to the left and around a prominent boulder.

"Whoa, Nelly," said the rider as the mare shook her head briskly and whinnied, tossing off saliva. She seemed excited, and the rider had to provide a disciplined reaction as he rounded Tory Rock on this late May day in 1781.

"Stop or I'll shoot a musket ball through your head," came a voice from the side of the boulder, requiring instant action by the rider.

He drew the reigns back, and the horse held up and came to a pause. The rider's eyes opened wide with fear. He stared at the two men standing near the boulder at the bend in the road. One of them seemed ready to shoot at any moment.

"Okay, okay," said the rider, with his full attention now on the matter at hand and no longer thinking of the warm tea he'd wanted just a few moments ago. He did hope he'd be alive to see his family, and perhaps fish again on a quiet stream someday.

"Get yourself off that horse and sit on the ground over there," said one of the men. The rider had been told to be on the lookout for two thugs who went by the names Moody and Smith. "We are going to go through the mail in your saddlebags."

The rider dismounted, removed his hat, and sat on a small rock near the stream after handing over the mail bag.

The short man with a rounded derby hat reviewed the mail and took a few he thought were of interest. "You can put your tricorn back on and get on your way," he said. "And boy, you look cute with that long, braided, blond hair flowing down your back." This was the rider who had seen Washington.

With that, the rider stood up and walked to his horse. Claudius took the butt of his musket and smashed him in the back of his head, with the tricorn falling to the ground, splattered with beads of red blood. The rider splayed with all limbs out and fell instantly onto the dirt highway, drooling into a hoof print hole.

"You idiot!" said the Moody. "There's no reason to provoke more harm. We have taken valuable information. You are going to get us both a long prison term or hanging. Claudius, you are a bumbling fool!"

With that remark, Claudius turned his view toward those fluttering leaves along the rock, and a flock of birds aloft, almost oblivious to the action on the road where the rider scooped up his tricorn and scurried to the horse, mounted, and trotted away as Moody stuffed the several pieces of paper in his coat pocket.

About a mile south on the road, the forlorn nondescript rider on the dull gray horse spotted a man with a musket. He was a tall and thin frontiersman, lean and fit, wearing a deerskin jacket and fringe dangling along the arms. He held a mighty musket vertically in front of him with both his hands, and a shining saber was ensconced safely from his hip. He watched the rider approach.

Dizzy from the butt swat to the back of his head, dried blood matting his blond hair, the rider drooped from the saddle, as his consciousness waned, and he began to slip away. The rider was caught in the arms of the frontiersman who had rushed forward. The frontiersman carried the messenger rider off the roadway and placed him under a tree beside the wooden fence of his farm. The rider was offered some water and regained his composure. He asked the frontiersman his name and was relieved that it was Colonel Seward[lvii], known as the "Terror of the Tories."

"Looks like you are woozy," said Colonel Seward.

"I'd been accosted by the enemy, beaten by those cowboys who robbed me of mail," said the half-conscious rider.

"It is the British who will get the results," said Seward. "They are making the most of the fact that our troops are stationed across the wide expanses of Connecticut, New York, and New Jersey, and also points south beyond Philadelphia."

"My head hurts," said the rider, who had deeply painful issues on his mind other than the British.

"Sorry, my friend. That is part and parcel to war," said Seward.

"Yes, sir."

"Communication is one of the most vital parts of a military

campaign," said Seward, as if the young man had no idea. "As the ancient Sun Tzu has said, 'a wise general will use the highest intelligence of the army for the purposes of spying, and thereby they achieve great results.' What you just encountered, my Patriot friend—unfortunately for you—is the enactment of gaining that information."

The rider was awake and listening.

"Colonel Seward, sir, my head is sore, really sore. That I can say for sure. I feel like taking rest against this tree."

Seward stood up over the young man who had, indeed, propped himself up against a tree.

"Here's some more water for you, son," said the colonel as he provided some cool water from his wooden canteen. "I refilled it earlier today from the stream, the same one that you passed by, as it crosses the road just around the corner from the Tory Rock. Now you can guess why it acquired that name."

Swinging his arms over his shoulder, he removed the etched powder horn and leather musket ball sack and put them aside, and then Seward grabbed the canteen. He handed it to the rider, who took a long swig. He began to talk as his horse munched on some tall, dry grass nearby as it was wavering in the breeze. The pain spilled out from the hit to his head and was broken loose with the salve of the cool water.

"I am a member of the mail riders, Colonel Seward. The riders begin the chain of expresses from the allied positions in Connecticut where Rochambeau and the French arrived a year ago. There are riders at about every fifteen miles. These might include protection with dragoons and French hussars. We ride every day and night to Peekskill, and the mails come over the Hudson River by boat on King's Ferry and up past West Point. Washington is staying in Newburgh, and the troops are sheltered at the cantonment in New Windsor just below there. We will ride down through Smith's Cove and the Ramapo Mountains, although there's currently been too many robberies using that route, so we are now coming down past your house, through Sussex County, and down to Easton and points below here such as Philadelphia and the South." He rubbed his head. "I didn't realize there were the enemy here also."

"Yes, my Patriot friend, they are here on Snufftown Mountain." Seward looked around, making sure that they were safe. "These days, Snufftown Mountain has been infested by Tories. They have tried to kill me, and an Indian has even tried to shoot me, but I wrestled the rifle from him. I have a bounty of twenty pounds on my head, so I have to be very wary."

"It sounds like quite a struggle up here in Sussex County, along the frontier."

"Just like it is everywhere these days, my son, everywhere. I had just reconnoitered around the rock and the stream. There is so much activity around the boulder you passed that the locals have been calling it Tory Rock."

At this, the rider wiped from his lips the fresh, clear mountain water and tried to get on his feet again. While a little slow, he stood up and raised his chin. He remained adamant about his duty.

"Colonel, thank you for the attention, the moment of rest, and the water. I will be on my way as the mail must get through for General Washington to Easton."

"Best of luck. The mail you carry can help save or lose this war!"

The rider mounted his horse and tipped his tricorn slightly, then winced with the still-painful blow to the head from Claudius. The rider then pulled on the reigns, and the horse trotted away to the south at a moderate gait, and the bloody, blond braid swung back and forth with the gait like the pendulum on a grandfather clock.

Chapter 33
Moody's Gift to Clinton

"Beware the man who comes bearing gifts and invoking flattering words."
– Proverbs 29:4-5

June 4th, 1781, and the British occupied City of New York awoke to another day. It was quite a scene along Broadway in southern Manhattan. Several well-dressed British guards were anxiously milling around on the sidewalk, with their blood-red uniforms and white, leather straps diagonally across their chest. As a carriage approached, they formed neat double rows of five men each, with the one row facing the other and their musket butts held by their left palm with the shiny, brass muzzles resting on their shoulders. They looked identical and moved with synchrony, like smoothly performing ballet dancers. Then, momentarily, they became frozen in their stance. As the carriage eased to the front sidewalk, the group leader shouted a command, and they snapped to salute the honored guest.

None other than Lieutenant James Moody jumped down from the carriage and proceeded forward through the invisible aisle that the British guards formed. He readjusted his round derby and saluted in reply to the guards as he jauntily went into the handsome front door of the British headquarters of Sir Henry Clinton.

Bounding up the stairs, Lieutenant Moody came to the main office and passed by the sentry guards and into the suite. General Clinton looked up from some notes to see his presence, smiled, and quickly stood and offered a handshake.

"Moody, my good man!" said the British commander of North American operations.

They shook hands and both sat down quickly, Moody on a sofa and Clinton back into his fine, leather commander's chair.

"In my estimation," said a satisfied Clinton, "you will have handed us victory over the Rebels."

"Thank you, sir. It was nothing but a little 'highway robbery' for the good general."

They both laughed heartily.

"Yes, literally, Moody."

"Right, sir. We know when and where the Patriots will send their mails. It is like taking candy from a baby."

"Oh, you are too modest, Moody," said Clinton. "I have eagerly reviewed the mails that you have recently obtained. Look at the number of messages you have gotten for us. Intercepts between General Washington and at least three of his highest general officers: General Sullivan, General Greene, and General Lafayette."

"Correct, sir."

"We have thought about these interceptions, and I have conceived the notion of what they represent."

Moody looked at Clinton with anticipation.

"We feel the messages clearly says that the Patriots will remain here and attempt to besiege New York."

Clinton then got up and walked to the window, brandishing his sword at his hip.

"It all makes sense. The Rebels have probed our lines north of the city. They will bring the large French Army contingent from Rhode Island to support their ill-trained troops. Their plan won't get anywhere because we have our open seas and the best navy in the world to keep us in plenty of food and drink here in Manhattan."

Clinton turned to Moody and said, "But our Southern Army, now led by General Cornwallis, will rest up from traipsing through the Carolinas and Virginia. He will then come up past Philadelphia to go behind the rebel Patriots. Yes, those unskilled country boys who haven't been paid by their new government, nor fed, and without much ammunition and with their clothing in rags and their energy near exhaustion, will be surprised at our British Army, the world's best troops, coming from behind them while they are lingering and awaiting the end of the siege. Ole' Cornwallis beat those Patriots the last time in New York, at the Battle of Long Island, where Washington got away by a gossamer thread."

Clinton rounded the room and dropped back into his cushy commander's desk. "Lieutenant Moody, I feel you have provided us British with the keys to end the Revolutionary War in success! This shall defeat the Patriots!"

"Thank you, sir. And I assume my payment will be gold doubloons as a reward?"

"No, no, no. This time, since you are successful, and victory looks assured, you will be given a greater prize. You shall go to England to live the rest of your life in luxury and glory."

"Thank you, sir!" said an amazed and proud Moody. "I took it on myself to do predatory incursions on the camps and gatherings of those troops, militias, and people who are in the so-called Committees of Safety. I have been watching the movements and uncovered the planning that the Rebels have been engaged in. I have lurked about the homes and residences of people of note, and people of character—like that 'Honest' Judge Ogden. In all my endeavors, I have risked many hazards, and I have narrowly escaped capture."

Clinton smiled. "Indeed, sir, you have been so cunning in all of your adventures that you have spread a great terror throughout the whole community of this region."

"And while I have been rewarded with acclaim for my work, they have been trying to capture me and put me in prison. I, in large part, avoided capture—only a couple of times."

"So for you," said Clinton as he cut off Moody from further musings about how great he was, "so for you, now, is the opportunity to go to England and live the life of a man of note, a man with a dignity and flare for the lofty life."

"Oh, sir, you know that I am your very humble servant," said Moody in response.

So it went for Loyalist James Moody. He came from defeat on his family's farm to become one of the most notorious (from the Patriot view) or successful (from the British view) spies of the Revolutionary War. Gold doubloons and fame and a voyage to England. He could not know the tragedy that would strike him or the way such promises would never come to fruition. How could he? Even Moody, who otherwise believed he had magical powers, could not, in the end, see into the future.

Chapter 34
Spy-GW Messages on Siege of NYC, around June 1781

"Ignorance is bold, and knowledge is reserved."
– Thucydides

A splendid mid-summer 1781 evening in Manhattan unveiled itself.

While the island was under siege, international ships had passage and came in from around the world. In a gorgeous mansion, a gathering took place, a party larger than the usual social scene in the city occupied by Loyalists and British soldiers.

A large and extravagant dinner was prepared by the kitchen staff and was being enjoyed by the officers of the British Army. The fine food had been handily consumed, and the flowing drinks were now being tipped. The spirits were taking their effect.

Waiters slid across the floor, bringing food and drink for the many requests. The officers and their lady guests spoke with raised voices and joked frequently, followed by laughter. The large room was filled with joviality and lightheartedness.

At the end of a long table sat the man in charge of the North American British operations, Sir Henry Clinton. He was well-dressed to the high level of his general's rank. He was enjoying his hearty steak taken from local farms and rich burgundy from the Portuguese Madeira Islands. Spinning the sparkling dessert sipper glass as it rested on the linen tablecloth, he looked around the room with an eye of satisfaction.

"This war has gone on much too long," said Sir Henry Clinton. "I miss the home country and family and friends back there in Britain. But to be honest, it is comfortable to remain here in Manhattan."

Into the doorway came a man in civilian dress. He removed his round, black derby and ignored the coat check clerk as he walked toward the long table of British officers.

"Ah, Lieutenant Moody," said Clinton. "I've been expecting

you."

They traded introductions with the officers who were present. Moody greeted each and then walked over and stood near the general.

"So, gentlemen, here's what we know," said Clinton.

The table became quiet. Although the meal was sumptuous and the wine of the finest grapes, the conversation would be so important that not a bite or sip was taken during the discussion.

"These are grave times for us here," said Clinton. The table was silent, and all eyes were upon Clinton. "A toast to our lost Major John André, hanged just north of where we sit."

"Here, here," the men said as glasses were raised and clanged.

Sips were taken. All eyes fell again upon Clinton.

Clinton waved to sentries who had stood guard over the festivities. He gave a signal, prearranged, that the guards were to vacate the room. This left only the British officers, and some accepted women, secured from prying eyes and ears. Clinton prepared to give some of the most sensitive discussions that he ever delivered.

"Here is the current Revolutionary War strategy: The Rebel American Army, the Continentals as they call themselves, or the Patriots, are at a standstill with us. Their country grows weary of fighting, their money is losing value. Their soldiers want it to be over with so they can go home to their farms and families, and the soldiers are growing so disenfranchised with their lack of pay or value to it that there's talk of mutiny.

"Dragging the war out, then, hurts their spirit. But, at the same time, Britain is also straining with fatigue at the time and costs. In addition, unfortunately for us Brits, the French have arrived here in America and are ready to help the Rebels."

Mumbles of disgust stewed up around the table, like a bad, gaseous stench brewing up from a swamp.

"We have our great British Army in two sections—one here in Manhattan, 'up north,' and one based out of Charleston, South Carolina colony, 'down south.' I have returned from the South having sieged and won the city of Charleston. The Southern Army under Lord Cornwallis has done a splendid job chasing those Patriots across the wetlands and lowlands and will one day catch them and crush them as they scurry northward toward Virginia, cowardly escaping direct confrontation with our illustrious troops."

Mumbles of agreement flowed, just as the wine flowed into fine, crystal glasses.

"We, up here in the north, have done a fine job of keeping Washington at bay, holed up in nearby Morristown. And since we almost got him with the Springfield expedition, he seems to have hidden his headquarters up the Hudson River in Newburgh."

"With the advent of the French troops here, there is the question, the large question, the key question at this time." He paused for effect, then continued. "Should we leave Manhattan and go to the aid of our Southern Army to create the combined army of our entire North American British expedition?"

Silence prevailed.

"We could, of course, stay here. But there is a strategic possibility that Washington, now with the numbers of French troops present, could bottle us in here on this island. They could lay siege on us here."

Manhattan certainly was a comfortable location—wine, women, song, and no cold nights in a tent on the campaign trail.

"Now, if instead of the siege, Washington decided to go south, then Lord Cornwallis might have a tough time. Cornwallis could leave by sea, and we have the best navy in the world, bar none."

"Let's prepare for the siege, if it comes," said one officer, munching on a steak cut from the stolen cattle from the *Morrisania* estate—owned by Morris, who signed the Declaration of Independence and who was now in hiding in Sussex County on his *Morrisvale* farm. He had been munching as several others were zealously sipping the fine wine of the great city. "And unlike our siege of Fort Ticonderoga and what happened in Boston and other places, there's no way for the enemy to roll the cannon closer or to get mortars into range, what with the broad Hudson River harbor distancing us from them."

Someone else added, "And there's the Hudson River and the Long Island Sound that they can't use to invade, and our navy would sink any platform that they'd bring!"

The officers laughed and considered the piddling Americans as unable to battle with as much finesse as the forces of England.

"We certainly don't want to act incorrectly like General Howe did."

Everyone knew that he had the major British Army come down from Canada with General Burgoyne and instead of sailing up the

Hudson to aid him and crush the Americans, he went to the south, to Philadelphia.

"I say let's stay here and not go south like Howe did before, and see what happens with Washington," said an officer with his arm around a pretty lady, obviously content with where he was. A lot of nods supported a decision to stay put, stay in the safety of the metropolis of New York City, and remain where good food, wine, and women abounded. There was also easy access to the British Navy should that be needed. There was the agreement to stay where comfort was in their hands.

"Okay then, gentlemen. I appreciate your consensus. This will be part of my decision-making."

A number of ayes and yesses followed as the officers more or less patted themselves on the back with their comments.

Clinton wanted to recognize the Loyalist spy from the New Jersey area. He raised a glass and said so.

"Lieutenant Moody here has done a grand job of intercepting the mails of Washington." Ayes and cheers came from the table.

Applause let out for Lieutenant Moody. He rounded the table and began eating the delicious food and sipping some wine. He sat with a beautiful woman and began to flirt. He believed he was finally getting the praise that he wanted, the appreciation that he felt was justified for his work for the British, and to be recognized for his risky escapades. The attractive, young woman's arm came near the hat, and Moody brushed it away. He took the hat in both hands as the long table of officers noted his rejection of the woman's encroaching hand. Moody clasped the derby firmly and then removed some contents from under the top of the derby. He took these, papers, unfolded them, and then handed them across the table to Clinton.

A couple of interesting jokes could be heard around the table. Several war stories were spoken of by officers at the table. The ladies were entranced by the victories that seemed to flow from the talk. But at the end of the table, Clinton was consumed by reading the papers. He looked at each several times, each of them for a few long moments. Around the table, the stories seemed to ebb and then cease as more and more of the attendees saw that the documents were being read seriously and at length by the general. All heads had turned in the general's direction.

Clinton finally allayed their concern. He began to slowly, and broadly, smile. He slid his chair back and stood up. He raised out his arm, at the end of which he clutched the papers.

"Here are a couple of letters that Lieutenant Moody here had snatched in northern New Jersey, up near that Patriot Colonel John Seward's fortified house." Sir Henry Clinton continued, "The contents of these letters leads me to feel that the Patriots are going to remain around the region; that they are intent to hold us under siege to keep us bottled up in Manhattan."

"Bottled up is right," shouted one happy officer. "Port wine bottles!" Many laughed.

Clinton chuckled in response. He appreciated that these officers were present for him. These were the British men who led the troops in the northern part of the western hemisphere. Clinton was their leader, and it was by his guidance that the war would be conducted.

Now he sat with Moody, the two men alone in a corner, their glasses full, and fine Cuban cigars had been lit.

"Not long after the French military leader Count de Rochambeau arrived at Newport in the Rhode Island Plantations, there was a meeting with the Patriots. Washington proposed a meeting on in Weathersfield, Connecticut. The two leaders, Washington representing the Continentals and Rochambeau the French, met to discuss strategy for continuing to prosecute the war. Washington and Rochambeau—our arch enemies." Clinton leaned forward as if to place an emphasis, and Moody understood. Moody thought back to his past, the torching of his family farm, the escape from prison, the knowledge that the Rebels wouldn't rest until they had him in the stockade and thence hanging from the end of a rope.

Clinton continued, "Shortly after their meeting, these letters were sent to the major armies of the Americans. Some of Washington's messages Lieutenant Moody 'acquired' and brought to me here in his derby."

Moody smiled without mirth, and Clinton pulled one of the letters out of the stack he kept in an envelope. Then he said, "This one is from General George Washington to John Sullivan May 29th, 1781. Sullivan has been in charge of the army in Rhode Island and was marching in the western reaches of the American coast. He said to Sullivan that confronting us in New York City would have the 'fairest prospect of success.'"

Clinton then drew another letter from the bunch. "Here we go," he said. "From General George Washington to another annoying Frenchman, Marie-Joseph-Paul-Yves-Roch-Gilbert du Motier,

Marquis de Lafayette. He wrote to Lafayette two days after that from the New Windsor cantonment, near his Newburgh headquarters, May 31st, 1781. In the letter, he said that remaining in the New York area was 'preferable to a Southern operation.'"

Clinton smiled cunningly at Moody. He said, "Lafayette is one of Washington's closest confidants."

The two men drank and smoked for a while in contemplative silence. Finally, Moody said, "What else have I brought you, sir?"

Clinton grinned. "I thought you'd never ask. This one is from General George Washington to Nathaniel Greene only one day after that, dated June 1st, 1781. General Greene is the army's leader in the South. Washington states that there is 'difficulty, I may say impossibility, of transporting the necessary baggage, artillery, and stores by land ...'

"All three of these documents state that Washington intends to keep his troops, and those of the French under Rochambeau, here in the North," said Clinton. He held up those three letters as if a proud man holding a winning hand of cards.

Some of the others in the room heard the news, and a hush fell over the diners.

"And I must say, based upon what we find from the Americans, the messages are indicative of being in support of preparing for a siege."

Clinton smiled with the look of supreme confidence that what he had said was true.

"What if this is a set up?" said one of the officers seated near the end of the table far from Clinton.

"We have been capturing various mails throughout the war. They have been found to be very useful," said Moody himself. "So far, not one has put us in the wrong place."

"That's right" agreed Sir Henry Clinton. "Washington has been up the Hudson River at New Windsor and needs lines of communication to run his war operationally. He has a chain of express[lviii] with mails traveling from the Connecticut region to his headquarters with riders at every fifteen miles, dragoons, and French hussars. In New Jersey, he has used regular riders of the mails. This is how he communicates with his American Army."

Moody said, turning to Clinton, "Washington used to run the mails through Smith's Clove and Galloway Grove, but my compatriot Claudius Smith and his gang have been so destructive to those Rebels that he had been forced to change the route of the mail delivery. He is now sending the mails farther west, where he may think they are traveling far from the British, too far to be intercepted. A typical delivery via the western route would be from Morristown directly on the road to Colonel John Seward's, then up through Warwick and then Chester to Newburgh where his headquarters are. It is along those roads I have been successful in nabbing rider after rider."

The table of officers were all looking at him at this point, in the warmth of this late August night. Moody spoke up on his own behalf.

"I have it on good authority that as of August 18, 1781, neither Washington nor his French colleague Rochambeau have moved out to the south. With the impending onset of autumn, I am sure it is not going to happen—I am sure that they will stay up north here to besiege New York."

Clinton outstretched his arms to intercede, almost like the Pope ready to recognize a cardinal. "Gentlemen, Lieutenant Moody has been so disruptive that Washington himself has been quoted as saying 'that villain Moody,' so we know how much of a threat our lieutenant here has been."

Moody bowed his head, as if humbled by the words.

"Why, our royal governor of New Jersey, William Franklin, has said that Moody is 'the best partisan we have.' We can trust Lieutenant Moody's words."

At that, down the table, a man stood up and gave a slow, deep bow of appreciation to Moody. It was the now-freed William Franklin himself, recipient of a prisoner exchange from his Connecticut prison to the luxury of New York City.

Smiles, aye-ayes, and a soft clapping expressed regards for the spy with the black, round derby.

Clinton continued, "These letters, I feel, are decisively describing, in no uncertain manner, that the American Army of the north will be preparing for a siege of New York City here. Because Washington believes he has found a route of the mails that is safe from us, he must surely be telling the truth. We, then, do not need to go south to support our British forces now in Virginia. We can stay here in the comfort of New York City."

All present cheered in agreement. "Comforts are preferred," said one as others nodded.

Clinton continued, "Cornwallis should be able to crush that fellow they call the Swamp Fox and the other Rebels from the South. If we find that the Southern Army needs our help, we can always call on the Royal Navy to pick us up from the city here and carry us into the Chesapeake and support him."

Roars of support erupted, followed with wine and song.

Clinton remembered how, in 1777, they sneaked past Washington to take Philadelphia by landing on the Chesapeake. That was only four years ago, and this was right at the mouth of the Chesapeake Bay, not way up the bay at Head of Elk like last time. Either way, he was certain that they would defeat the Americans and save the colonies for King George.

Chapter 35
Yorktown Secret Information

"Fortune favors the brave."
– Pliny the Elder

General Washington pulled off his glasses with one hand and rubbed his eyes with the other. "My vision is going."
"I wouldn't say that," responded Lord Stirling. "You have great vision in this message."
Washington dipped his head down with a slight smile.
"Soldier!" yelled Stirling.
A young man came forward.
"Yes sir," said the man, not much more than a boy, with braided blond hair partway down his back, contrasting nicely to the blue Continental blazer. His outfit also was attractive with the white leather sash running diagonally across his torso, front, and back.
"Take this message," said Stirling. "We are aware that you have been stopped and robbed before. But you are valiant and brave, and you have survived. We will do whatever we can to ensure that you are not hurt in your duty. But your courage attests to the fact that you are doing dangerous and heroic work. It is imperative that this message be sent immediately."
The soldier stood taller. "Yes, sir," he said. He grabbed the document with a hint of reluctance—he'd already been robbed twice and had heard of many other messengers who'd been similarly dispatched. But his fear was superseded by his Patriotic zeal. He knew this would be a dangerous mission for him.
It was only one sheet of white paper, but it had been folded and secured with red sealing wax and had now become an official military correspondence. He deposited the important mail into his leather saddle bag and mounted his horse to depart the Hasbrouk House at Washington's headquarters in Newburgh, New York. He pulled the leather reigns to the horse so he'd head for the road to the south and then prepared himself as best he could to move toward the

threat of British capture or Loyalist thievery.

Washington and Stirling exchanged glances. They both knew that the letter was a fake.

"I hope the boy makes it out without getting hurt," said Washington.

Stirling, who hadn't been thinking that same thought, quickly agreed.

Washington felt weary, but he roused himself and said, "We have nothing but to wait, and we shall see what comes of the messenger."

Just then, the door to the Hasbrouk House opened, and a number of general officers and staff came in.

These key officers were attending a scheduled special staff meeting. They greeted General Lord Stirling, chatted briefly, and shortly thereafter, all gathered round a table and sat down. Slowly, General Washington arose from his study desk and came over to the table. He removed his glasses and rubbed his eyes while gaining his composure, looked up, and welcomed the men.

"Our broad strategy for this year is shaping as we speak. As you are well aware, there are two large British forces which make up their North American presence. There are thousands of men in New York City, just a few miles to our south, directly down the Hudson River, from Newburgh here, to New York City. There is also the southern force, which had captured Charleston, South Carolina but is currently encamped along the tidal waters to the ocean approaches in Virginia after chasing our army, led by General Nathaniel Greene, around the Carolinas. Our small spotting group, led by my friendly French protege General Lafayette, inform us that those British are digging in there. Our allies, the French, have their thousands of men in Newport, Rhode Island and are ready to assist us. Another key force is the French fleet under Admiral Compte de Grasse, which I have just been informed is sailing up the Atlantic Ocean from the Caribbean Sea."

One younger officer spoke. "We have been sending forays of men to probe the northern defenses of Manhattan. We have gone south of here to White Plains, for example."

There was mixed opinion on this.

"The British may think that this is where we are building our effort—to dislodge them from New York City like we did in Boston," said Washington.

The senior officers present were very intent and understood. It seemed like all the set pieces in a chess game were ready for a major movement.

"So," said Washington, "we are ready to make a final and decisive effort." He leaned over the table and rolled out a basic map. The plan he was to describe was very different from this attack on Manhattan; it was an ingenious deception and a large, pivotal change of position.

"The French troops will move to the west from Rhode Island, and we will depart from our large encampment here in the Newburgh and New Windsor Cantonment. Both of us, the French and our Continental Army, will join up and move south toward Virginia. Since the southern British force seems to be digging in there, they will remain in their position as we approach them, as a combined French and American force. And we will be aided by a large force of militia from the nearby Virginia farms."

This was a major, gigantic, effort that would be done in secrecy, as best as possible, and the senior leaders of the military knew this. Some even gasped when they realized just how large this plan was. Some officers, keen as they were, felt that this could be a leaky plan.

"But that would mean our Continental Army would have a direct confrontation with the great British Army," said a learned young officer. "We have experienced that we are not a match for the well-trained enemy army when on a balanced field of battle. They whip us when we do."

Grumbling took place.

"It is so far away to take our whole army on travel," said another.

"And we have not been paid, are short on good clothing and weapons," said yet another.

Heads looked at each other with consternation.

"Sir, why go all the way down there, leaving the north undefended, when the Brits could just have their navy come down and remove the troops?"

"Good point, officer. That French fleet communique that I just got states that Admiral de Grasse will be coming north and move into the area in dispute, in the Chesapeake Bay, and keep the British navy away so that they are unable to help the troops there. The French fleet will be available, for a short time period, to support us by denying the British navy of supplying their Southern Army."

"Quite a plan," said another officer, "and so what about the undefended north?"

The men nodded in assent.

He added, "And more importantly, the northern British Army could then come behind us and catch us in a pincer movement and destroy our whole American and French armies?"

Great attention was drawn toward Washington.

"I just sent a letter, a message."

A collective inquisitive look appeared on the officers' faces.

"Blond braids riding south on a country back road," said Stirling with a grin.

The heads all rotated toward Stirling, but the inquisitive look remained. Then their gazes went back to Washington as he began to speak.

"The message is a deception. We hope that our chain of messaging, that has had robberies before, will again have stolen our correspondence. I am sending messages to my commanders around here to the effect that we are digging in here and will besiege New York City. Hopefully—and this is a largest of hope—Sir Henry Clinton, their commander, will take heed of the message and prepare for the siege and assume and continue to believe that we are here around New York City and here is where we will remain."

"Ah," said one officer, now understanding the plot. "I get it. The British in New York City will remain right where they are while we go and then besiege the other British Southern Army and defeat them."

"Brilliant!" was a collective response.

"But," said Stirling, "it all depends on whether the 'fake' message is captured, and then believed, by Clinton."

The meeting adjourned, and the officers went back to their commands. Stirling approached Washington as they stood looking southward.

"General," said Stirling, "I have my hopes for Lieutenant Moody, the Loyalist, intercepting the letter."

"He is a smart one for sure. From a human attribute's perspective, I believe that to use his cunning against him would deliver us a victory."

Stirling, raising some red wine to his lips, said, "Good luck to our blond-braided messenger."

Chapter 36
Battle of Yorktown 10/1781

"Success is to be measured not so much by the position that one has reached in life as by the obstacles which he has overcome."
– Booker T. Washington

    The noise was tooth jarring. It was the boom that shook the ground.
    In the death and destruction that is war, men scurried about in the rounded mounds of earthen berms and the shallow trenches cut into the ground. The mortars created the most deafening sound. Each time the mortars fired, the ground seemed to swell up and lift the dirt. You could see dust emanate from between what scrawny grass there was remaining on the battlefield. Then some trace of yellow flame appeared near the mortar, followed by dirty, white smoke that was belched from the iron carcass that was the mortar body.
    This vivid but deadly action took place from many mortars and cannon which were assembled up and down the line, all aimed at the enemy in a barrage of fire. The Yankees' Continental Army were raining death on the British troops, in the town nearby, where the enemy were cowering for cover as the iron balls fell from the sky onto them below.
    The Redcoats were only six hundred yards away, in the village of Yorktown. While the day dimmed, the barrage did not. Shortly after the boom of the cannon sounded, the Americans could hear the screams and shrieks which cut the night's darkness and indicated the terror in the town nearby. All troops knew the pain and suffering that the cannonballs were eliciting. And the mortars kept up the shelling of the enemy.
    Behind the redoubt, a small but constant yellow flame could be seen. A candle produced a pointed light, waving slightly, and was mounted upon a dark dirt wall. The redoubt was a reinforced structure made of earth that protected the American troops who, in turn, had the Brits pinned in at the village of Yorktown. The candle

flickered at the sound of each mortar firing, and the mortar ball would explode down the line in the enemy's encampment and produce a compression wave.

Coming from the American encampment beyond the battle line, a young man had worked his way across the no-man's land to the battlefront of the siege of Yorktown. He moved quickly and silently, wary that death was prowling near in many forms. Jogging swiftly, he held his hat in hand to avoid losing it in the darkness. He traversed the muddy depressions and avoided the spikes meant to pierce a soldier's foot and impede an assault, and then clambered up the steep embankment and quickly entered the redoubt and toward the flickering candle.

Out of breath from the rough approach, and clutching his tricorn hat, he then looked for a familiar face. He scanned many men on the forward berm that looked toward the enemy; most men were sleeping except for one or two staring ahead as if in shellshock from the din of battle. On the far side of the redoubt next to that candle, he noticed an officer leaning on the forward wall, consumed with searching the landscape ahead with a spyglass. The young man made his way to him.

The glowing candle produced a yellowed look to the faces of them both. The young man, still holding his tricorn, took notice of the officer as he was steadying the telescope and keeping still, lying prone on the dirt rise, most of the way up on the wall. He was eyeing the town through a spyglass. The younger man looked at him with respectful review.

"Captain Ogden?"

The officer glanced over at the young breathless man, and he put the spyglass at his side and turned to speak. "Yes?"

The younger officer just smiled and stared.

"What are you looking at?" Ogden said.

"Well, sir, I am admiring you and your capabilities."

"Ah well, I hope that I am worthy of your gaze," he said, returning to the spyglass as another round of cannon fire exploded in the distance.

"Yes, sir, you are, sir."

"Kind words, young man. Hopefully I live up to them. Right now, though, it is my duty to observe the effects of our cannonade on the enemy's fortress."

Later, the two men paused for a cold drink of water that was passed to them in tin cups. The younger man said, "Tell me about the capture of the enemy ship, *Blue Mountain Valley."*

Captain Aaron Ogden made a face, half smile, half frown. He didn't like to talk about his battles. And as they were in the midst of one at the moment, it seemed grandiose and arrogant to speak now of his triumphs.

"Please," said the young man. "Just to pass the time. It has been a long and wearying battle. I am trying to forget all that I have seen."

Ogden looked at his new friend and smiled. "All right," he said. He peered into the night as if he were back in time. "This all began back in 1776, in January. My father, Robert Ogden, was chair of the Elizabethtown Committee of Safety, and he helped scheme plans against the British. There was one plan of some note, that Father produced, along with Lord Stirling, who would own the zinc mine adjacent to Father's farm in Sussex County."

The young man was watching the night sky, waiting for the next percussive boom.

"My brother Matthias took the small boat in a strong northwest wind with Lord Stirling and captured the enemy ship *Blue Mountain Valley* early in the war. Later, when British General Howe's army was moving toward Philadelphia, I was under my brother's command at the Battle of Brandywine, and later in the Battle of Springfield."

"I heard you were a life guard for General Washington."

This time Ogden smiled broadly as it was clear he had enjoyed protecting the great general. He nodded. "Yes, that was while in Morristown."

The young man said, somewhat breathlessly, "Those are experiences that I would like to have."

"Well, that you should get good experience if this war lasts much longer. But we have surprised the Brits this time, that is for sure. Here, in the South, as the British chased our southern troops around and then the enemy came to rest here, in the Chesapeake, we surreptitiously came these many miles from the north. This is one of the greatest feats of the war—Washington's duping of Clinton. Our general had snuck away from Clinton in New York, where he was tricked into thinking we were getting ready to assault him in Manhattan. This was a twist on an earlier deception by the Brits, where they went on ships supposedly to Charleston but got off them near Philadelphia yet again here on the Chesapeake. We tried to stop him at Brandywine. How surprised they must have been when our French allies came up from the Caribbean to confront Admiral Howe's fleet as he came and tried to resupply Cornwallis here."

"Yes, your great experiences and the highlights of Washington and Stirling certainly are colorful."

Ogden smiled at the young officer's descriptions of the war.

Then the young man said, "So, you and your brother have done much to help us get where we are today." He fumbled with his hat.

"Yes, with my brother, Matthias, we have fought the war in the army and in battle. And with Colonel Lewis Morris too. His father was a signer of the Declaration of Independence and who has the farm near my father's, a farm they called *Morrisvale* in Sussex County. And my own father, like Morris, lost his home in the city and was robbed and in death's grip. They both have been important men. There are many who have aided our cause, such as another of Father's neighbors, Colonel Seward."

"And General Washington with his exploits and ruses has worked with Lord Stirling to help create victories," said the young man, rolling up his tricorn snugly.

"Yes, Howe got us then, in the beginning years, but General Washington and the French got them this time by surprise. Now, their main force of troops is trapped. Those men before us have been cut off from food and supplies for much too long. They are sure to give up soon."

"Tell me about the French allies that we have, if you don't mind. I want to learn as much as I can."

Aaron Ogden stared at the young man and wondered for a moment why he wanted the information. A moment of suspicion passed through him as his training kicked in. Then he saw the young man's upright posture, the Patriot symbols on his uniform, the way he held his tricorn with pride. He saw that the young man wanted to follow in the footsteps of Patriots as himself. Ogden nodded and said, "With our French allies cutting off the seaways, and the fact that Cornwallis can't get any supplies, it will only be a matter of days before our incessant bombing of him and his lack of food or reinforcements will make him yield to us. The British deserters have told us so."

"Yes sir, Captain Ogden."

Ogden stood up and returned to the telescope. The young man brought up a cloth for Captain Ogden to clean the telescope lens.

Aaron wiped the lens and peered out. He said, while watching for lights in the sky, "On this very battleground, there's been quite an assault. We came forward, four hundred men, into the teeth of the enemy's defense."

"Even tougher than that, Captain Ogden," said his admirer, seeming to know more than was thought. "When we attacked this fortress, we encountered an entrenched professional army. With overall command of General Washington, under the responsibility of Lafayette, under the field command of Colonel Alexander Hamilton, and our group moving forward into battle being led by you, Captain Ogden. We assaulted this mighty indominable earthen works, where they were being protected by sharp spikes and earthen defenses. You quietly approached this fearsome place, and your men only with bayonets, against the cannon and musket fire available to the British. People would say that you crashed against the teeth of the great warriors' defenses; here in this earthen structure, Yorktown's Redoubt #10. That feat, I believe, will one day be a sign of our great glory, and of yours, sir."

Ogden pondered the past. Then he looked at the young man, registering his passion for justice and glory. He felt flattered and strangely hopeful. "It was a moonless night," he said. "Bayonets on the muskets but no power or balls for our guns since we were on the quiet."

He moved the telescope from his face and said, "Be that as it may, we tried to minimize casualties on both sides, and if the bayonet was needed, it would not give away the position nor the surprise attack."

Both men stood in silence. Ogden then sighed and stood straight, the sky his forefront, the frame around his strong figure. The younger man remained where he was, then said, "May I?"

Ogden turned and saw the corporal gesturing toward the telescope.

"Be my guest," he said with a smile.

The young officer said, "Yes, how about that rallying cry as we approached the redoubt?"

"You remember?" asked Ogden.

"Rush on, boys. The fort's ours." Smiling, the young man looked for a response. "You remember, sir, don't you?"

"Yes, of course." Then Ogden said, "I was gifted a contusion here." He touched his arm and winced. "It still has yet to heal. But these are the outcomes, sometimes, of war. It is not just any war, it is our freedom war, young man, and worthy of dying for. This small pain is but nothing in the larger sacrifices of my men. These are the price we pay for winning."

"The price of glory for you, Captain Ogden."

Ogden smiled. The young man reminded Ogden of himself when he was younger. A boy, then a young man who wanted to sever the ties to England so that America could govern itself away from tyranny. He said, "The assault, led by Alexander Hamilton, was in the newspapers all around our country."

"I am delighted at having helped the cause," the young man said.

"I am much gratified by your dedication."

"You have great experience, sir, on top of your education at Princeton. I can see you being the new governor of our great state of New Jersey."

"Oh, that's kind of you; maybe someday, someday," Ogden said. He rubbed his chin, thinking, and said, more to himself than the young man, "And Morris' great grandfather, also Lewis, was the New Jersey colony governor back in 1738. Small world. It could happen."

Ogden returned to the concerns of war and began observing the town. Sometimes it felt to Ogden that in all his life moving forward, he would be on the watch, even in peace, should peace ever come.

"My brother," Ogden said, thinking of Matthias, "is also of high esteem. He volunteered, along with his cousin, Aaron Burr, to go with a force to Canada early in this war, and was wounded in the Battle of Quebec and was with General Montgomery as he died. He was captured and released by the British and conceived of the plan to capture the future king. And he may, if this war ends, go to Europe and perhaps bring back the treaty."

The young officer nodded. Enthusiastically he said, "Yes, he may be called a brave and gallant soldier." He scanned the land ahead. "General Lafayette is fond of him, and one day he may go to France, and perhaps be received by King Louis XV. Maybe, if luck would have it, he will bring back the good news of the end of the war."

There was a sullen silence. Not to be driven to reminisce about the glorious victory but to get back to business, Ogden repositioned himself against the dirt embankment upon which he was holding his observation of the enemy in town. One could see more at this time for the day was brightening with the coming dawn. Daybreak was close. But Ogden dutifully went back to observing through the spyglass.

"Oh my!" said Ogden.

"What is it that you see, Captain?"

"My goodness! Oh my!" Ogden reiterated.

"What is it, sir?" said the young man.

"I see two figures coming from the enemy position in Yorktown. I see a bugle boy and an officer coming our way. They carry a white flag."

"They're surrendering!" shouted the young man, elated at the prospect.

"We are about to begin a new adventure as the United States," said Captain Ogden.

Chapter 37
Abduction of Admiral Digby & Prince William Henry, March 28, 1782

"I think the King is but a man as I am: the violet smells to him as it doth to me."
– Shakespeare

    With the stiff wind coming from its rear, the ferries sped under sail across the choppy Hudson River from the Jersey shores near Hoboken. Back and forth all day with business to be done.
    On this busy passageway to the large city, four whale boats journeyed eastward. Moving against the wind was a much slower journey, but the whale boats had strong rowers aboard who were punching through the wind and waves toward their goal, Manhattan Island. Two men were in the lead whale boat, and they were wearing new clothes. They were trying to force fit the seemingly tight suits over their frames. The men, Colonel Matthias Ogden and his third in command had recently donned civilian clothes. Ogden stood at the helm and looked once again at the folded document in his vest pocket. He made sure that it was secure. Then, certain that no one was near, he pulled it out, unfolded it, and read it one more time.

> *To Colonel Ogden of the 1 Jersey Regiment*
>
> *Sir,*
>
> *The spirit of enterprise so conspicuous in your plan for surprising in their quarters, and bringing off the Prince-William Henry & Admiral Digby, merits applause; and you have my authority to make the attempt in any manner and at such a time as your own judgment shall direct.*

> *I am fully persuaded that it is unnecessary to caution you against offering insult or indignity to the persons of the prince or admiral should you be so fortunate as to capture them; but it may not be amiss to press the propriety of a proper line of conduct upon the party you command.*
>
> *In case of success, you will, as soon as you get them to a place of safety, treat them with all possible respect, but you are to delay no time in conveying them to Congress and reporting your proceedings with a copy of these orders. Given at Morristown this 28th day of March 1782.*
>
> *Your obedient servant,*
> *General George Washington*[lix]

After he read the note again, assuring himself again that his plan to kidnap Digby and the prince was approved, Ogden looked ahead into the wind. Across this choppy water was the home of the enemy. The sun was beginning to set, and the evening was about to lessen the light level, good for any prying eyes. As the boats came to Manhattan's shore, Ogden became quite apprehensive. He looked up to see a large British first-class ship with almost one hundred guns sticking out the side in long rows and several rows high. It looked like a giant porcupine with quills at attention.

Matthias quickly folded up Washington's orders and stuffed it into his pocket. As the boats passed by the massive ship, the stern heaved around toward them as the ship rode the anchor, showing the placard "*HMS Barfleur.*"

The other officer standing beside Mathias quietly, but with great excitement, said to Matthias, "Sir, that is the British flagship!"

"I know, and we'd be dead men if they knew who we were and what we are doing."

The whale boats continued to the Manhattan pier head. Fighting against the headwind, the vessels finally bumped into the wooden pier, and some of the men acted as stevedores and helped tie the stay ropes to the hold down cleats.

***

The playful group looked like children though they were all

adults. Admiral Robert Digby watched with growing impatience as the young men and women played hide-and-seek and chased each other across the ice playing tag. They were running back and forth, some of them skating and giggling frequently. Prince William Henry seemed to chase girls more so than the other boys did. He was also laughing with wild abandon. He was easily spotted because, instead of skating, he was in a chair with blades at the bottom, being pushed across the ice by another child.

Two military men looked intently on the boy. Admiral Digby spun his eyes about as he tried to follow the antics of the laughing boy. His lips hung low at the corners, as if this were the last thing that he'd want to be doing at this time.

"I have had enough of this childish foolishness," said Admiral Digby[lx]. "Here I am, the commander of the fleet, and I am babysitting this horseplay."

"I know, I know," said Commodore Edmund Affleck[lxi] who was standing beside him. "This Prince William Henry[lxii] is quite an annoyance. As his 'roommate' at our quarters in Hanover Square here in Manhattan, all I see is an adventurous youth barely out of his teens."

"Right. He is young and spoiled. It is a pity," said Digby.

The two senior officers of the British Royal Navy looked on as the prince stood up near the edge of the ice and grabbed one girl who had a pair of long, blonde ponytails and kissed her squarely on the lips.

"My gal, Charlotte!" the prince said, full of brazen, immature manhood. She ran away from him, screaming in disbelief.

"How long can this go on?" said Admiral Digby

Just then, the principal officer in North America, General Clinton, walked up behind them, quickly and with a very serious demeanor. He had a couple of words with the two men.

"You men come with me. And bring the prince with you."

"Yes sir, General Clinton," said Admiral Digby, sighing. The three men briskly saluted each other. All three alighted into a nearby carriage to swiftly leave the area, along with the prince, whom they dragged along.

**

Meanwhile, Colonel Ogden and his officer were being thrashed about in the whale boat. When they anchored, Ogden said, "Well, that was a rowdy ride. Howling wind and a tossing boat in the waves off Manhattan." The small boats bounced about trying to loosen themselves as if wild dogs on a short leash. Ogden looked around. "We are here safely."

"Yes, sir," said the officer with him. They were at Coenties Market slip, between the coffee shop and the head of the old slip. "Sir, you have kept us in the dark all this time. We have risked our lives to come over to the bees' nest of Manhattan. We understand this is serious business, and we want to perform our best. But we need to know what we are doing. Can you tell us the plan now?"

Ogden got the men onto the street and then looked both ways, and he made sure that no one was behind the nearby building. He leaned in on the team of men and spoke softly but earnestly.

"We have about ten or eleven men in each of the four boats. We're heading to Prince William Henry's spacious accommodations on Hanover Square," said Ogden.

"That's about two hundred yards from our Lord Stirling's old quarters on Broad Street," said the other officer.

"Yes," said Matthias, focusing back on the urgent problem at hand. "The prince has two sentinels that must be seized. There are forty or so men guarding nearby, near City Hall."

Ogden's men began to jump off the whale boats. Some had knives and darkened lanterns. Some had crowbars, some had axes with which to force the doors. Others had muskets and were fitted with bayonets. Some were carrying four large oil clothes to capture their valuable prey.

"Officer, once the deed is done, you will follow about a half-gunshot behind."

"Yes, sir."

Matthias was confident that he might take the most valuable British possession this side of the British Isles—the prince who would become king! The men were quiet and professional, but they were full of enthusiasm too. The deadly work and combination of brilliance and daring would be among the most prominent in the Revolutionary War. The plan was going well. The whole contingent of men stealthily moved along the cobblestone until …

"Colonel Ogden!" shouted to a man. All forty men froze in place.

The man was dressed darkly and appeared of medium height, thin, and otherwise nondescript. He turned slowly, observing closely his surroundings, and then provided a combination of a whistle and several claps of his hands.

Ogden smiled. This was the secret signal.

All of a sudden, a young girl appeared, coming from the north.

While the darkly dressed man was the one who'd shouted, it was the girl with the blonde ponytails who drew the attention of the assault party who were on their way to one of the most exciting captures in the history of the world.

Matthias ran up to the man, whom he recognized as a Manhattan spy for the Patriots. "Hello," said Matthias, eager with enthusiasm, being anxious about his mission.

The darkly dressed man said, "I am undercover. Please lower you voice, sir."

"Yes, sir. We are ready to make the abduction, sir," said Ogden.

"Colonel Ogden, there's no one here. They have all left."

"What?"

"The plot to capture the prince has been found out by Sir Henry Clinton," said the spy.

"You mean, there's no one here for us to capture?"

"Correct, sir."

"Where? What?"

"Someone spying for the Brits let the story out. Word has it that there was spying in Washington's camp for the benefit of the British. The prince has been known to be very public, in hard-to-protect adventures, predictable and foolhardy. Clinton took him away."

"Where are they now?"

The girl with the blonde pigtails, energized, wiped what seemed to be dirt from her lips with her right palm and threw up her left arm, quickly pointing several fingers west toward the Hudson River, toward the biggest ship in the harbor.

"Sir," said the girl, "Sir Henry Clinton and Admiral Digby had left the play area where they were watching."

"And they took Prince William Henry," the spy added. "They are on a ship now, the *HMS Barfleur,* and are at this moment sailing out of the New York Harbor," said the spy.

Colonel Ogden looked around and saw the huge ship-of-the-line moving downstream from where he saw it anchored. They had apparently just loosed the shorelines from the cleats, and the seamen aboard were unfurling its sails into the strong headwind. She was sailing safely away.

"Well, men," said Matthias Ogden. "Our plans are off. The prince is safely aboard a British warship."

They all returned on their small boats to New Jersey.

Chapter 38
Smith's Clove

"Everything takes a different shape when we pass from abstractions to reality."
– Carl Von Clausewitz.

On the easterly side of the Ramapo Mountains was a mysterious place called Smith's Clove. There was a settlement here where the Smith family resided, which included Claudius. Smith Clove was located in a remote hollow nestled within the rounded and stony mountains which rose above the land. The Ramapos were majestic in their own way. They generally followed the southwest to northeast run of the Appalachian Mountains as they drifted toward the east. Many of the mountaintops were noticeable as a single giant knoll. Smith Clove was a human presence in a largely wilderness area.

The Ramapo Mountains had been the home of the Ramapough Indians who had been there, it is said, from prehistory. Interestingly, the Ramapo Mountains began only a score or so miles north of the spot where the Atlantic Ocean meets the Hudson River basin at the city of New York. The Ramapos were similar to those mountains on the other shore, the eastern side of the Hudson River, an area known as the Highlands. The Hudson River split the green knobs of earth as if searing the landscape from the north directly downward to the south; as if both sides were a large, long stick of butter and the Hudson River a hot knife through it. And nestled within this western mountainous area along the Hudson River, the Smith Clove was a marker, a dirty stain, an evil presence on the green, luscious, and innocent wilderness.

The Ramapo Mountains were considered one of the most beautiful parts of the new country. Sometimes the prevailing winds from the west would submit white cumulus clouds that would slide alongside the Ramapos and drift in to hover over the prominent staid summits on their lazy way to the east. Many clear days abounded, allowing for a view of at least fifty miles. The evil men who resided in Smith Clove were known to clamber over these mountains and hillocks to take advantage of the majestic view for many miles.

Rocky outcroppings burst from the rounded peaks and were smooth surfaced, almost the color of pink in certain light. Granite facing on these rocks would warm in a summer sun and make for a cozy spot for the weary mountain climber to rest, sitting up with one's hands palm down behind him, providing distant views of other mountains that spread out along the vast countryside. The evil men from Smith Clove took advantage of the camouflage that the varied and busy landscape made to hide themselves within it.

The mountains made difficult passageway from the rich lands and resources to the north as the English colonists, and the Dutch landowners before them, fashioned their way forward, carrying their produce to the great commerce center in New York City. Because of the impediment caused by the rugged mountains, over the years of the 1600s and 1700s, much produce and commerce traveled by boat up and down the Hudson River. But the Patriots could not use the river due to the presence of the British fleet, the greatest in the world, and their ability to block and arrest any Patriot attempt to utilize the waters of the Hudson River.

With the onset of the Revolutionary War, this made control of the river very important. The British held the southern part, from New York City up to West Point, where the Patriots had placed a giant chain across the river to impede travel by water. So, there was the chain across the river at the fortress West Point. The giant mountain known as Storm King was very steep and immediately descended into the water, preventing land travel just to the north of the chain. Then there was the all-important place of Washington's Newburgh headquarters, which was just around the Storm King bend of the river and to the north.

Thus, because of the limits of river travel because of the war, much of the personal travel took place by primitive roads through the Ramapos. These roads also carried the ever-crucial messages that Washington might send from Newburgh to points south. Success in the war depended upon these messages being sent, having secure transportation, and then finally getting through to the intended recipient. The Smith Gang from Smith Clove knew this and took advantage of this for their own personal gain at the cost of lives and goods of the Patriots.

The mountains represented a nearly impassable terrain. On the easterly shore of the Hudson River, the Highlands, and on the western side of the mighty river, the Ramapos, were like giant thorn bushes holding back the traveler. Movement was slow with the winding roadways, around one knob, and up one hill and down another. The roads were difficult to maintain, steep and stony. With nary a house proximate to the steep hillsides, no one was nearby. A hamlet or town would be many miles away, making help or support virtually nonexistent. This all presented to the Smith Gang an easy opportunity to rob and steal.

The difficulty of travel, and importance of any load that was onboard the wagon or horse, was a thought not lost on those who might be drawn to nefarious acts. The general remoteness left those who suffered assault by bandits to wait out a day or so, assuming they were not injured and could travel on before authorities could be called upon to offer some sort of reciprocal force. At that point, the robbers would be far away and indistinguishable from others in the country and town.

Politically, there were several distinctions in this mountainous place. On one side was the territory held by the British. The British tended to hold onto an area that had an opening to the sea, and because of this, it was thus a commerce center. Examples beside New York City were like those of Boston, Philadelphia, and Charleston. These cities also tended to have the comforts and entertainment that were normally found in a large city in Europe. The British held high value in the leisure life afforded to living in the city.

North of New York City was a middle ground. It represented a land where no one could be sure of the person they met along the roadway. It also might be frighteningly true that the person they met was a robber looking to steal personal possessions. The neutral territory was a land of terror where anyone you met might be sharply suspect. No one felt safe, and everyone was afraid. The robbery and thievery that took place during the Revolutionary War generally took place in a neutral area. On the other side of the neutral territory was the land of the Patriots—those lands which held most of the rest of the American colonies. Standing out as notorious thieves were Claudius Smith, the Smith Gang, and James Moody.

Lovely mountains, treacherous terrain, foreboding travel, and isolation characterized the Ramapos. They also were an island in the middle of the Revolutionary War. The Ramapos were remote but important, ambiguous but weighty, of little tangible value but ranking high in the strategy of the war.

The British were befuddled by the existence of the Ramapos and the Highlands as they impeded travel of the many soldiers who would be necessary to knock out the Colonist Patriots. On the other hand, they liked the idea that there was some sort of wall, an insulation from the dangers of the Rebels to the set piece structure of living on a small island. Boston had been within cannon range when Washington and Knox surprisingly obtained them, and the British had to leave the city as indefensible. This was similar to what happened at Fort Ticonderoga. For the British, the mountains to the north of New York City had mixed benefit, and the difficulty with the mountains added to the British's decision to stay put in the haven of the city.

For the Patriots, these mountains created a safe separation from the enemy to the south. General George Washington was satisfied with holding the fortress of West Point and being able to fire cannon down on any British ship trying to ply northward. Just beyond West Point was the giant chain across the Hudson River which would prevent the passage of ships. Then, safely around the corner of the massive Storm King Mountain was Washington's Newburgh headquarters in the stone Hasbrouck House.

And in between, in the neutral area, what was the status? There were people who leaned toward the Patriots, looking for freedom in a new country. Some of these people had joined the Continental Army and had a uniform, and for the most part, those men were away with the Patriot Army, encamped somewhere to the south in an arc of some hundreds of miles. A portion of the Patriots were part of the militia and were citizen farmers, or commercial people, who were ready to answer a call to arms for the Patriots. Additionally, there were common citizens who, if prodded, would side with the Patriots. The Patriots also had a stealthy council in most areas, groups of men who were known as the Committee of Safety.

Then there were the Loyalists, or Torys, who wanted to continue to be governed by the British as they had in the Colonies for over a hundred years. These men also had similar gradations of commitment to sides in the war. They might be part of the British

Volunteers and many of them were under the command of British Brigadier General Cortland Skinner. Others were less conspicuously faithful and would lean toward the British if pushed. Both sides had people who were faithful to even a lesser degree, who would not be too committed but who would send word along if information was obtained about someone's loyalty to one side or another.

Finally, there were those who were out for themselves. Men who would rob and plunder, kill and maim, solely for the purpose of gaining substance and making money.

These men would congregate with others of similar nature and taste. One of the foremost groups out for themselves and who were willing to destroy and engage in thievery for their own gain was the Smith Gang.

Chapter 39
The Smith Gang

"Sometimes history takes things into its own hands."
– Thurgood Marshall

The countryside of America was a beautiful sight to behold. Purple mountains and valleys and plains full of produce. The human factor—Loyalist versus Patriot—painted a mixed color over the landscape, affixing a factor of help or hindrance, depending upon one's point of view in the war. Such were the dominant Ramapo Mountains. To the Loyalists and cowboys, they were an opportunity for robbery and hiding. To the Patriots, they were a large area infested by thieves, fugitives, and runaways. It was a primitive place of wilderness and mountains, legends and lore.

Atop the tallest peak in the Ramapo Mountains, he was flat on his back with his head propped up with his crumpled hat.

"Lying out on this warm, flat rock is the way a day should go. Just sitting here, doing nothing, lazing in the sun; yes, that is the life for me." Claudius Smith seemed to be speaking to the sky, but his friend in arms was beside him, just a little farther down a gentle slope on his own rock.

Relaxed and cushioned by thoughts of an easy life, Claudius Smith looked self-assured as he lay on the whaleback, the hard rock outcrop. Claudius picked his head up slightly so that he was able to watch the white cumulus clouds drift by on their way toward the east. The fluffy white against the dark blue sky was a soft and pleasant view, as Smith watched the afternoon roll by. The clouds passed between the big toes on his left foot and then passed the toes of his right foot as he viewed the brown of his worn and tattered leather boots, now glistening with the brass buckles, stolen from an unlucky traveler.

His comrade smiled at his comments and looked out to the

distant horizon beyond the rounded mountains of the Ramapos.

"We just park ourselves up here and wait for some innocent traveler to pass below down on the roadway. Down where we can prey on them."

"Come on, Claudius," said one of his sons, William. "You gotta watch for the travelers too. Why do we have to do everything?"

"Kinda funny if ya ask me," said Claudius. "I like to look up at the geese passing overhead when we are out on a robbery. But when we are up here, atop the Ramapo Mountains, I see those same geese now flapping below us. This is the life here, where even the birds are beneath me."

"Enough of your drifting mind, Claudius," said the other, a Hessian with a heavy German accent. "You need to work too. You can't just hang out and sleep!" said Franz[lxiii].

"Franz, recall yesterday when we pulled over that Dutchman heading south on his painted pony?" he asked.

"Yes," said Franz. "Can you believe his fear? Pulled out his wallet before he got off his horse."

"He sure let the money drop when I pointed the gun at him," said William, shining a flintlock pistol. They all laughed.

"But he didn't have much money," Franz said.

"No, but I love his boots." Claudius admired the buckles he now had on his classic tall boots he'd stolen from a man they robbed long ago.

Such was a day of spying down, from aloft, looking for innocent people they could stop and rob.

The man with the German accent spoke up again. "Claudius, come on over. You have your three sons, William, Richard, and James[lxiv], doing all the work here."

"Hah," said Claudius. "That's the way I trained them."

He sat up from the rock and turned to look at the group. This was the band of robbers, or freebooters, a dozen or so rowdy men who rode with Claudius on the notorious raids that he would make upon innocent small farms and citizens. Claudius and the Smith Gang would take their stolen loot and turn it in for money to the British Army when they were stationed at nearby Stony Point and at Fort Lee. The gang would steal so many cattle that they became known as "cowboys" when they took the food to the British for their use. If chased, they would flee to deep glens and caves and recesses in the Ramapos and Highlands. One cave was close to Man-of-War Rock near Tuxedo, a cave near Indian Kill. The boys knew them well, but most people trying to follow would get lost.

One son of Claudius, William Smith, acted like a sergeant and made sure that the band of thieves were all at work, contributing to the planned highway robbery that they were inclined to do. He had a mean streak in him and was always bossy. And William Smith meant business too.

Richard was peering over the edge of the rock ledge, looking for travelers going up and down the roadway in the distance. Richard was short and thin. He was a jokester, always laughing and playing tricks on people. He seemed jovial at first, but when he lost his temper, he was known to slash and stab men, painfully injuring them. Then he laughed about it. He had killed John Clark[lxv], who didn't give him what he wanted. He shot Clark in the back, a cowardly act, just outside of Clark's little log home.

James, the youngest of Claudius Smith's sons, was looking after the horses. James was not much more than a child, about sixteen, and looked younger than that. He was not very knowledgeable and followed orders without defiance or question. He tended to the horses and made sure they were groomed and bridled and ready to ride. James was checking that they were tied properly, rested, and fed at the small cave on the mountainside where they were all located, just below the outcrop observation post.

"So, you let your sons do all the work?" said the German, again, to Claudius. The German was new to the gang. "Is that how your parents brought you up?"

Smith stood up. He had a length of dried straw dangling from his lip.

"My parents?" said Claudius. He spit on the ground.

"That is what I'm asking," the German said.

Claudius paused. "We lived on Long Island, and they were always out for themselves. I never trusted them. My father beat my mother with a cane. He taught me to steal."

Claudius stood there high atop Schunemunk Mountain, the highest mountain in Orange County, New York, looking down from the 1,664-foot summit onto the town of Blooming Grove. He was visibly very uncomfortable with this prying into his early life. He looked afar.

"So, do you see anybody coming?" said Claudius to the lookout.

"Nobody yet," said Richard.

Franz walked over to where Claudius was standing in the sunlight.

"It is worthwhile that you have provided me with information we can use to rob and plunder."

"Well, it should be obvious."

"Agreed. Our worse enemy is Major Nathaniel Strong."

"What will you do about it?" asked the German.

"Me?"

The German nodded. "What will you do to get rid of him?"

"Well, I am comfortable here."

"But he's the source of our troubles. If he is gone, then we can do as we wish."

"Yea, that'd be good if he were gone. He has been the most active Patriot in intercepting our Tory brothers and other Loyalists on their way from Albany southward to Manhattan."

"So, Claudius, as our leader, what will you do about it?"

Just then a shout came out from Richard on the observation ledge. "Rider on the roadway!" He turned to talk to the gang. "It's Major Strong."

"Gear up, men," said Claudius as he quickly gathered his hat and his own pair of flintlock pistols. They went down to the nearby cave where the horses were kept. Young James made sure that they were saddled and ready to go.

They journeyed down to the valley. As the Smith Gang proceeded toward Blooming Grove, there was Major Strong on a horse, trotting toward them. The men picked up their firearms and jostled their way down the slope and into the valley. The major sat high in the saddle, a proud and accomplished man. He worked feverishly to defend the Patriot's cause, and as a result had made a positive impact for the Americans to win the war. Because of this, he was well-respected in the community. But he was hated by Smith and other Loyalists.

He had heretofore impeded their ability to rob and plunder, and every member of the Smith Gang placed high importance on his removal.

Shots were fired, and Major Strong saw the dozen or so Smith Gang members blocking his way. He retreated about six miles to his home. The Smith Gang followed him.

"We will get him once and for all," said one of the boys. The Smith Gang sped off, with Claudius holding back as he saw a flight of geese overhead. He paused for a moment to watch their graceful flight. Claudius remembered when he'd stolen Colonel Ebenezer Woodhull's mare. Woodhull was a brother-in-law to Fletcher Matthews, one of the trusted followers of Claudius himself. When it became clear to Woodhull that Claudius wanted to take his beautiful mare, Woodhull moved the animal from the barn to his cellar. But Smith remembered the evening he stole the mare, how one of Woodull's guests stood up to shoot him. Smith smiled to himself now as he recalled what he'd been told. How Woodhull stopped the man from shooting. "If you shoot Smith, I will be dead," the other man said in dread of repercussions.

He then caught up to his gang. There they found two merchants from the nearby village. They weren't carrying much, but Smith took what they had and returned to Schunemunk Mountain.

This was only one of their hideouts, here atop of Schunemunk Mountain. Additionally, there was a place called Horse Stable Rock that was used as a hangout and where the horses would be kept nearby one of their surveillance spots, so they could ride off quickly—either to capture some innocent victim or to speed off from capture themselves as they rode away, riding near the quaint Wesley Chapel.

"You sure have secure hiding places," said Franz.

"We have several hiding places in the Ramapos," said Claudius.

Another hiding place was at Smith's Den, or Smith's Cave, just north of the New Jersey border and located in the proximity of Tuxedo. This was a sizeable climb up the steep mountain, where there was a narrow space that was of tactical importance, and then it provided a good look from the nearby Smith's Rock. This was a great place of a *roches moutonnees*, also known as a sheepback or rock knob to those in the gang.

From here, the vigilantes could look down at the passing public. This was a favorite lookout for the Smith Gang, just as it had been a favorite camping and hunting location for the Minsi Indians many years before. The caves were not deep, but rather long, horizontal shelters made of rock at the foot of the successive cliffs. Claudius' men improved the caves over time, rolling huge boulders to keep the cave that Claudius favored sheltered from wind and rain and snow.

"Ah, this is one of my favorite abodes," said Claudius, acting like an expert as he reviewed the dirty and cold stone shelter as if it were a king's mansion. He went on, energized.

"The lower cave is a crude shelter for horses and cattle and for the various silver and other precious goods our men have stolen. But most importantly, a spring runs alongside the mountains between the two caves, providing water for the men and the livestock."

Though not often enough, the men also washed in the frigid water, when even to them, their own stink had become intolerable.

The large whaleback, Man of War Rock on Fox Hill, above the Episcopal Church was another place with a good lookout for the prey and a broad escape from capture. A similar and nearby location was on Pine Hill, where there were large blocks of rock on gentle slopes.

The Smith Gang would sometimes rendezvous at a spot near Augusta Falls and Augusta Works, the Ringwood Iron Works, and Sterling Furnace. They supposedly stashed treasures near there.

One crisp, cold afternoon, Claudius and his sons, William and Richard, and his trusted followers, John Brown and Thomas Delmar, were taking a needed rest in the caves. They had just finished stealing a dozen horses and managed to drive them to the British Army. On the ground of the cave where they were currently hiding out lay a tattered *New York Gazette.* A fifty dollar reward was being offered for the capture of Claudius Smith, who'd recently escaped from the Goshen jail.

Claudius picked it up and said, "They describe me as having a white beard, gray complexion, short hair, and powder burns under the right eye."

"That's pretty close, Father," said William.

"They also tell everybody that I use the aliases James Reed and John Wright. But look at this here," Claudius said, beginning to read. "They say I'm 'a great bully and will fight wherever he goes, being very conceited of his strength.'"

Everyone laughed loudly. John Brown lit his pipe. Claudius slipped some chaw into his cheek, then spit.

Brown was picking at his teeth with the shaft of a weed when he said, "People are sleeping in their barns now, they're so scared."

"Aye," said Claudius with a satisfied grimace. He thought back to last heist, and how they had amassed so many cows and horses that they'd had to build temporary pens to shelter the animals until they could get them to New York City for the British.

"They hide in the corn cribs too," said William, and for some reason everyone laughed.

Claudius sat back. "I like to think back to my escape from jail."

"Ah yes," said John Brown. "Those oxen. If they'd gone a little slower …"

"But alas, we were caught. Can't make a dumb animal walk faster than it will," said Claudius.

"It is your own greed, Father," said Richard.

"Shut up, boy, before I smack you," snapped Claudius.

Another round of rough laughter erupted. Claudius remembered how they'd been held at the jail in Orange County and then he and John had been ordered by the sheriff to be moved to Goshen.

"We have good allies, eh?" said John Brown, who was also thinking back to their escape from Goshen.

"Papa," said Richard. "Tell us again about the guard."

Claudius and John Brown exchanged glances, and with a wicked smile, Claudius said, "A number of our followers converged on Goshen, and when they got there, they grabbed the sheriff and put a rope around his neck."

"Aye, Richard," said John Brown. "He was scared to death. The message to him about our quarters was not at all unclear."

Claudius laughed. "Yes, my sons. He was terrified. And knowing he would not survive if we were not released, he let us go discreetly."

"I'm sure they all thought he was a coward," said Richard.

Claudius and John Brown laughed hard.

Richard looked confused for a moment. Claudius had always wondered about his son's intelligence. Richard seemed confused very often and questioned their moves too much. He worried that one day his son might even do something stupid, get them caught, or get captured and in exchange for a lesser sentence, rat him out.

"Well, we have amassed much treasure and have supported our allied," said Claudius.

Now Richard said, "Is that why our grandmother said you would die like a trooper's horse, with your shoes on?"

Claudius stood up and towered over his son. He kicked the boy hard with his boots. "Shut yer mouth afor I smash it with my own hands."

"We aren't called the cowboys for nothin'," said his other son, William, the spitting image of Claudius and of equally bitter heart.

The men spent the rest of that day and on into the evening drinking and sleeping before their next forays to rustle much needed cattle for their Loyalist troops. Later, Smith, drunk and ornery, left his favorite hideout in search of a woman.

With all these places to hide themselves, stash their treasures, and run away, the Smith Gang felt invincible. The fact that the messengers and public kept coming down their isolated pathways, like the Ramapo Pass, made it seem like the good times would never end.

***

As he had many times before, the Cowboy of the Ramapos went searching for cattle, and was caught and charged with stealing heads of oxen which were owned by the Americans near Kingston, the capital of New York at the time. The authorities then transferred him to Goshen. A spy let the gang know, and they took Sheriff Dumont as a prisoner and would hang him. There was a prisoner swap, and the Smith Gang left Goshen with a significant plunder of booty and goods.

The Smith Gang had it made and would all be rich, swimming in gold doubloons gained in their notorious and devious work. Even the well-known Loyalist Lieutenant James Moody from New Jersey was jealous of the gold that the Smith Gang was acquiring—fame and fortune fighting against freedom-seekers.

Chapter 40
Claudius on the Gallows, January 22, 1779

"...the agony of my soul found vent in one loud, long and final scream of despair."
– Edgar Allan Poe

"Where's my gal, Katharine?" questioned the excited Claudius. He had the poor, old woman known as Aunt Hester slammed up against the outside of her log cabin.

The girl that Claudius loved with abandon was gone. He could not find her, even though he searched high and low. He was getting desperate and was showing his proclivity to be randomly wild, like a racoon with rabies.

Aunt Hester had been quietly playing cards at her pine table when she got up and answered the incessant loud knocking at the door. Claudius grabbed her by the shoulder, pulled her outside, and shoved her against the round, wooden logs that made up the wall of the cabin. The wind was howling, and the hemlocks swayed and bent, as if in protest to this ghastly act. This was a screaming storm, with lightning, thunder, and a deluge of rain—as if the clouds could hold back no more. Hester's hair quickly became soaked.

Aunt Hester was a mysterious, crotchety woman who no one wanted to befriend. But she seemed to know what was going on in the area, much like a soothsayer of old. She mostly kept her eyes open and her mouth shut.

Claudius kept pushing her against the wall, now with one of his flintlock pistols pinned to her chest. He had fallen in love with Katherine, a girl of golden curls that he could recall fondly while high above the Ramapos, aloft in his dreams of villainy. And now she was gone. He had never been so animated and mad. "I want my woman back, you witch!"

Aunt Hester smiled. "She left you of her own accord."

"You are a fortune teller, and you can tell me where my gal is, the love of my life, my gal with the golden curls," insisted the Cowboy of the Ramapos. "Where have they taken her? I'll get'er back from them!"

"Okay, okay," said the old woman. "Black George, the slave boy, found out that his master's daughter, 'your' Katharine, had disappeared. It was not that they took her away, but that she didn't want to be with you. You, a friend of the British and enemy of freedom-seeking people. It was not someone stealing her away, but it was because of your association with the British that she has run off to be away from you. It is your choice in opposing their family, all of whom supports freedom and the Patriots."

"I should tear your old heart from your shrunken body," growled Smith. He couldn't believe that it was his own actions that were the cause of his love now being lost. "You are just a weather-beaten hag!"

These were Smith's last words as he suddenly pulled back quickly, turned toward the angry trees, and made off into the sheets of drenching rain. Shaking his head in disgust, he left her to her potions and whatever else she did.

As Claudius retreated into the copse of evergreens, the woman shrieked in anger, "And as I see in a vision, your future appears dangerous and deadly, like a burning building with the flames shooting skyward!"

He blended into the soaked, swaying trees as they wavered back and forth, almost like a chorus vacillating in solemn unison, and then he disappeared into the black of the night.

Lightning flashed and ignited the darkness, revealing just for a second, the shiny polished brass handles on Smith's two flintlock pistols as they bounced away and faded into nothingness.

At this point, Claudius felt himself becoming more violent, like a man who had been embarrassingly struck, a lover forsaken, and a loser in the game of life. He became a man on a mission. It was like a fuse was lit that would end in an inevitable and deafening explosion of destruction. Thereafter, the Ramapos vibrated, Smith Clove quaked, and blood flowed freely with a deadly combat that ensued between the Smith Gang and the Whigs of the Clove, in the valley and the environs of Schunemunk Mountain and of Ramapo Pass.

Soon afterward, Claudius convinced his Smith Gang to burn down the entire house and farm of Katharine's family. All their worldly goods were gone up in smoke, and the only possessions left were their cows. The Smith Gang drove the herd of cattle to the British lines and obtained much gold for it.

"With this, I will gain her love, now that I am rich with the gold doubloons to match her sweet curls!" said a bedeviled Smith, to no avail.

The Smith Gang's marauding continued, with more thievery, blood, and death. Claudius began to take more drastic steps. For one, he was fed up with the militia intruding on their messenger route robberies. And the key was Major Nathaniel Strong.

Smith was growing impatient. He felt that getting Nathanial Strong was taking too long. One day the Smith gang were on their way back to the Woodhull home to steal what they thought would be many silver artifacts and valuables. When they got to the door, they knew that Woodhull wasn't there.

Mrs. Woodhull was no dummy. She realized who was at her door, demanding that she open up. But she would not. Instead, she quickly fetched all her silver and hid it in the baby's cradle, under the baby. When the door finally gave, the men raided the home and looked around but found nothing. All the while, Mrs. Woodhull sat near the cradle, trying to comfort her crying infant. She ignored the men and allowed them to do what they needed to do and be done. When they left with nothing, Smith was in a rage.

As the gang left the Woodhull residence, Smith noticed a beautiful horse in the meadow near the house, and they knew it belonged to a relative of the Woodhull's. They took the horse, as they always did when such opportunities arose, and galloped away. Mrs. Woodhull watched them disappear into the night, shaking but relieved that she, her baby, and the silver remained intact. Having lived at such a time and in such hard conditions, Mrs. Woodhull was not prone to give in to the plunderers. Like many of her women acquaintances in the area, such a life had taught them to be strong, to shoot if they must, to ride quickly to escape, and devise whatever plan they could in the moment to save their lives and the lives of those they loved.

Following this event, Smith decided it was time to pay a call to Nathanial Strong, who they believed was a hindrance to their goals as robbers and to the goals of the Loyalist army. They were going to murder the man, and unlike their last event, this time the man was home. However, since the hour was late, Nathanial Strong was asleep in an inner room. When Smith and his gang broke in, they woke him, and Strong had an inkling that this might be his last night on earth. Nevertheless, he would not go down without a fight, and he armed himself with a musket and a pair of pistols.

After the gang smashed their way into the home, they broke their way into the room by tearing down the outer room. When they got there, they saw Strong, armed and looking very ready to kill.

Smith cursed under his breath. Then he said to Strong, "Sir. We will not harm you. We've only come for your valuables. Allow us to finish our job here, and we will be on our way. We ask that you lower your weapons. You can trust us—though we may have plunder and theft on our minds, we do not murder unless first attacked."

"There is no reason that I should trust you," said Strong.

Smith said, "Aye, sir, but we come to you not in violence. We are here just to rob. Please now, sir, lower your weapons."

Strong, a gentleman to the core, a man who took the word of other men, paused then lowered his guns.

"Thank you, good sir," Smith said. But then as the men approached the door to the inner sanctum of the major's house, they all raised their pistols and shot at him through the window to the room, mortally wounding him. They watched as Major Strong fell slowly to the ground, uttering no dying words.

Smith realized, perhaps too late, that this act might well signal, in time, his own death.

"Come, men, grab what you can, and let's take our leave."

The other men seemed cowed. They went about their business, stealing what they could find of value. Then they returned to their hideout.

Days later, a chorus of protest and outrage erupted. Citizens demanded that Smith and his gang be caught and hanged. So, on October 31st, 1778, Governor Clinton responded to the outpouring by placing a $1200 reward for the apprehension of Claudius Smith, and $600 for the capture of his two sons, Richard and James. This,

Clinton believed, would show Claudius the price he would pay for passing on the family occupation to his two naïve sons.

New York Governor George Clinton issued a proclamation. Clinton was a colonial militia brigadier general and a lawyer. He would become a vice president of the new United States. He was experienced at defending the Highlands against the enemy and created the chain across the Hudson River.

Claudius was depressed upon his return to the mountain. He banished his sons from the mountain cave, and he sat glumly. He had heard already about the price on his head. He drank from a bottle of whiskey that he'd taken from the major and then made a decision. In the morning, he fled from his old haunts in The Clove and made his way to Long Island where he took up residence with a widow adjacent to Smithtown.

***

"Smith, eh?" said the major.

"Yes, that is he," said the merchant. "He was here getting some dry goods for his journey. He was a tall, skinny man with the most noticeable feature of his footwear. He had big boots, boots that were worn but were almost up to his knees. While he gave me some good conversation, he took those good and then tried to leave without paying."

"Claudius?" asked the major.

"Yes, that's right!" exclaimed the merchant. "One of his buddies said for Claudius to get out of there. When I demanded that he pay for what he took, he pulled out the biggest belt knife I had ever seen and pointed the sharp and shining blade at me."

"That was Claudius Smith, Cowboy of the Ramapos," said the major. "He has a bounty on his head."

"So, you know Smith then?"

"I am Major Jesse Brush, and I am an ardent anti-Tory farmer. I had left my property in Long Island for Connecticut where the environment was more, let us say, sympathetic to Patriots. I have, though, occasionally come back to Long Island, secretively since I am not a Loyalist. I have come back to check on my property."

"I will tell you where he is holed up if you get me my dry goods back," said the merchant.

"Deal," said Major Brush.

Major Brush returned to Connecticut and told his ally, a Mr. Titus, to go with him to capture the scoundrel and get the reward for doing so.

They asked three other men to join them in their mission. They armed themselves with muskets and pistols and took a whale boat across the sound to Long Island on one dark night and anchored at Smithtown. Leaving one man on the boat as a sentry, the rest of the men went to Smith's lodgings and walked directly into the house, fearing that a knock would wake and warn Smith of their arrival.

"Good evening, my good woman," said Major Brush as he removed his hat to the room attendant. "Pardon our interruption, but we have come looking for Claudius Smith, whom we know is here," said Major Brush.

The old woman was somewhat surprised. She nodded. "He's asleep. I shall go and get him."

Major Brush realized there might be something fishy here in addition to the seaside scent. "Where is he? Tell us what room he is in."

The woman was puzzled but also looked protective of her boarder. She didn't know about the reward on Smith's head. She said, "He's upstairs."

She pointed to the stairs and stepped aside.

Major Brush gently took the candle from the old lady, tilted his head and looked at the stairs ascending before him. "You," he said to one of his men, "stay here with the woman and guard our rear."

Major Brush and his men quietly worked their way up the stairs. They came to the door of Smith's room. One of them tried to pull up the latch ever so quietly, without success. As they looked at each other they put their shoulders into the door, whereby it came open with splinters flying. Startled awake, Smith quickly sat up. As Brush's men approached him, Smith threw a wild punch, and they drew back. Smith grabbed something from behind his pillow as the men moved in again.

"It's a pistol, look out!" exclaimed one of the men. Smith pointed the gun at the speaker and began to pull the trigger as another fell upon the pistol and arm. The major's men dragged Smith to the floor.

"Tie him up, and let's get him back to the whaleboat," said Brush. We'll get him back across the sound to Connecticut, put him in shackles, and get our reward."

The next day, Brush alerted Governor Clinton of Smith's his capture and brought him through southern Connecticut to Fishkill Landing, gave him to guards, including Colonel Isaac Nicoll, and collected the reward money.

Smith was bound up for trial in Goshen. Once at Goshen, he was cast into jail and his hands and feet were ironed and chained to the floor. Guards were stationed around the clock outside his cell. They named his cell in Goshen the "grief hole."

***

Friday, January 22nd, 1779, saw the sun come up around Goshen. The golden beams stretched from behind Shewenuck Mountain and swept across Slate Hill as the light seemed to quietly envelop the town and the surrounding businesses and houses.

A small stir occurred in the jail at Goshen. In a corner of the building, a man looked neatly attired in a broadcloth suit, finely made, with noticeable silver buttons on the outer coat on this winter's day. Down at his feet were tall boots, time-worn but with fancy, gold buckles atop them. The beams from the sun seemed to make the buckles shine, a charm normally indicative of a well-dressed man. The man in the suit grinned as he looked eastward toward Slate Hill.

"They'll be coming," said the guard to Claudius.

Then the guard began to laugh.

The guard put his musket down and unlocked the door of the jail cell. He pulled out another key and unlocked the shackles that bound Smith, who'd dressed in this fine suit.

Claudius walked out of the cell, through the open door of the jailhouse, and into the morning sunlight as the day was beginning, seemingly free as a bird. But the muzzle of the long-barreled musket was jammed into his back, and his hands were chained behind him. As they walked forward, the guard said, "Look around you, man; this is it for you."

As the guard pushed the musket barrel into his spine, Claudius got the hint and stepped forward. They rounded the corner of the building. In front of them was the biggest crowd that Claudius had ever seen. Thousands of people stood in silent awe of the man who had terrorized them for months and months. They were all there to witness his execution in the makeshift gallows, erected for Smith.

Claudius looked at the guard and thought he recognized the man walking him to the gallows. The fellow had a reddish look, with a cut wound, now healed, near his lip.

"Where have I seen you before?" he asked the young man.

"I am Private Red Sullivan. I had been a messenger rider for General George Washington, and years ago, you stopped me at a bridge and punched me in the face. Remember?"

"Yes, I do."

The guard pulled back his jacket to show a big, shiny hunting knife. "Well, I have my precious knife back now."

Just then, he saw his younger son, James, who saw Claudius and caught his attention. Walking right next to him was another son, Richard. They both looked at their father. With the three looking at each other, Claudius smiled. He thought that another plan was being hatched to free them all. Claudius was waiting for a signal from Richard or James, a sign that the Smith Gang was here to release him, just like the last time when they were here in Goshen and had broken free in exchange for the sheriff. Claudius could smell freedom, and he was just waiting for the signal to make a run for it and be on the loose again.

But Richard put his head down and kept walking, and James kept moving along as he had been, a step or two behind his brother. They didn't say anything, just kept on walking, going around the corner and out of sight with some others who appeared to be guards but perhaps were Smith Gang members in disguise.

Walking a few feet, and having been prodded by the rifle, Claudius put his knees up onto the wooden flooring of a small cart. He crawled on all fours and sat in the corner of the cart. Then another person caught his eye. It was his younger son James. They looked at each other but did not say anything.

The rickety, little cart started moving forward from the jail and bounced on the rocky ground, which was now very firm from the hard freeze of the winter. As it moved slowly along, Claudius saw that a large crowd had flocked to a nearby site.

He looked around to see where the men of his gang would be located. There were a lot of people gathered around and watching. Most of the folks were from the town of Goshen but also some from his home, at or near Smith Clove in the Ramapos.

The cart swayed back and forth on its way onto the Goshen Town green, which at this time of the year was a misnomer as the grass was brown and stiff with the frost.

The guard came alongside the cart. "Just to let you know, Claudius Smith, moments ago your associate Thomas Delmar was hanged for housebreaking and burglary. Your friend in crime, James Gordon, was also just hanged for horse stealing and housebreaking."

Another man in a militia uniform approached and said, "In case you hadn't heard, your eldest son William has been shot, up in the mountains, his body eaten by wild animals and his bones left to bleach in the sun over the coming years. Your son Richard has been hanged. And just shortly before you came around the corner, your son James was hanged, right here in Goshen at the green." The guard said with no emotion whatsoever, "And now, you are next."

A familiar woman ran up to the cart. "Smith, where are the papers you took from me, and the calico frock, that you ripped from my hands? Where have you hidden them?"

Faint words came from Claudius. "This is no place to talk about papers; meet me in the next world, and I will tell you all about them."

The woman covered her mouth with her hand and stood aghast as the little cart rolled on.

As the cart came by, one of the townspeople asked another standing near him "Did this man have anything to say at his trial?"

"No," said the other. "Judge Bodle at Goshen asked the scoundrel if he had anything to say in his own defense, and Smith said, 'No; if God Almighty can't change your hearts, I cannot.'"

Someone else said, "He sure looks good in that fancy suit."

As Claudius lay in the cart with his hand on the flooring and his arm propping him up, a figure from the crowd approached him: a man in black, with a white collar—a "man of the cloth." He walked slowly but directly up to the cart from the middle of the crowd. His eyes were trained right on Claudius. He raised a cross up in front of him from his pocket. He then said very clearly, a passage from Numbers 32:23: "*Ye have sinned against the LORD: and be sure your sin will find you out.*"

Claudius raised his head a little higher and scanned the many people in the front rows. There were men and women, some holding the hands of children. He couldn't see any members of the Smith Gang; although he still expected them to lurch forward with weapons and take him away on an escape plan. His eyes went behind the first row to the second row of onlookers. No gang members there. He tried to see if any of those who were wandering around the back of the crowd were his associates, but there didn't seem to be any in sight. He looked again toward Slate Hill, now more visible from the outside as it were. No activity, no fires, nothing.

Frequently it seemed that one would appear to mumble something and point his hand in Claudius' direction. All the people were standing nearly motionless. There was a quiet spell that then crept into the throng watching the event taking place. It seemed that almost everyone was looking at him.

Not soon afterward, the little cart wobbled and came to a halt. Claudius comprehended the reason. As he looked up, he could see a primitive scaffold with new wood that looked like it was constructed only hours ago. Ah, the sweet smell of fresh pine.

As he looked up higher, he could see a rope dangling down from the cross beam of the scaffold, high above his head. At the end of the rope was a neatly tied noose. It swayed ever so slightly in a tender breeze.

Then the guard commanded, "Stand up."

Claudius felt several hands under his arms, picking him up before he could think, before he could make a motion himself. He was now standing on the rickety, little cart. Never had he felt so alone.

"Any last words?" said the man in black.

"I, I," was what he could muster.

The guards tied his hands behind his back while the executioner looped the noose around his neck and tightened it.

Claudius remembered his mother telling him, "Claudius, you will die like a trooper's horse, with your shoes on."

He was too proud to make his mother's words true. In a bitter rebuke to her prediction, he asked that his boots be removed, and it was done. The man wearing a black hood then placed the rope around Claudius' neck, then patted the noose down gently to make sure it was a tidy job. He jumped down off the cart. He picked up the boots, put them under his arm, and walked away.

Claudius, whose life had been punctuated by little in the way of education, and a lot in the way of hunger and rough training for a harsh world, seethed in anger. Under his bare toes, he felt the cart buck a little bit; he felt the slight prick of a splinter in his toe from the floorboard sliding beneath his frame and then the flooring of the cart move off to his side. He felt the chill in the air from the January cold. The cart beneath him squealed as it left, and Claudius looked toward Slate Hill once more, and then saw a flock of geese flying overhead toward the south, above the scaffold. Then a tight grip of manila hemp around his throat electrified his eyes and brain.

***

When his body stopped wiggling and his frame ceased twitching, one of the guards cut the rope that was tightly choking his neck. His body dropped to the ground, lifelessly in a lump just like cow manure in a field outside of town. All that was left was his remains near a small cart beneath the gallows scaffold. He had done a lot in his short forty years of hard living. Nothing good, though, came of his time on earth.

Near the scaffold, a man with a shovel dug through the hard frost. Claudius Smith was buried in a shallow grave near the scaffold, set back from the green and in the First Presbyterian Church Park in Goshen.

Some years later, his bones protruded from his shallow grave. It is said that his skull became part of the ornaments at a meat market, as if it were a trophy. When the Goshen Court House was completed, it is said that his skull was put in the mortar above the entrance to the building. His bones laid on the green only yards away from those militiamen's bones, recovered from the Battle of Minisink of 1780 that were recovered forty-three years later and brought back to be honorably rested near the Presbyterian Church. All the bones of all the men, good and bad, deteriorating to nothing in the centuries past. Only legend retains the stories and events that were so important in those days.

Chapter 41
Matthias Ogden in France, Aaron Ogden as Governor, and the Judge

The large sailing ship slowly swayed to port. A faint rippling sound could be heard from the slight buffeting of the sheets aloft as they moved in the fresh breeze. Then the huge, wooden hull slowly shifted to starboard, with a low-pitched creaking sound from the large timbers as they flexed and groaned and shouldered the burden of the voyage. All this repeatedly occurred as the gentle ocean swells rolled by from bow to stern. The green water looked like moving hills, and on the foamy surface could be heard a soft popping as the bubbles burst, as if the sea were speaking to the sky and spitting salty breath while doing so. This elicited a fresh spiking of the senses that was evident on an otherwise calm day. With the continuing rocking and swaying, the natural motions became repetitive and then routine to a seaman as the sun slowly swept overhead and the day wore on. An alert sailor's sense could discern the smell of the ocean in his nose, fluffy cumulus clouds passing by in his eyes, the rocking motion in his sense of balance, and the warmth of the sunny day on his skin. In sum, the crew of the ship knew that landfall was imminent. Standing at the ship's wooden rail, taking all this in calmed his body, and it seemed like a time to think for Colonel Matthias Ogden.

"Ahoy, mate," came the call to Ogden from the poop deck, aft on the vessel, near where the helmsman stood, with hands on the large wheel that was steadying the rudder.

"Yes, Captain," said Colonel Ogden as he held the rail with one hand and turned to listen.

As he put down the sextant and viewed the compass, charts, and the distance, the captain replied, "We should reach the American continent sometime today, sir."

"Good," said Ogden. "We have been to sea much too long, at least for me."

While he had been aiding the Patriots from the beginning, even going on the expedition to fight the British in Quebec with General Montgomery, Ogden had been granted a leave by Congress in April 1783. The purpose was to visit Europe on a mission to try to build a business relationship with the French, who had been allies and benefactors to the neophyte nation. After the anticipated end of the war, the inevitable need for partnership in industry would be anticipated, and a good relationship with France and its commercial and manufacturing base would be highly beneficial.

"Aye, sir," said the captain. "I realize that you are eager to get the news to America."

"That is true," said Ogden as he again took hold of the rail with both hands. "I have news, good news—great news, in fact. Perhaps the most significant news that was ever delivered to America."

"That you do, Colonel Ogden."

The grizzled, old captain walked toward Ogden. He had a long, gray beard and a slim appearance. Although the deck heaved back and forth in its dance with the ocean, the captain maneuvered well.

"Aye, Colonel Ogden," he said with a grin and a spit as he lit up a cigar from a smoking lamp astride the mizzenmast. "You're being reluctant to trust the deck of the ship," said the captain as he eyed Ogden holding on to balance.

"Two hands for me."

"Hah," said the captain. "So, what was it like to meet the King of France?"

"Quite an experience," said Ogden. "King Louis XVI was lavishly dressed. I approached where the king sat, surrounded by his entourage. I strode up several stairs to meet him where he sat on his throne."

"Amazing," said the captain, unaccustomed to such gentlemanly niceties. "What did you talk about?"

"I was in France working with several of the business-oriented aristocracy. The king was keenly interested in this because this meant commercial benefit with our country. He and his staff have been very involved in helping our cause in the Revolution, and the king had spent much of the wealth of France for us to fight and build toward our success."

The colonel paused. He heard something thump against the hull of the ship.

"Did you hear that?"

The captain cocked his head, then shook it.

Ogden nodded. He said, "The king provided me with an honor known as the *honor le droit du tabouret.*" The colonel again paused, as again he heard thumping against the hull. But he thought he must have been hearing things since captain said nothing about it. He looked at the skipper.

The captain laughed and then said, "Keel hauling a sailor who became drunk out of our keg of rum without permission. Fortunate for him, it is only short, and we are pulling him back in now." The captain then looked at Ogden. "So, tell me more."

"The king was also obviously fully aware of the negotiations for ending the wars around the world between the English, Americans, French, and Spanish. Needless to say, he was delighted to know the agreement to end the war. The same word that I am reporting to the new nation of The United States of America."

Then the captain's eyes seemed to shift in his interest to another topic.

***

"Land ahoy!" came a scream from the crow's nest atop the mizzen mast a short time afterward. The captain pulled out his spy glass, opened it up to arm's length, and viewed the trees and shoreline.

"We are at America," he said.

"And what news I have," said Ogden, "about the end of the Revolutionary War."

Ogden brought back news of the Treaty of Paris upon his return to America. He was breveted as a brigadier general by Congress in September 1783 and was described as a "brave and gallant soldier."

***

Aaron Ogden was wounded at Yorktown. He went on to be a lawyer and was described as "a genteel young fellow with an aquiline nose."[1] He later became a member of the New Jersey Assembly and was elected New Jersey's fifth governor in 1812.

Chapter 42
Ogden's Redemption

"Action is redemption."
– Emily Dickinson

It was a cold winter's day with snow on the ground. A picturesque scene it was, while quiet and starkly white with snow and black or gray trees. Between the trees stood a grand site here in the rural landscape around the town of Sparta. A surprisingly large crowd of people had gathered together. Before them stood an immense wooden church with a high roof, and the steeple above it went to great heights and seemed to scratch the gray skies that slowly passed by. It was a long sought after structure, a place to finally center what was gatherings in homes, religious service in family abodes as what was known as a meeting house. This was now a home for the Sparta Presbyterian Church.

From the north, along the road covered in white, came a horse trotting at moderate speed and pulling behind it a sleigh. The two runners ran smoothly along the hard pack on the road, making an easy sliding pull for the horse. Holding the reigns with a firm grip was a heavily clothed man, and beside him was his wife. They were cozily covered by a white, fur blanket seemingly matching the blanket of snow.

The head of the man, clothed in a fur hat, was that of Judge Robert Ogden II. His white hair, blending in nicely with the snowy scene, showed his years. He was, at age seventy, showing the length of time on the earth. It was an apt display of the wisdom he held within. As the sleigh approached the crowd, the judge spoke to his wife.

"Phoebe, my dear, the day has finally come. We can see how our hard work has resulted in establishing the Lord's sanctuary."

"I know, my dear, that this is such a goal that you have had over the years. From the lifetime of effort that you gave in Elizabethtown, before you were rejected due to the political differences, to the years out here in the country where you held many services at our home as we struggled during the Revolutionary War, to now, in 1786, when you have given so much to see this church built."

"Yes, I watched each step of the fabrication of this wonderful structure. I recall that we came out here to watch Noah Talmage as he chopped down trees to provide the timber for this church. It has given me, in a large way, a reprieve, a redemption, to the difficult dilemma that I wrestled with those turbulent years during the war."

"I believe that is true, that the moral issue of telling the truth versus protecting our family brought to you—a good and moral man—the internal angst." This, Phoebe felt, was a very true statement.

"I know now that this was the best course of action, and the Lord has provided. Our family has regained their stature in the community, my heart has been calmed, and our children are shining stars to carry on the Ogden name in great numbers and in similar benefit to society that we have strived for these several centuries in America. I am at peace."

Robert Ogden II, the "Honest Lawyer," continued to live in Sussex County. He was a major influence on the construction of the First Presbyterian Church of Sparta and is buried right behind the structure with his wife.

Chapter 43
Moody's Reflections

"Youth is to all the glad season of life; but often only by what it hopes, not by what it attains, or what it escapes."
–Thomas Carlyle

The Sissiboo River wandered amongst planters' farms as it made its run to the sea, carving its path in the cool climate of Nova Scotia. Another harsh winter had just begun to loosen its grip and allow the first flowers of spring to emerge. But its presence continued the burden of life of the residents of the coastal community along the Bay of Fundy in the Canadian northland.

Two children laughed as they approached what appeared to be a crouched over, ancient fisherman who was holding his pole calmly along a mud bank as the tide drew down the water level.

"Hey, old man," shouted one of the boys. They laughed again as they teased the innocent-looking figure, benign and nonthreatening. They must have been energized by boyish enthusiasm as they were enjoying the first hint of spring in the salty air.

"Where's all of your catch?" shouted the other boy as he grinned at his accomplice, knowing that there were no fish beside the man. He had nothing there to show for the time he had put in since dawn.

The white-haired fisherman slowly looked toward the boys. He had a good crop of hair—receding from his forehead but hanging long down his back, almost as if someone had put his hand over the peak of his head and slid the crop backward.

"No, boys, no fish. I guess it's not my day," he said to his youthful tormenters.

"We see you here fishing a lot. Sitting your life away, not moving much and with not much reward for your passive labors." Both inquisitors looked at each other, seemingly proud of their incessant interrogation of the old man.

"Well, I have had a life of adventure. It is my time to take some consideration resting on this bog here, to be reeling slowly for sea bass along the mud banks as the tide comes in and goes out. This happens six times a day. Have you boys noticed this, six times a day?"

"We know that there is a tide change. It happens every day. Day in and day out," said one boy.

"One day is the same as the next," said the other. "Tides are a part of life."

"Hah," said the old man. "Now we have agreed on something. Tides are a part of life."

Not to be outdone and not to give ground to their senior, the kids continued. "Tides and life are ways to see things happen, to mark time and gain progress. What have you done? An old man like you must have story." This was followed by a laugh. "Tell us about it." The boys sat down on a nearby bog, sneakily tempting the white-haired man to speak to them on this rather unexciting day.

"The tide comes in and goes out. Such is life. You may be poor, there's opportunity to become rich, or famous, or successful. But, often as not, each period in your life comes to pass. Time goes on, and you may become blessed or cursed." Seeing that the boys were paying attention to him, he laid down his fishing pole, turned on his marsh bog toward them, and eyed them.

"So, what's your name, old man?"

"Moody. James Moody."

"Hey, aren't you a captain in the regiment here?" said one boy.

"And aren't you a ship builder here?" said the other.

Moody gave a huff. "Well, yes, I am. I guess that is what I am known for. I am both a shipbuilder here in town, and I am also a captain in the Royal Nova Scotia Regiment. I am also the representative for our county in the Nova Scotia House of Assembly," he said calmly, in almost a hushed tone.

"That sounds like a lot that you've done."

"True, but now I am in my final days, I can feel it."

"So, this has been your life. Interesting."

"Well, not really. This has been my life here for a quarter century. But I have come from afar and suffered much setback. I come from way back in New Jersey to the south."

"Tell us," said both boys in unison. "We have the time. And it sounds like you were one of the Patriots who tore away from the Crown to be independent."

"Oh, no. I was a Loyalist. I still am, for what that's worth." He fidgeted on his marsh bog, an uneasy cushion that would waver back and forth on its wet, muddy base interwoven with sea grass roots. He fidgeted with handling his pole in an anxious fashion. "I worked for the British."

"There were so many Colonists who wanted to break away from England; you were not one of those?"

"As it turned out, I was one of the most successful spies in the whole war, the American Revolutionary War. I have been told that I am quite the noted man."

"So that's what you mean about the ups and downs in life?"

"Yes, for sure. I began on my father's land in Little Egg Harbor. It was a place very similar to this, near the sea, with natural tidal basins and salt marshes."

"And the tide going in and out."

"Exactly. I loved to fish with my brother. And I farmed with my family back in the days before the war. Then, due to Dad's vocal siding with the British, my farm was burned, but I escaped. I worked against the Rebels and helped the British in New York City."

"So, you were a noted British spy?"

"Yes, I brought many secret messages back to General Sir Henry Clinton who was in the city; military mail stolen on their way to George Washington. I made a significant difference for Britain."

"So, from poor to a hero?"

"Yes, and as you know, the Americans won the war. And before we left, I got the recommendations from what seemed to be all the leaders from our country of Britain. This ending had me go to Britain, where I was told I would have a hero's welcome."

"Did that take place?" said one.

"Was this a high point for you?" said the other.

"Not really. I published my memoirs. But I didn't gain money or prestige, and I didn't get a sizeable pension or recompense. And my brother, with whom I loved to fish in the tidal waters along the shore, he was gone, hanged for participating with me in an attempt to steal their Declaration of Independence." Moody mentioned several other notable experiences.

"No big reward?" said one.

"And the loss of many things?" said the other.

"No reward of any size. I lost my wife and remarried. And now I am here, back on the North American continent but far from the home I knew."

"Boy, Mr. Moody, your life did have ups and downs," said one.

"With your escapades—possibly changing battle outcomes, almost getting the governor or New Jersey, grabbing people from prison, and almost stealing the Declaration of Independence—you may have changed the course of history, several times," said the other.

"Yes, I might have altered history. Close, but not there. I did exert my energy. I did give it my best. Well, either way, now here I am. In my final days. Fishing like I did when I was young, when I was your age. I have the sea which I used to contend with but now which gives me comfort. And I have the tides, ebbing and flowing through the salt marshes of my life. Right now, we are at neap tide, and the water is standing more or less still, paused while I chat with you boys. But change will occur, you can be sure of it. While I wait, I will fish."

"That is what we can want, Mr. Moody. To be able to sit and fish."

Thinking about what the boys said, he felt satisfied. He looked up with a grin and said, "I guess this is a successful Loyalist's life," as his silver tooth glistened in the cold, salty, morning air.

What's next?

Honest Ogden is book one of a series that includes two other stories from the American Revolutionary War. Book two is the story of Colonel Seward and Mohawk Chief Brant and concludes in the Battle of Minisink. A third book explores the virtue (or not) of Lewis Morris III who signed the Declaration of Independence for New York (reputedly the last to sign) and his escape to the wilderness of Sussex County in New Jersey and his building of *Morrisania*.

More to read…

Here's a listing of my other books that are on the shelf or under construction:

Sparta: Head of the Wallkill
Franklin, Hamburg, Ogdensburg, and Hardyston – Images of America
Mining for America – The Story of the Great Zinc Mining Operation that Strengthened America
Louis Larsen – Country Roads and Portrait of a Century Past
Sussex Wantage – Images of America
Honest Ogden -- Amazon
Seward & Brant – *(In Process)*
Morrisvale and the Declaration of Independence – *(in Process)*
The Commodore and the Mucker – *(In Process)*

Acknowledgements

"We stand on the shoulders of giants" – Sir Isaac Newton.

Those who came before me and influenced me in several ways are to be credited. Those who provided input and feedback are appreciated.

For gaining an interest in history and in learning, I'd like to include my grandfather Sydney Hall and my father Wilfred Truran. They gave a comfortable surrounding and a nurturing feeling along with their learned wisdom. This also includes the rest of my loving family.

I was schooled in Franklin, NJ. I only went to one building—that's kindergarten through twelfth grade. And both of my parents did too. Small town, good teachers, continuity in well-founded basic foundational education. A particular influence with spark and energy was Mr. Bach, teaching high school physics and the concept of passion for academics and energetic pursuit of for answers and the truth.

With this foundation, I was enflamed to be educated. This included BS Electrical Engineering at University of Tennessee, MBA at Fairleigh Dickinson, MS in Industrial Engineering and Operations Research at Columbia University, and a PhD in Engineering Management at Stevens Institute of Technology. Additional academics were required in fine arts with a Creative Writing Certificate from the online program associated with University of California Berkley. Though there's a diversity of programs, concentrations, and
specialties, the good environment of each of these institutions kept the flame alive and aided me to consume the material. Thank you.

Stretching my legs continually, with writing five books and now some more my way has been guided by the likes of Mary Carrol Moore, Jane Friedman, Keith Smith, Christina Chiu, and Pauline Harris.

May the knowledge, friendship, good will, and guidance that the above have provided to me be extended to others to help the world be a better place.

The life of an author

Hello, reader, let me tell you about myself.

I have spent half a century as an engineer and technology professor. Making order out of chaos has been a calling for me, my job and career. After getting my Ph.D., I wanted to alter my viewpoint to explore the depths of history. In particular, my area of Sussex County, New Jersey has its own unique history—as does any area in the world.

For me, I could see the "minerals, mining, and miners" aspect of my county. I have had the good fortune to be the Sussex County Historian for a few years now, and to help guide our young people, and older ones too, to our heritage. One lifelong aspiration was to honor our school tree—The Old Oak Tree—now well-labeled and celebrated. I helped to get the local mineral to be honored: Franklinite is the New Jersey State Mineral. We worked with students in the local schools to write to the state legislators and "get 'er done" so they could see that they could make a difference, as Margaret Mead said, *"Never doubt that a small group of thoughtful, committed citizens can change the world; indeed, it's the only thing that ever has."* Another important commitment I find is to partner with the Smithsonian Institution to bring the Franklin area to national recognition as a place where poor locals and ragged immigrants came from around the world to find a good home for their families.

In addition to bringing artifacts and landscape to life through identification and writing, I see deeper meaning to be had with my work. While science and technology—my career—helps to make order out of chaos and helps relieve basic burdens from our lives, understanding history and our heritage can make our quality of life more attractive and interesting. Writing with depth on a journey into one's head might give insight to how we tick and what might ease the mind of its own internal burdens. How? How might I be able to help make the world a better place?

Perhaps I can make a difference by providing examples on how these local Revolutionary War men thought and reacted in their human ways might give others guidance and meaning to their own actions. This I try to do through the American Decision Series.

Perhaps I can by documenting the immigrant miners' dangerous jobs and earnest work ethics that gave value to themselves and their families. This I try to do through working with the Smithsonian Institution and several books and videos I have done.

Perhaps I can by teaching the youth. In the last couple of years, I have had the great fortune of working with local school kids to help them gently remind legislators of good stewardship and this succeeded in getting the local mineral Franklinite to become the NJ State Mineral. Judge Ogden making the right choice in his deadly dilemma. These can be examples, portraits in character if you will, that can help make the world a better place.

Perhaps I can through highlighting good qualities of people I have known, encountered, or read about. These I call, on my Substack **Inspiring History** site, as *Portraits of Character*. These projects represent a passion that I possess to help make the world a better place through exploring, identifying, writing, and interpreting during my time on this planet.

References

- Haines, Austin Alanson *Hardyston Memorial and the History of the Township and the North Presbyterian Church* by Alanson A. Haines, Pastor, 1886.
- Moody (Journal of the American Revolution) References https://allthingsliberty.com/2020/11/contingencies-capture-and-spectacular-getaway-the-imprisonment-and-escape-of-james-moody/
- Moody, James
- Walton, Jean https://njpostalhistory.org/media/featuredcoverspdf/2012AugustFeaturedCover.pdf
- Enneagrams https://rmfw.org/2018/11/20/character-building-with-the-enneagram/
- Ogden to Washington
- Ogden to Washington https://www.gilderlehrman.org/collection/glc04386
- Ogden to Washington
- https://books.google.com/books?id=NHMHDAAAQBAJ&pg=PA200&lpg=PA200&dq=Ogden+to+Washington++digby&source=bl&ots=LHbXY9eQcw&sig=ACfU3U2gir0EfcOOIEl310gV4F9E_BWQlw&hl=en&sa=X&ved=2ahUKEwjInvP52MrpAhX1l3IEHQ1JCqUQ6AEwAHoECAQQAQ#v=onepage&q=Ogden%20to%20Washington%20%20digby&f=false
- Abductions McBurney, Christian. Abductions in the American Revolution https://books.google.com/books?id=NHMHDAAAQBAJ&pg=PA72&lpg=PA72&dq=Kidnap+Gov+Livingston&source=bl&ots=LHbX_5dP8q&sig=ACfU3U01e4PTq7hGX1xitWDDUzYRpns-rw&hl=en&sa=X&ved=2ahUKEwjmtq3dqM_pAhVdknIEHUfbANcQ6AEwAHoECAcQAQ#v=onepage&q=Kidnap%20Gov%20Livingston&f=false
- Kidnap future king

https://allthingsliberty.com/2014/01/washington-authorizes-plan-kidnap-future-king/
https://www.neatorama.com/2014/12/19/The-American-Plot-to-Kidnap-the-Future-King-of-England/
- Governor Franklin release **https://www.newenglandhistoricalsociety.com/william-franklin-bens-son-spent-revolutionary-war-connecticut-jail/**
- Washington papers **https://www.archives.gov/founding-docs**
    - Villain Moody **https://founders.archives.gov/documents/Washington/99-01-02-07686**
    - Moody capture Hackettstown 8/4/1780 **https://founders.archives.gov/documents/Washington/03-27-02-0380**
    - To Washington from Benedict Arnold and reply from GW **https://founders.archives.gov/documents/Washington/03-27-02-0495**
- https://allthingsliberty.com/2020/11/contingencies-capture-and-spectacular-getaway-the-imprisonment-and-escape-of-james-moody/

Index and Endnotes

Characters (via "INTROs" will show major/minor/flat characters)

[i] INTRO Robert Ogden II
[ii] INTRO Phoebe Ogden
[iii] INTRO James Moody
[iv] INTRO Lowery
[v] https://allthingsliberty.com/2020/11/contingencies-capture-and-spectacular-getaway-the-imprisonment-and-escape-of-james-moody/
[vi] https://allthingsliberty.com/2020/11/contingencies-capture-and-spectacular-getaway-the-imprisonment-and-escape-of-james-moody/
[vii] INTRO Private Patrick "Red" Sullivan
[viii] INTRO George Washington
[ix] INTRO Lord Stirling or General William Alexander. A corruption as Sterling may also be included
[x] INTRO Governor William Franklin
[xi] Washington letter to Livingston 1/12/1782
[xii] INTRO Billy Lee
[xiii] INTRO Major Matthias Ogden
[xiv] INTRO Lewis Morris III
[xv] INTRO Colonel John Seward
[xvi] INTRO Rverend James Caldwell
[xvii] INTRO Reverend Isaac Watts
[xviii] INTRO Benjamin Franklin
[xix] INTRO Aaron Ogden
[xx] https://www.google.com/books/edition/Biographical_and_Genealogical_History_of/LU5KAAAAYAAJ?hl=en&gbpv=1&dq=how+many+children+did+robert+ogden+and+wife+phoebe+have&pg=PA825&printsec=frontcover#v=onepage&q=how%20many%20children%20did%20robert%20ogden%20and%20wife%20phoebe%20have&f=false
[xxi] INTRO Cuffee
[xxii] INTRO Joy
[xxiii] INTRO Michael Rorick
[xxiv] INTRO Molly
[xxv] INTRO Pastor Constant Hart
[xxvi] INTRO William Johnson
[xxvii] INTRO Claudius Smith
[xxviii] INTRO Joseph Brant
[xxix] INTRO Robert Morgen
[xxx] https://www.njherald.com/news/20161218/with-a-history-of-indian-raids-and-captives-fredon-now-known-as-a-safe-and-affordable-town-for-families

xxxi INTRO Daniel Talmadge
xxxii INTRO Nathaniel Wade
xxxiii INTRO Reverend Jim Hawkins
xxxiv **https://en.wikipedia.org/wiki/New_Jersey_Volunteers**
xxxv **https://en.wikipedia.org/wiki/Cortlandt_Skinner**
xxxvi INTRO Governor William Livingston
xxxvii https://allthingsliberty.com/2020/11/contingencies-capture-and-spectacular-getaway-the-imprisonment-and-escape-of-james-moody/
xxxviii Moody, James, 1783. Moody's Narrative of his Exertions and Sufferings in the Cause of Government since the Year 1776, pg 15, Richards and Urquhart at the Exchange. London.
xxxix INTRO Scotsman Robert Maxwell
xl INTRO General Horatio Gates
xli INTRO Benedict Arnold
xlii INTRO the Sheriff
xliii INTRO Sir Henry Clinton
xliv INTRO General Sullivan
xlv INTRO Governor Livingston
xlvi INTRO Major Aaron Ogden
xlvii INTRO Colonel Matthias Ogden
xlviii INTRO Knyphausen
xlix gorget
l To Washington from Benedict Arnold and reply from GW
https://founders.archives.gov/documents/Washington/03-27-02-0495
li Benedict Arnold
lii Major John André
liii Beacon atop Sparta Mountain
liv Ogdensburg
http://freepages.rootsweb.com/~normansofmiltonnj/genealogy/fileman/historyofsussexnwarrencounty.htm
lv Ogdensburg.
http://freepages.rootsweb.com/~normansofmiltonnj/genealogy/fileman/historyofsussexnwarrencounty.htm
lvi Ogdensburg. https://www.facebook.com/SpartaNjHistoricalSociety/posts/well-done/839637276092114/
lvii INTRO Colonel John Seward
lviii Chain of Express mail delivery
lix Letter from George Washington to Matthias Ogden
lx INTRO Admiral Digby

lxi INTRO Commodore Edmund Affleck
lxii INTRO Prince William Henry
lxiii INTRO Franz, Hessian soldier with Smith Gang
lxiv INTRO William, Richard, James of the Smith Gang
lxv INTRO John Clark https://allthingsliberty.com/2019/03/terror-in-the-ramapos/

www.ingramcontent.com/pod-product-compliance
Lightning Source LLC
LaVergne TN
LVHW041659060526
838201LV00043B/497